HOW LOGICAL ARE YOU?

Thunder Bay Press

An imprint of Printers Row Publishing Group

10350 Barnes Canyon Road, Suite 100, San Diego, CA 92121

www.thunderbaybooks.com

Printers Row Publishing Group is a division of Readerlink Distribution Services, LLC. Thunder Bay Press is a registered trademark of Readerlink Distribution Services, LLC.

All notations of errors or omissions should be addressed to Thunder Bay Press, Editorial Department, at the above address. All other correspondence (author inquiries, permissions) concerning the content of this book should be addressed to Carlton Books Ltd, 20 Mortimer Street, London, W1T 3JW, United Kingdom.

Publisher: Peter Norton
Associate Publisher: Ana Parker
Publishing/Editorial Team: April Farr, Kelly Larsen, Kathryn C. Dalby
Editorial Team: JoAnn Padgett, Melinda Allman, Dan Mansfield

ISBN: 978-1-68412-933-1

All images: © iStockphoto & Shutterstock

Printed in Dubai

23 22 21 20 19   1 2 3 4 5

HOW LOGICAL ARE YOU?

Test your aptitude for deduction and examine your ingenuity with 400 puzzles

Tim Dedopulos

THUNDER BAY
P·R·E·S·S

San Diego, California

CONTENTS

Introduction   5

Easy Puzzles   9
Medium Puzzles   91
Difficult Puzzles   173

Easy Answers   257
Medium Answers   267
Difficult Answers   277

4

INTRODUCTION

INTRODUCTION

Welcome to *How Logical Are You?* – and to 401 logical puzzles of every conceivable variety. Inside, you'll find mental problems to test your powers of reasoning to the limit. Even the toughest puzzlers will find themselves scratching their heads from time to time. But then, what else were you expecting?

Every society on Earth knows of puzzles, and makes use of them for entertainment and education. Likewise, through history, every period we have reasonable archaeological or documentary data for shows evidence of puzzle use, even as far back as the ancient Babylonian civilisation. Curiosity and challenge are powerful motivators, as is the drive to compare our abilities to those of others. Some of the earliest bits of writing we've found are maths puzzles inscribed into clay tablets. The urge to solve puzzles is hard-wired into us.

It's no surprise really, when you think about it. We're a curious species. Our intelligence and imagination have brought us the modern world. If we didn't like to experiment and find answers to the things that were puzzling us, humanity as we know it would not exist. Our physical adaptability is important, but it is our mental flexibility – the ability to ask "what if?" – that really defines us.

Over the years, puzzles have taken many forms, from tests of manipulation right through to highly abstract mental reasoning. At its core, a puzzle is a test of analytical ability – if I am given a set of initial condititions X, then what is the correct way to find an end-state, Y. This is true whether Y is the solution to an equation, a plausible situation that could have led to X, or simply an understanding of what X means.

Our capacity for logical analysis – for reason – is one of the greatest tools in our mental arsenal, on a par with creativity and lateral induction. Logic is the very backbone of our scientific method, and despite our everyday assumptions, it is not necessarily obvious. When obvious event A always causes obvious event B, the link is clear to all, even birds and animals. But looking at A and B and asking why the one inevitably brings the other is a relatively recent development, even in terms of human history. This is the very core of scientific thought, of reason itself.

The human brain gives meaning and structure to the world through analysis, pattern recognition, and logical deduction. We understand our sense input by categorising things, and looking at what those categories imply. The more accurate our mental models, our categories, the better our understanding of the world. Our urge to measure and test ourselves is an unavoidable reflex that results from that drive for greater understanding. So what could be more natural than spending time puzzling?

The logic puzzles contained within this book will definitely let you put your brain to the test. There's no guesswork required, but that isn't to say that you won't need to do a little work for the answers. A core method of the scientific process is to form theories from the data, and test them against the evidence. When your theory is contradicted, you go back to the drawing board. In this book, all the data is in front of you. All you have to do is piece it together.

Humans get a very pleasurable sense of achievement from succeeding at things, particularly when we suspect they might be too hard for us. But it also turns out

that working out a complex puzzle is one of the most important things the human psyche can achieve. Recent advances in the scientific fields of neurology and cognitive psychology have hammered home the significance of puzzles and mental exercise like never before. We now understand that the brain continually builds, shapes and organises itself all through our lives. It is the only organ to be able to do so. Our brain continually rewrites its own operating instructions and alters its very structure in response to our experiences. Just like the muscles of the body, our minds can respond to exercise, allowing us to be more retentive and mentally fitter. And while exercise can often be a chore for many of us, a good brain workout can often be achieved from the comfort of your own sofa.

Let's be clear – solving these puzzles won't be easy. But it will be fun.

Happy puzzling!

EASY
PUZZLES

Can you divide up this board to correctly show the 28 dominoes listed below?

2	0	0	6	5	3	3	0
3	6	5	4	0	1	1	3
2	0	2	2	4	5	3	6
4	6	5	5	2	5	5	0
2	2	1	0	4	0	6	3
6	6	3	4	4	2	1	5
4	1	3	1	4	6	1	1

0	0

0	1	1	1

0	2	1	2	2	2

0	3	1	3	2	3	3	3

0	4	1	4	2	4	3	4	4	4

0	5	1	5	2	5	3	5	4	5	5	5

0	6	1	6	2	6	3	6	4	6	5	6	6	6

Answer see page 258

Answer see page 258

Can you match the fragments to reassemble the names of several Hollywood celebrities?

MC	MIN	IGAN	HANN
GEL	JU	DRI	TORN
THEW	OW	VER	NIE
DREY	AN	LIA	FUS
WIL	ERL	KIE	INA
UGHEY	SUTH	SON	GIB
LIE	SON	SON	ALY
JO	CONA	AND	MEL
EN	FER	RIP	MAT

Following this set of simple instructions is supposed to help you cross the road safely. There is an error, and if you follow them exactly, you might never cross the road. What is the problem?

1. Walk to the pavement where you want to cross.
2. Face the direction that you want to cross in.
3. Look both ways, and remember if you see any vehicles.
4. Are there any vehicles within 75ft? If yes, go back to 2, else proceed.
5. Walk across the road briskly.
6. Get onto the pavement in front of you.
7. Stop.

Answer see page 258

Can you insert the mathematical operators + – * / ( ) to make these equations valid?

Answer see page 258

A 7 ◯ 6 ◯ 5 ◯ 15 ◯ 18 = 23

B 9 ◯ 7 ◯ 7 ◯ 3 ◯ 13 = 13

C 8 ◯ 9 ◯ 12 ◯ 14 ◯ 5 = 4

The following grid operates according to a specific pattern. Can you fill in the blank section?

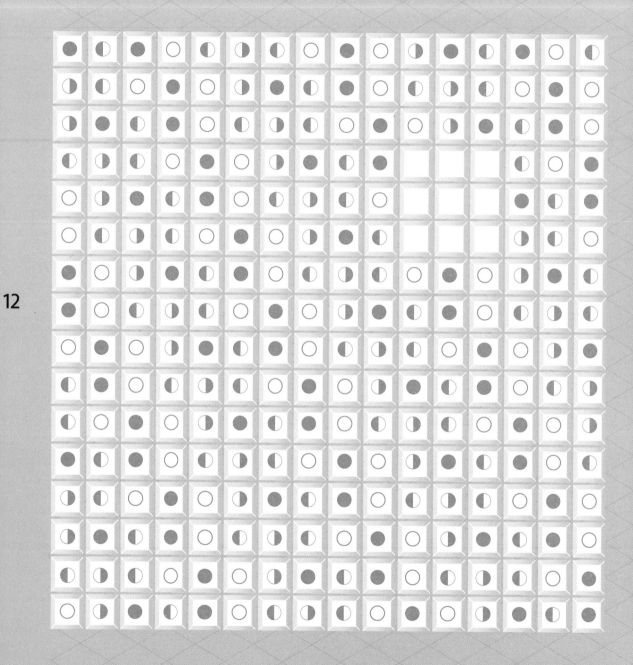

Answer see page 258

You are faced with two doors, either of which might be wired to kill you as soon as you open it. Each door bears a sign. One of the signs is true, and one is false.

Which door should you open?

Sign A: This door is safe, but door B is deadly.

Sign B: One door is safe, and the other is deadly.

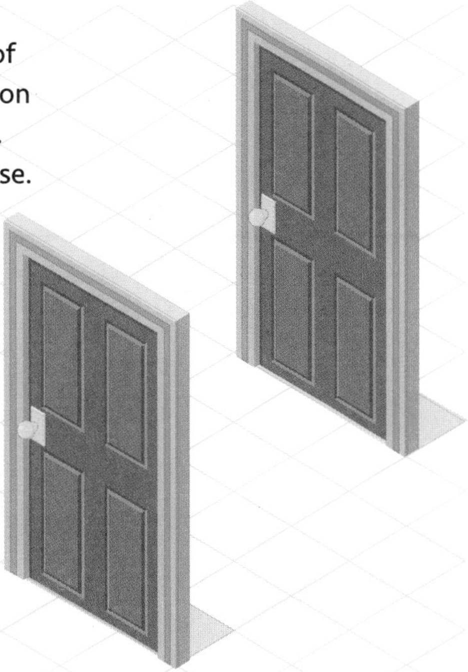

Answer see page 258

These triangles follow a specific logic. What should replace the question mark?

Answer see page 258

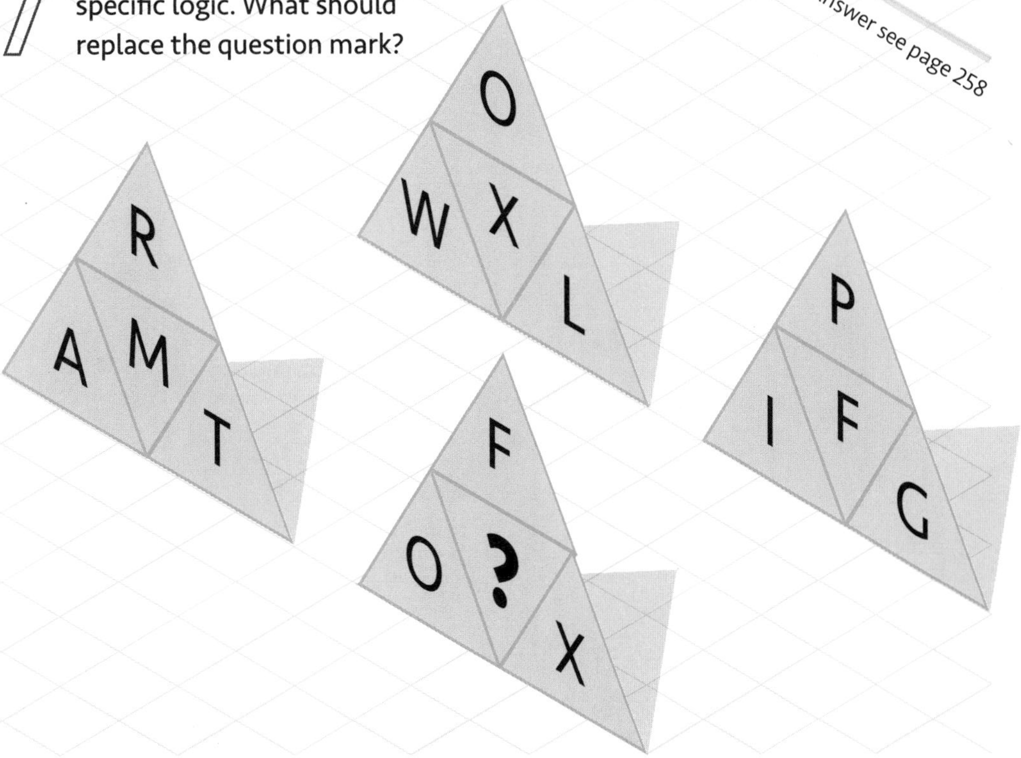

O
W X
R
A M
T
L

F
O ? X

P
I F
G

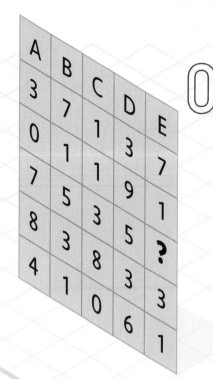

A	B	C	D	E
3	7	1	3	7
0	1	1	9	1
7	5	3	5	?
8	3	8	3	3
4	1	0	6	1

The following numbers obey a certain logic. What number should replace the question mark?

Answer see page 258

09 Three archers were practising their skills. After each had fired five shots, they paused to compare scores. Examining all three targets, each person made three statements, one of which was incorrect. Who scored what?

Answer see page 258

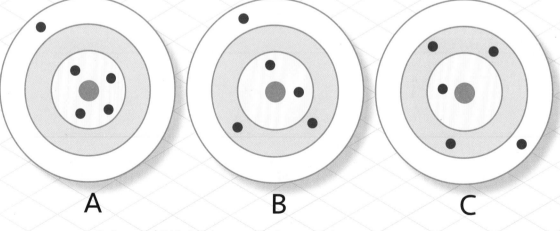

A   B   C

A: I scored 260. I did not score lowest. There were 40 points between C and B.
B: I scored 40 less than A. I scored 200. I scored 20 more than C.
C: I scored 60 less than A. I scored 200. B scored 60 more than A.

Answer see page 258

10 A is to B as C is to V, W, X, Y or Z?

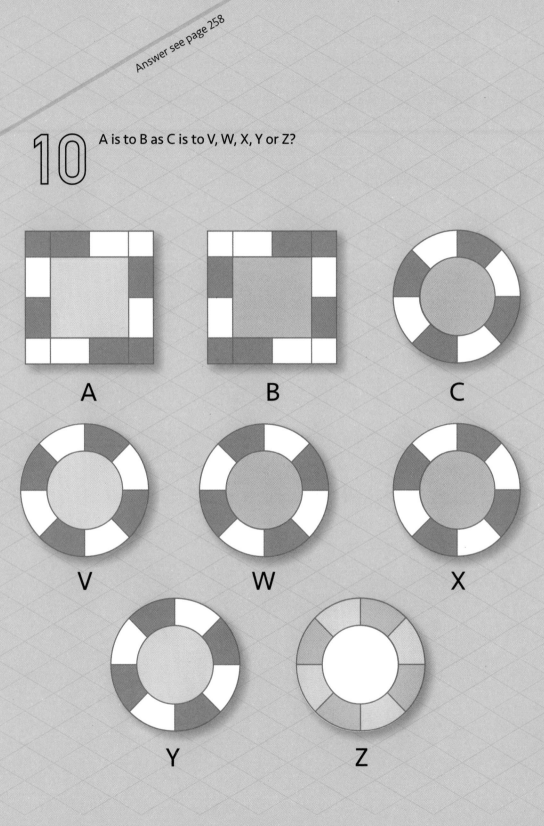

A

B

C

V

W

X

Y

Z

15

11

The following tiles have been taken from a five by five square of numbers. When they have been reassembled accurately, the square will show the same five numbers reading both across and down.

Answer see page 258

Can you rebuild it?

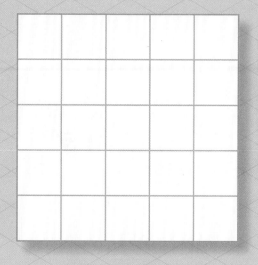

16

4	9	4

5	7

5	7

2	8	5

3
0
2

4
9
4

0
2
8

6
3

2
3

3
5

12

Can you draw three circles within the box so that each one completely encloses exactly one triangle, one square, and one pentagon? No two circles may enclose exactly the same three elements.

Answer see page 258

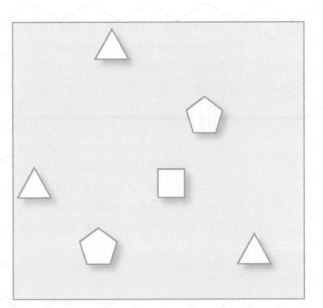

13

Ten people are in different locations in the city center, and want to meet up. Which street corner should they pick to minimise their total combined journey?

Answer see page 258

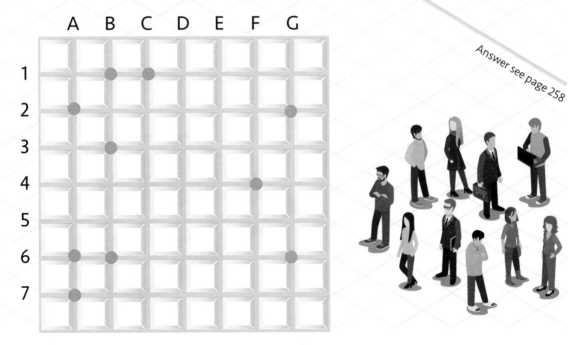

14

Ten people are sitting in two rows, facing each other, men on one side, and women on the other. From the information given below, can you say which desk Pip is at?

Pip is next to the woman opposite Richard. Adam is next to Tom. Alice is three desks away from Emily. Graham is opposite the woman next to Anita. Either John or Richard are at desk 8. The woman sitting next to the woman opposite desk 10 is Alice. Anita is opposite John. Tom is three desks from John. Adam is opposite Emily. Either Alice or Cassandra are at desk 3 and desk 1 is opposite desk 10.

Answer see page 258

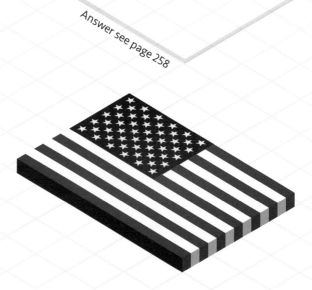

Answer see page 258

15

The following five items are all famous US states. Can you decrypt them?

DMZUWVB

SMVBCKSG

WZMOWV

VMJZIASI

WSTIPWUI

16

Using six straight lines that each touch at least one side of the box below, can you divide the box into sections containing 1, 2, 3, 4, 5, 6, and 7 shapes?

Answer see page 258

17

Can you tell what number comes next in this sequence?

Answer see page 258

2 3 5 7 11 13 ?

18 Two people are playing chess. Under the rules, a win is worth 2 points, a draw is worth one point, and a loss is worth 0. They both start at 0 points, and after three rounds, A has four points, as does B. How is this possible?

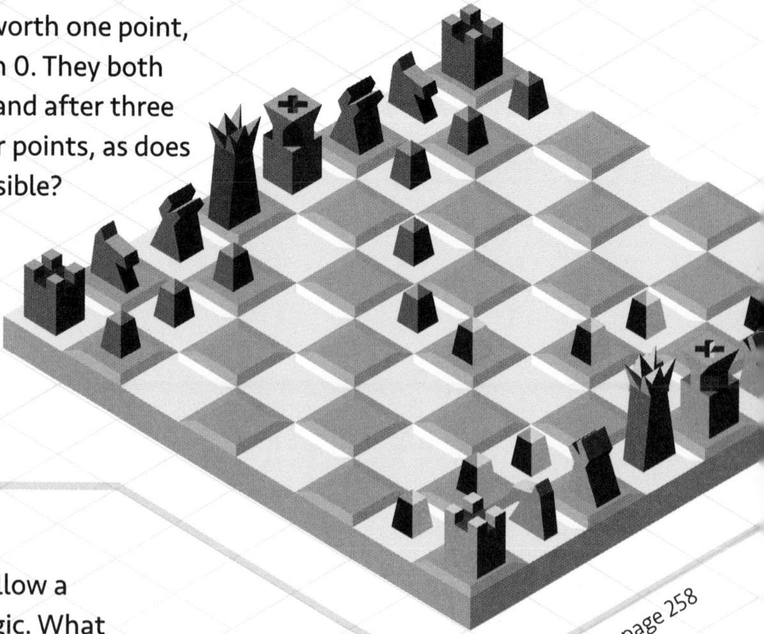

Answer see page 258

Answer see page 258

19 These triangles follow a certain specific logic. What number should replace the question mark?

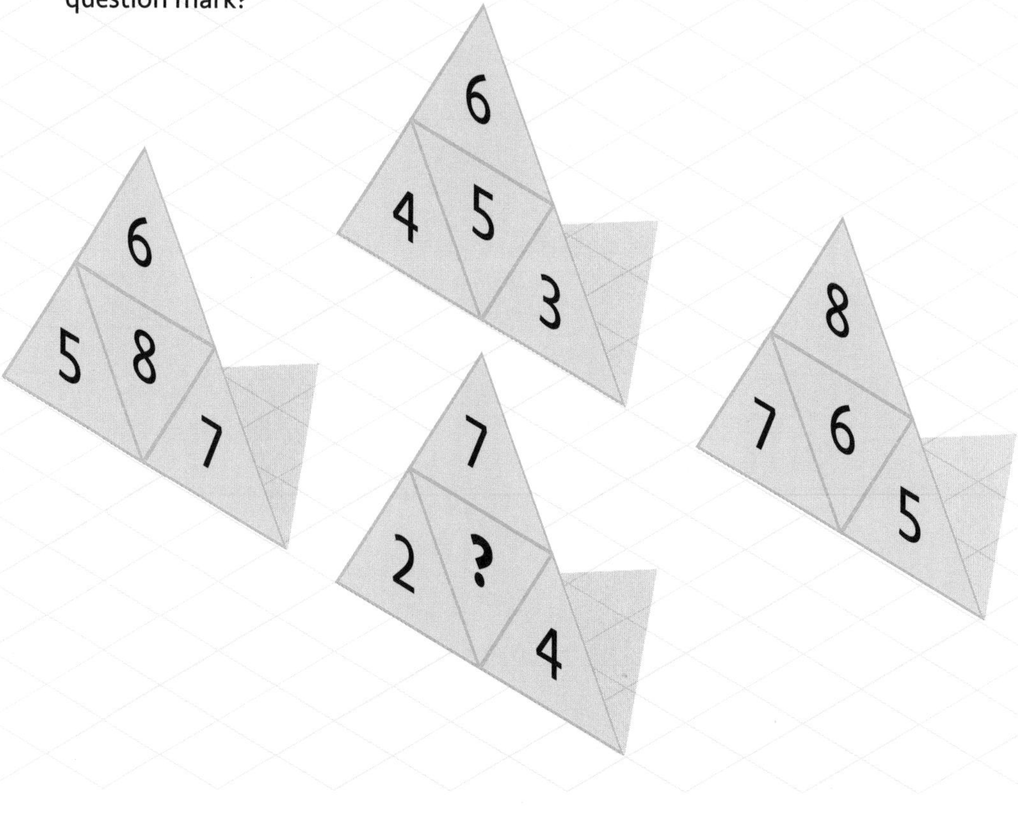

20

20 Can you divide this square into four identical shapes, each one containing just one of each of the five symbols?

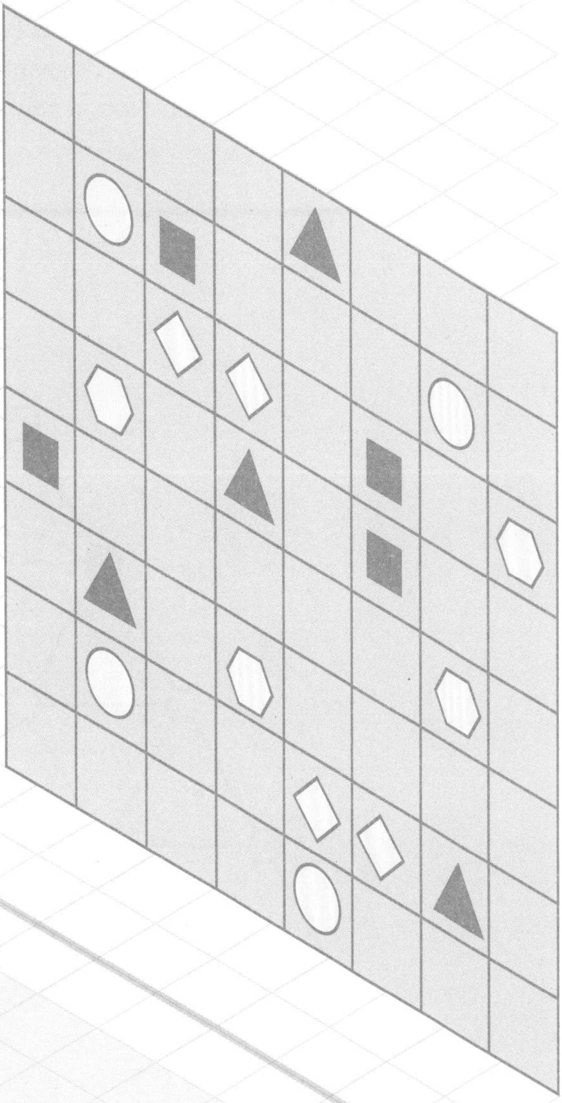

Answer see page 259

21 The following numbers obey a certain logic. What should replace the question mark?

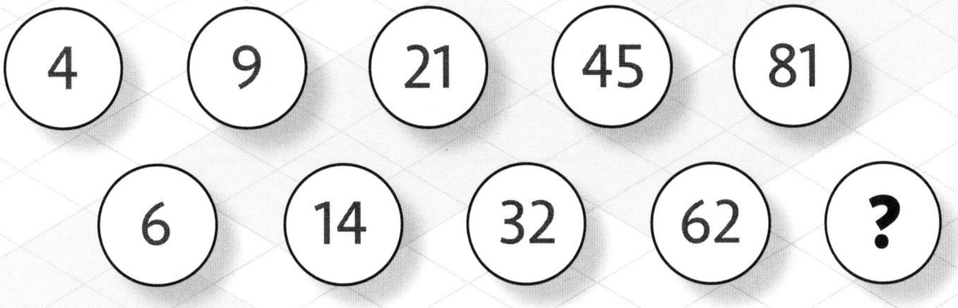

Answer see page 259

21

(4)   (9)   (21)   (45)   (81)

(6)   (14)   (32)   (62)   (?)

Can you place the segments below the triangular grid over the grid itself in such a way as to ensure that every node is covered by an identical symbol? Not all connecting lines will be covered.

22

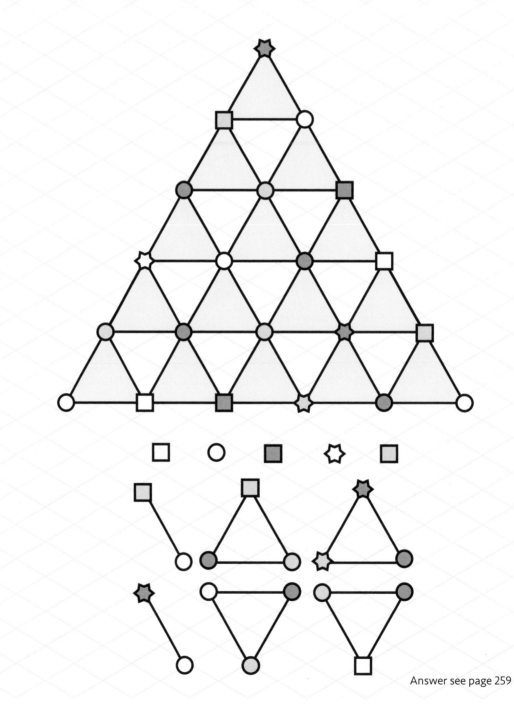

Answer see page 259

Can you fill in the numbers provided to correctly complete the grid?

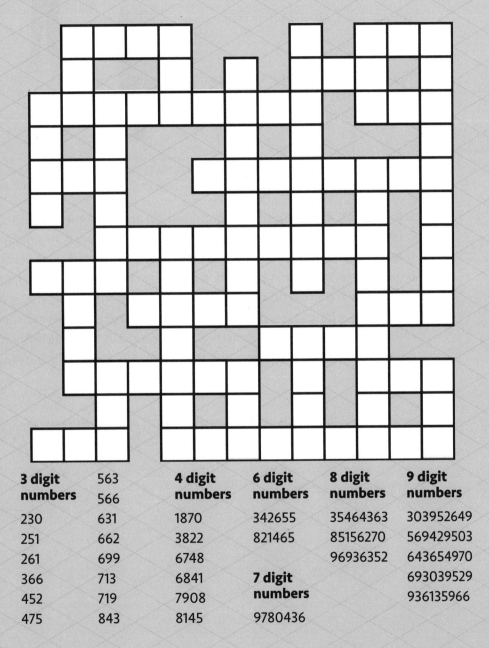

23

3 digit numbers	563	**4 digit numbers**	**6 digit numbers**	**8 digit numbers**	**9 digit numbers**
	566				
230	631	1870	342655	35464363	303952649
251	662	3822	821465	85156270	569429503
261	699	6748		96936352	643654970
366	713	6841	**7 digit numbers**		693039529
452	719	7908			936135966
475	843	8145	9780436		

Answer see page 259

You are faced with three men, A, B, and C, who know each other. Each of the three either always lies, or always tells the truth. Each makes one statement to you.

Which, if any, are definitely telling the truth?

You are unable to hear A's statement.
B: "A said that he is a liar."
C: "B is lying to you."

Answer see page 259

Answer see page 259

Signs – symbols in a specific position – which appear in the outer circles are transferred to the inner circle as follows: If it appears once, it is definitely transferred. If it appears twice, it is transferred if no other symbol will be transferred from that position. If it appears three times, it will be transferred if there is no sign appearing once in that position. If it appears four times, it is not transferred. In instances where signs with the same count are competing, then from high to low, priority runs top left – top right – bottom left – bottom right. What does the inner circle look like?

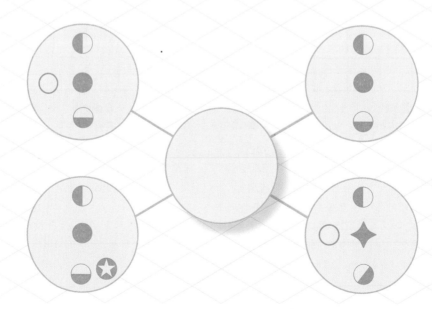

26 These circles function according to a certain logic. What number should replace the question mark?

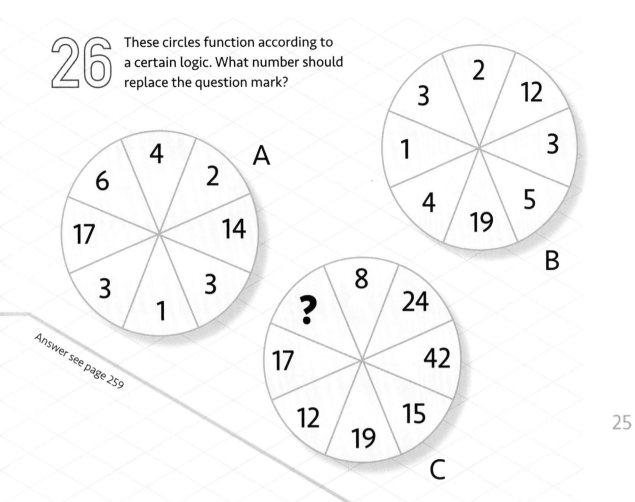

A

B

C

Answer see page 259

27 This diagram obeys a certain logic. What is the missing number?

Answer see page 259

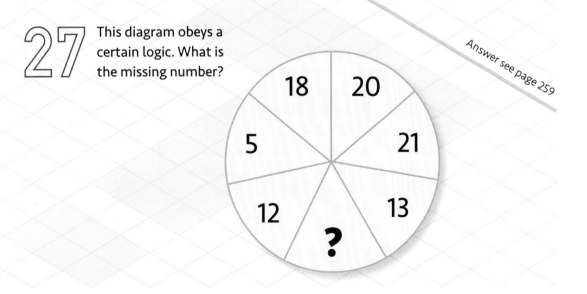

28 In this long division calculation, each digit has been consistently replaced with a symbol chosen at random. Can you discover the original calculation?

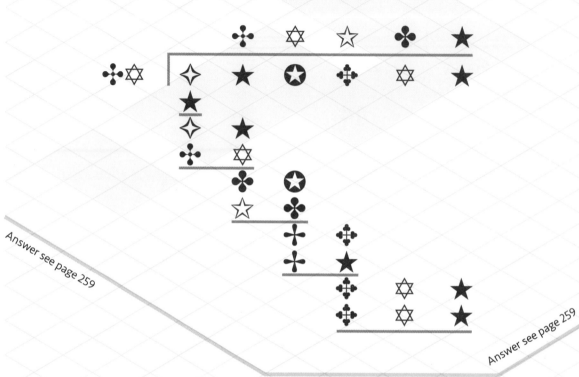

Answer see page 259

26

Answer see page 259

29 You come up with a theory, and ask three entirely separate scientists to evaluate how likely it is that you are correct. Each one works independently of the others, and there is no communication between them. After some time, you receive their reports. The first one says that the likelihood that you are correct is 80%. The second one also says that the likelihood that you are correct is 80%. Finally, the third one says the same as the other two – that the likelihood that you are correct is 80%.

What is the actual probability that your theory is correct?

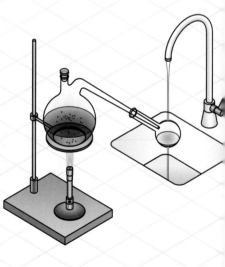

30 Which group of shapes, A-D, most closely corresponds with the
conditions of the large group of shapes above?

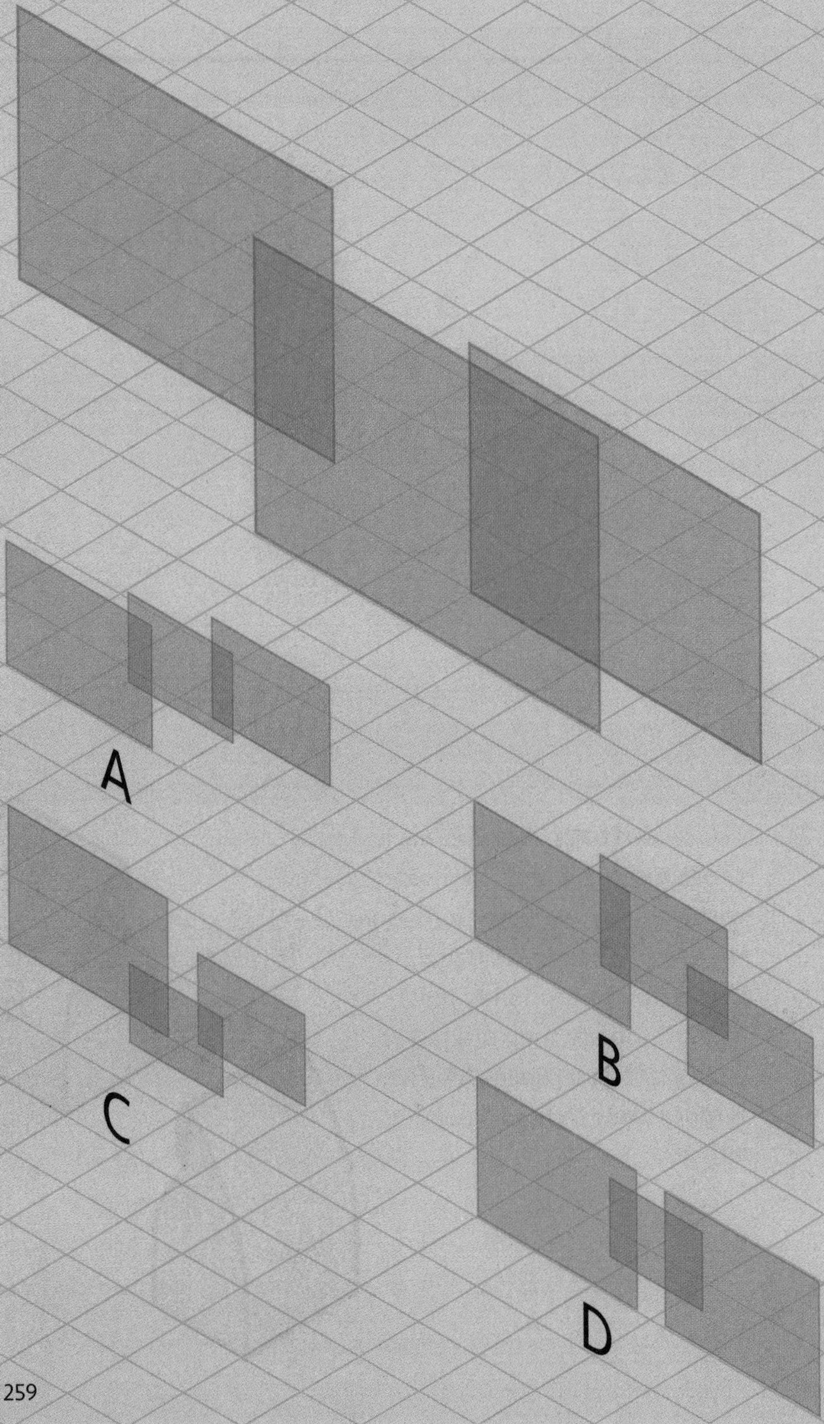

A

B

C

D

Answer see page 259

Following the logic of this diagram, what symbols should the triangle at the top contain?

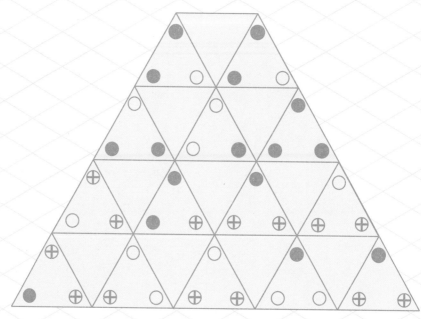

Answer see page 259

Answer see page 259

Two sealed bags, A and B, each contain either a bead or a pearl with equal probability. Someone then puts a pearl into bag B, shakes it, and randomly pulls out a pearl. You are then offered your choice of bag to open. Which is more likely to hold a pearl, if either?

33 The letters and numbers in this square obey a certain logic. What number should replace the question mark?

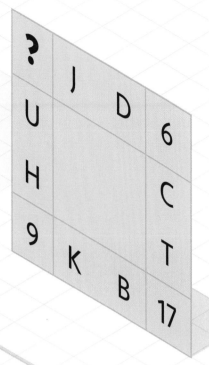

Answer see page 259

34 Imagine a very large piece of very thin paper, its thickness one tenth of a millimetre. Cut it in half, and place the two halves on top of each other. Then cut the two halves, and restack to make four pieces. Continue in this fashion until you have cut a total of fifty times, assuming one cut is always enough to halve the stack, and that you are likewise tall enough to combine the two resulting piles back into one stack.

Approximately how tall is your stack after fifty cuts?

Answer see page 259

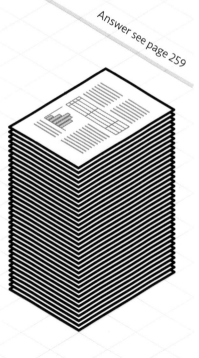

35 The following list of numbers represents cities whose letters have been encoded into the numbers needed to reproduce them on a typical phone dial. Can you decode them?

772 483

227 235 662

452 746 9

274 722 63

826 268 837

382 24

Answer see page 259

36 The word TROTTING is located exactly once in the grid below, but could be horizontally, vertically or diagonally forwards or backwards. Can you locate it?

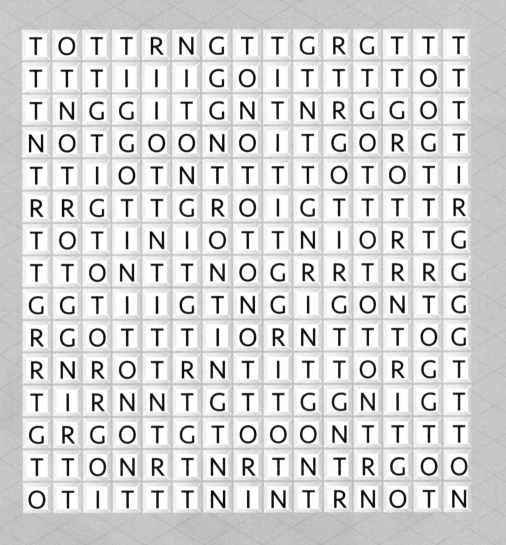

T O T T R N G T T G R G T T T
T T T I I I G O I T T T T O T
T N G G I T G N T N R G G O T
N O T G O O N O I T G O R G T
T T I O T N T T T T O T O T I
R R G T T G R O I G T T T R
T O T I N I O T T N I O R T G
T T O N T T N O G R R T R R G
G G T I I G T N G I G O N T G
R G O T T I O R N T T T O G
R N R O T R N T I T T O R G T
T I R N N T G T T G G N I G T
G R G O T G T O O O N T T T T
T T O N R T N R T N T R G O O
O T I T T T N I N T R N O T N

Answer see page 259

Can you uncover the logic of this grid of letters and replace the question mark with the right letter?

D	I	B
C	E	G
H	A	?

Answer see page 260

Answer see page 260

These 12-hour digital clocks follow a specific logic. Can you work out the time of the fifth clock?

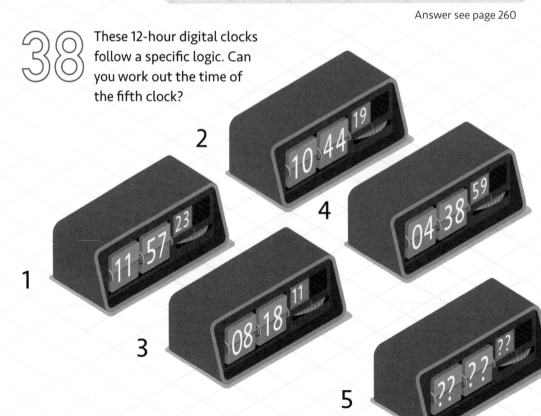

1 — 11 57 23

2 — 10 44 19

3 — 08 18 11

4 — 04 38 59

5 — ?? ?? ??

Look at the diagram to the right. What is the largest version of the same shape that can be drawn within the box so that none of its edges touch any other edges, or stray outside the box?

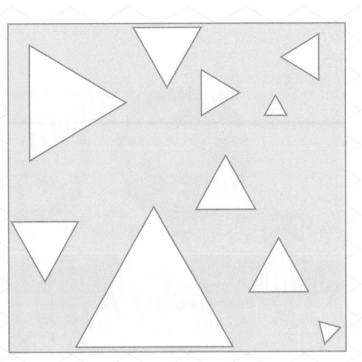

Answer see page 260

Answer see page 260

Three crooks are accused of a robbery. Each gives a statement, but only one of the statements is true.

Which one is telling the truth?

A: "B is lying."

B: "C is lying."

C: "A and B are both lying."

Figure #1 is to figure #2 as figure #3 is to which figure?

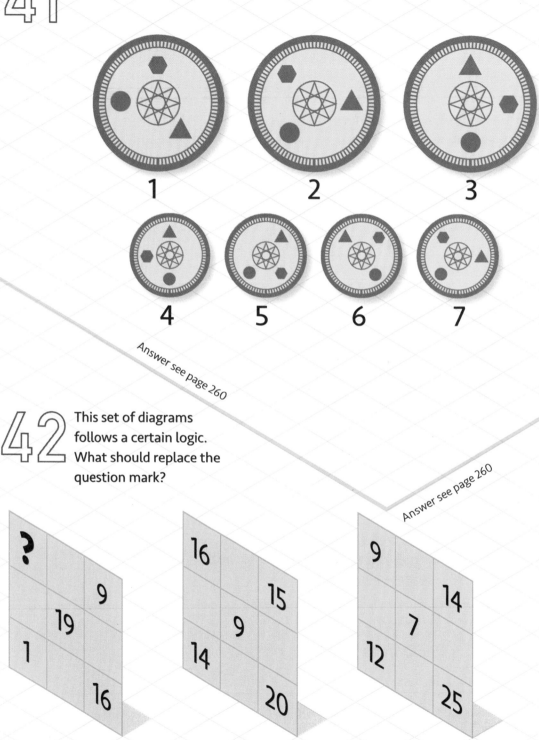

1   2   3

4   5   6   7

Answer see page 260

34

This set of diagrams follows a certain logic. What should replace the question mark?

Answer see page 260

?		
	19	9
1		16

16		
		15
	9	
14		20

9		
		14
	7	
12		25

43 To which of the lower shapes, A-E, could a single ball be added so that both balls matched the conditions of the balls in the upper shape?

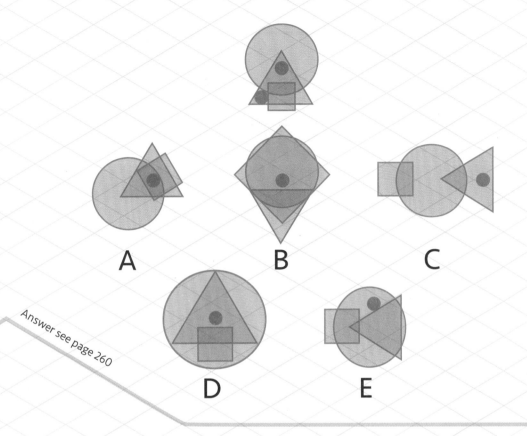

A

B

C

Answer see page 260

D

E

Answer see page 260

44 In a chess club of 60 people, 32 are female, 45 are adult, and 42 wear either glasses or contact lenses. What is the least possible number (not including zero) of people who fit all three categories?

45

Five people meet at a conference, and get talking.
What is the favourite food of the person who was born in Oregon?

The person from Vermont loved cherries, and was neither Margaret nor Otis. The person who said duck was their favourite food was an engineer, and was not named Bobbie, who was born in Ohio. The botanist was not named Hersh or Angie. The person who loved lamb was a researcher. The person who was born in Louisiana did not love chocolate. Angie, who was born in Arizona, was not an engineer. Margaret was a doctor, and was not born in Oregon. One of the group was a farmer, and another had bread as their favourite food.

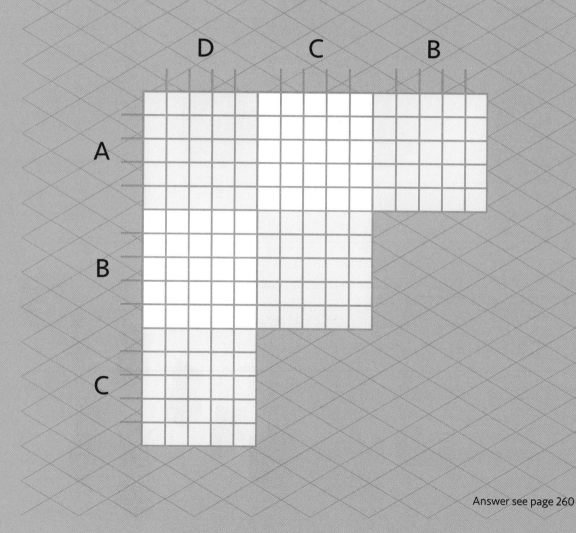

Answer see page 260

The diagram below operates according to a specific logic.
What should the missing square look like?

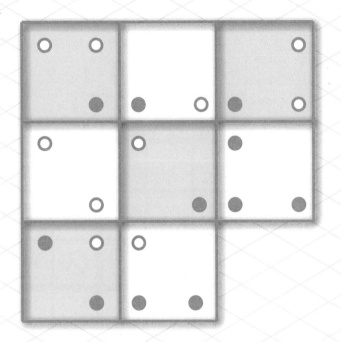

Answer see page 260

This set of diagrams follows a certain logic.
What should replace the question mark?

Answer see page 260

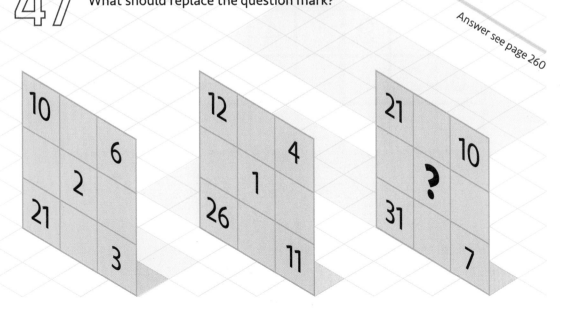

Answer see page 260

 Complete the grid so that:
- Each 9x9 row and column contains each digit from 1 to 9 once only
- Each 3x3 box contains each digit from 1 to 9 once only.

38

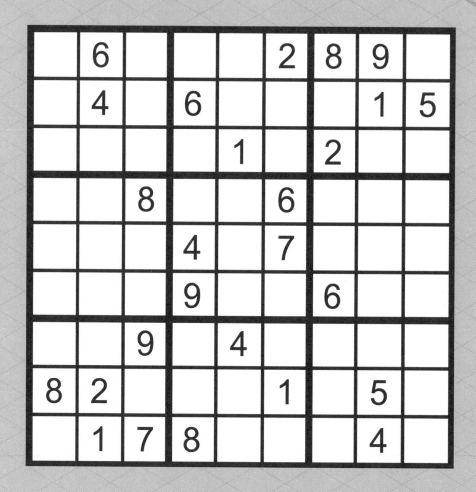

The following playwrights have had the vowels and spaces removed from their names. Can you untangle them?

STPHNPLKFF

SCRWLD

JHNNWLFGNGVNGTH

FDRCGRCLRC

LLLNHLLMN

GRGBRNRDSHW

NKLGGL

RSTPHNS

CHRSTPHRMRLW

SRHKN

Answer see page 260

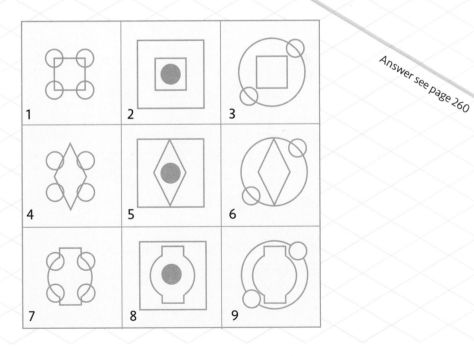

One of the squares in the 3x3 grid is incorrect. Which one?

Answer see page 260

1 2 3

4 5 6

7 8 9

Can you rearrange the digits in this equation to make it correct, without adding any mathematical operators?

4 2 6 = 1

Answer see page 260

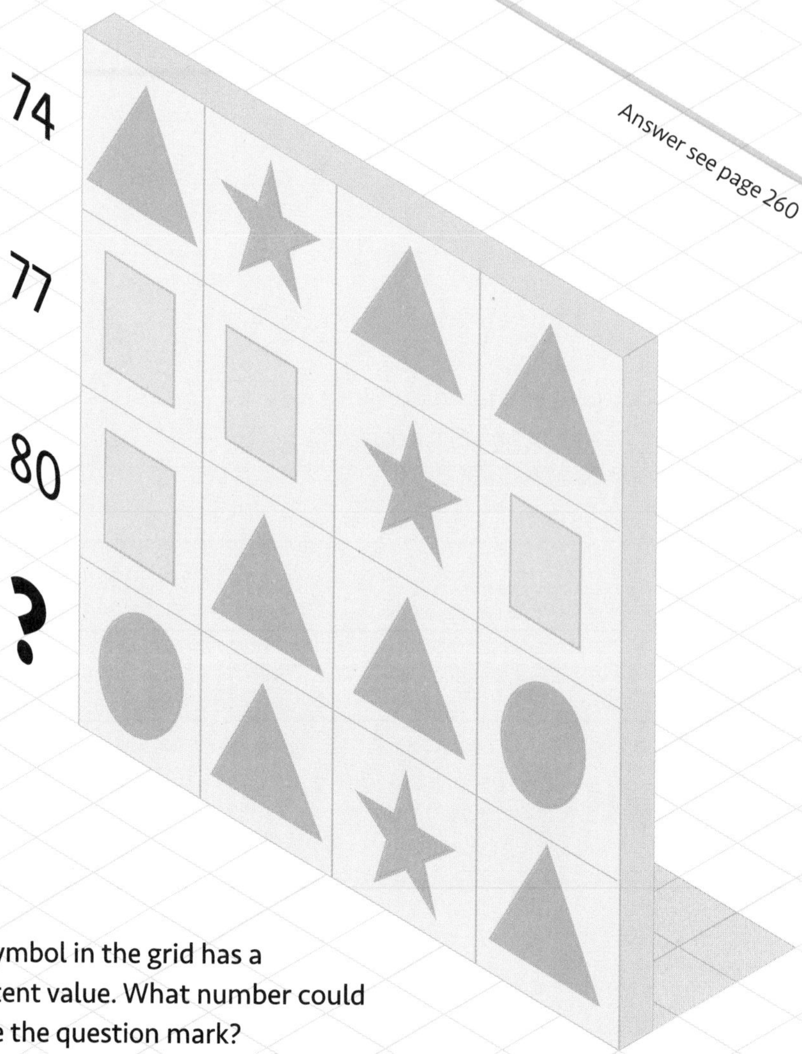

74

77

80

?

Answer see page 260

Each symbol in the grid has a consistent value. What number could replace the question mark?

Each square on this grid shows you the move you must make to arrive at the next square in the sequence, Left, Right, Up, and/or Down. So 3R would be three squares right, and 4UL would be 4 squares diagonally up and left. Your goal is to end up on the finish square, F, having visited every square exactly once. Can you find the starting square?

3R	1D	1L		
3D	3R	2D	2L	
2R	1UR	2L	3D	1L
3U	F	3L	3L	
1R	3R	2L	1UR	3U
	1U	1U	1R	2L

Answer see page 260

These clocks obey a specific sequence. What time should the missing hour hand on the fourth clock be pointing towards?

Answer see page 260

3

2

?

Which of these shapes is the odd one out?

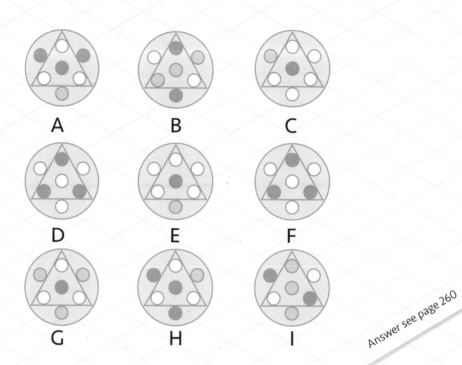

A

B

C

D

E

F

G

H

I

Answer see page 260

42

Answer see page 261

The following numbers obey a certain logic. What should replace the question mark?

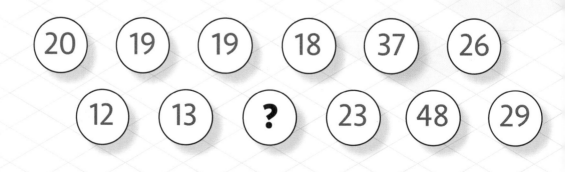

Starting at any corner, follow the paths until you have five numbers, including the one where you started. Do not backtrack. Add the five together. What is the highest number you can obtain?

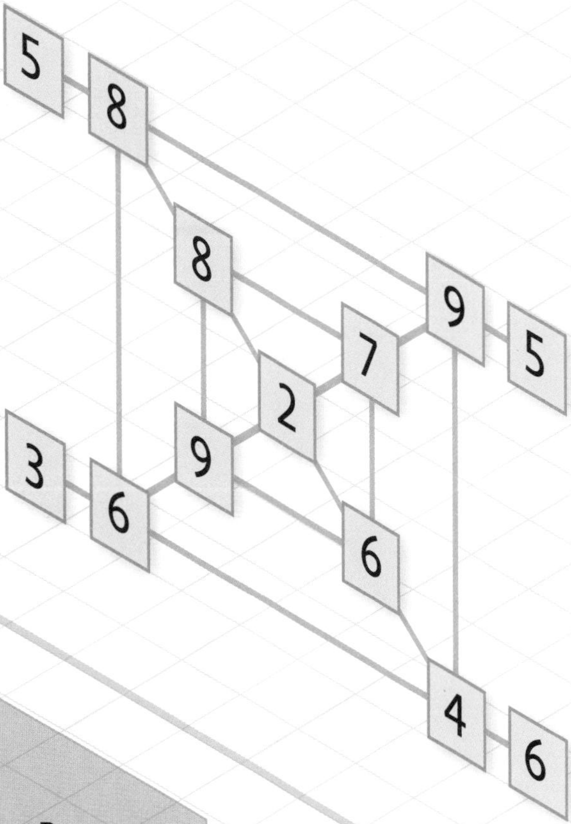

5 8
8
9 5
7
2
3 6 9
6
4 6

Answer see page 261

 The following design works according to a certain logic. What number should replace the question mark?

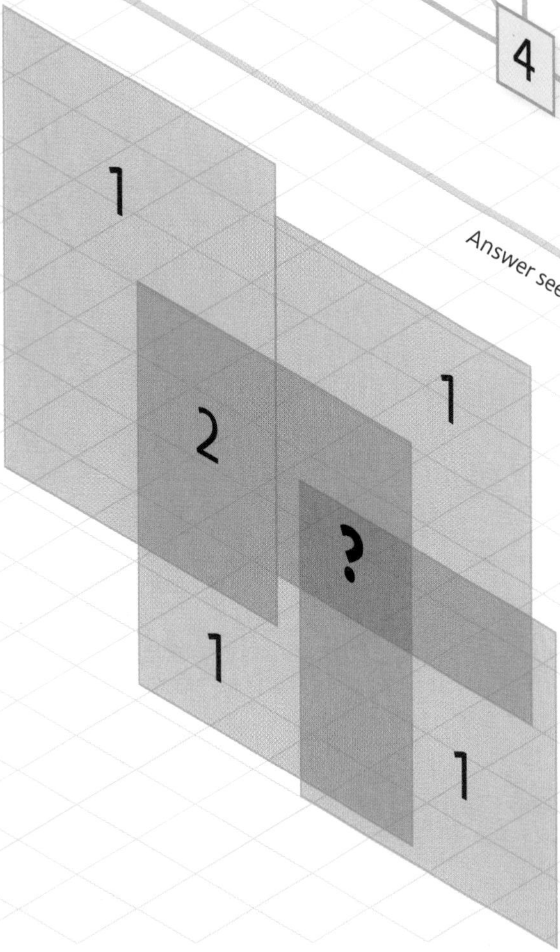

1
1
2
?
1
1

Answer see page 261

Answer see page 261

59

Four of these five pieces fit together to make a regular geometric shape. Which one is left over?

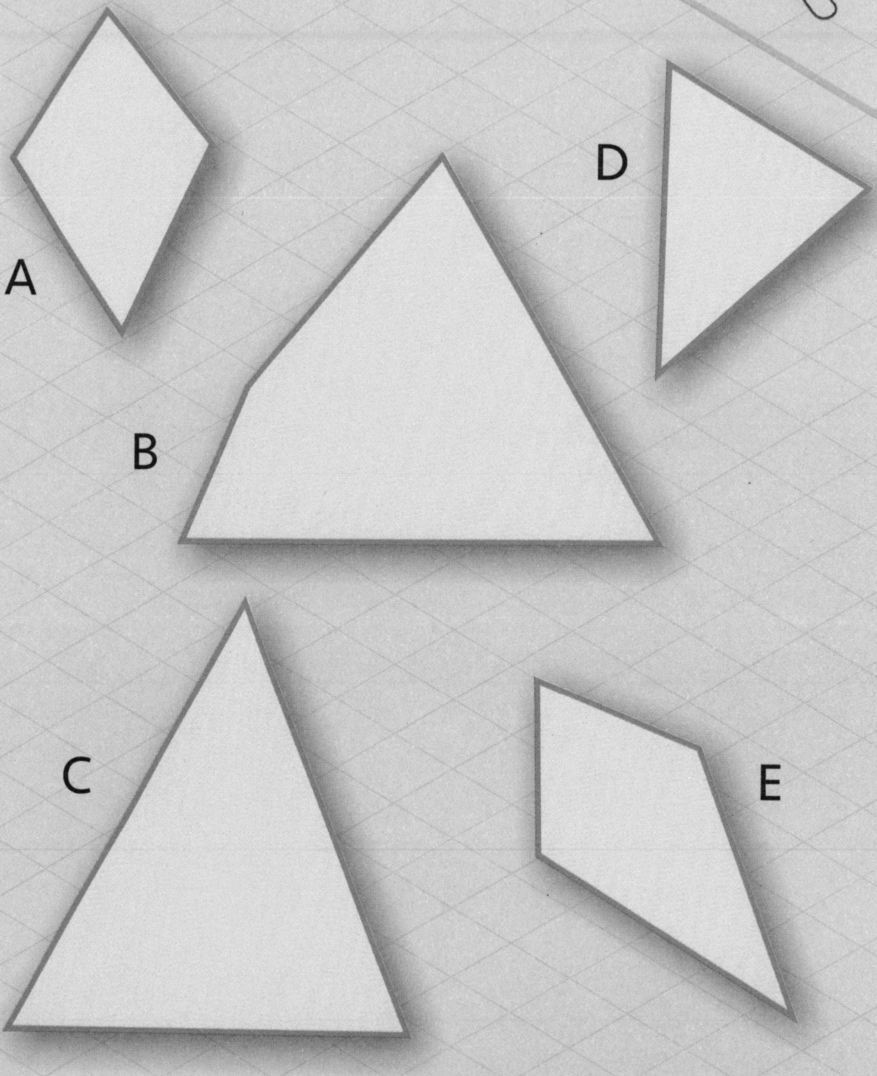

44

A

B

C

D

E

60

A race was run in four legs. Given the distances in kilometres of each leg, and the average speed in meters per second for that leg for the top five contestants, can you work out who won, and in what total time?

	Leg	A-B	B-C	C-D	D-E
Runner	Distance	4.5km	2.7km	3.3km	1.3km
V		4.4	3.3	4.8	5.1
W		4.7	2.9	4.4	5.0
X		4.1	3.7	4.3	5.1
Y		4.6	3.3	4.9	5.2
Z		4.5	3.4	4.6	5.1

Answer see page 261

61

Can you insert the mathematical operators + and – to make these equations valid?

Answer see page 261

12 ◯ 17 ◯ 9 ◯ 6 ◯ 14 = 12

26 ◯ 10 ◯ 4 ◯ 17 ◯ 11 = 14

15 ◯ 17 ◯ 9 ◯ 8 ◯ 13 = 16

62

Each of the circles below contains the name of a work of literature and its author. Can you unscramble them?

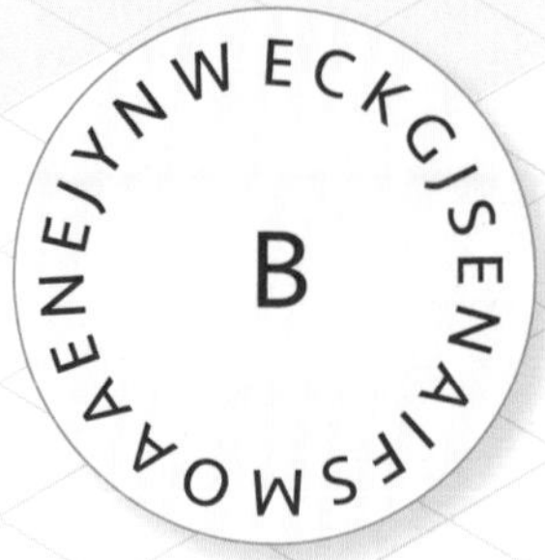

C

A

B

Answer see page 261

Answer see page 261

46

63

If Kelly likes rugby, Amarantha likes decathlon, and Jocasta likes sailing, which sport does Millie like?

A. Athletics

B. Snooker

C. Football

D. Tennis

E. Surfing

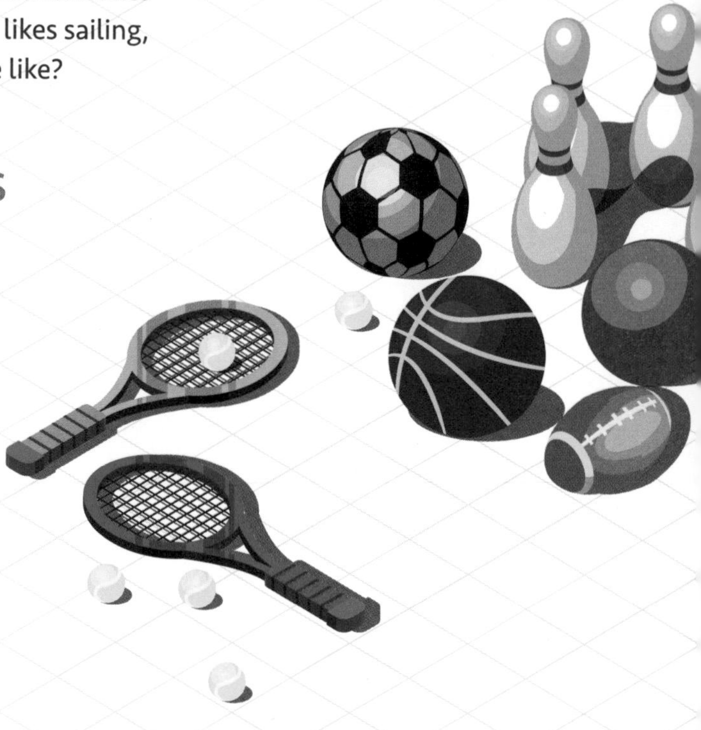

64

What weight will balance the beam?

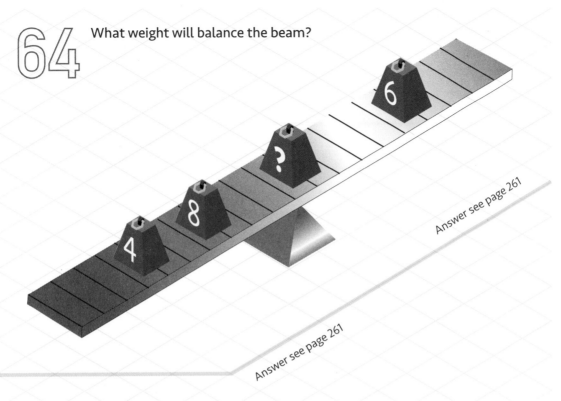

Answer see page 261

Answer see page 261

65

The matchstick diagram below shows five equal squares.
Can you move 2 matchsticks to show just four equal squares?

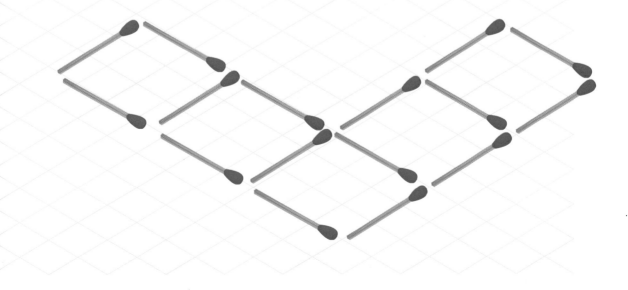

Examine the top three shapes.
Which of the five options A-E
continues the sequence?

Answer see page 261

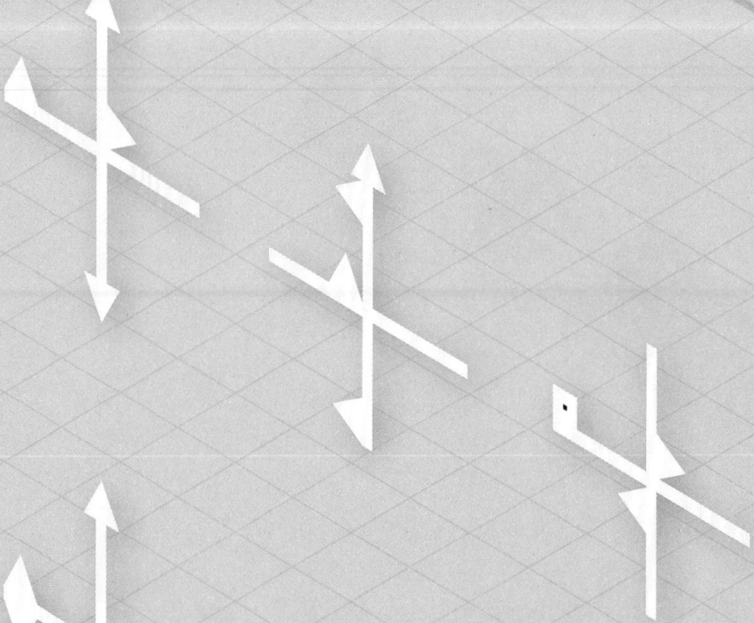

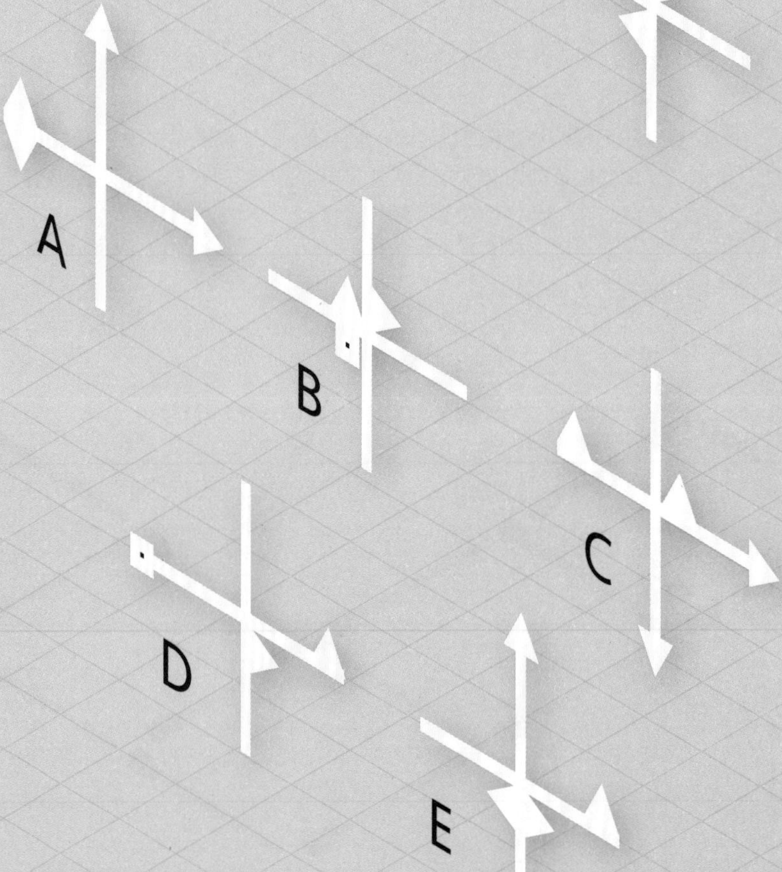

48

A

B

C

D

E

67 These rings obey a certain logic. What number should replace the question mark?

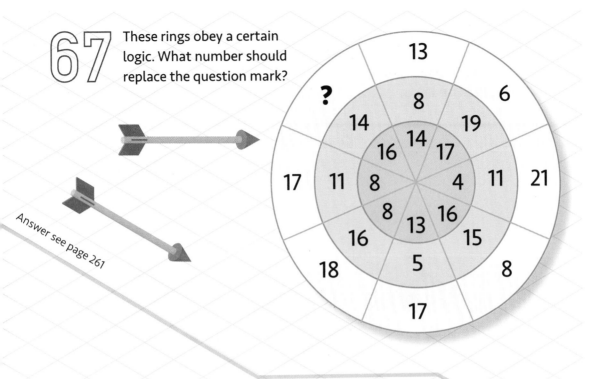

Answer see page 261

68 These triangles follow a certain specific logic. What number should replace the question mark?

49

Answer see page 261

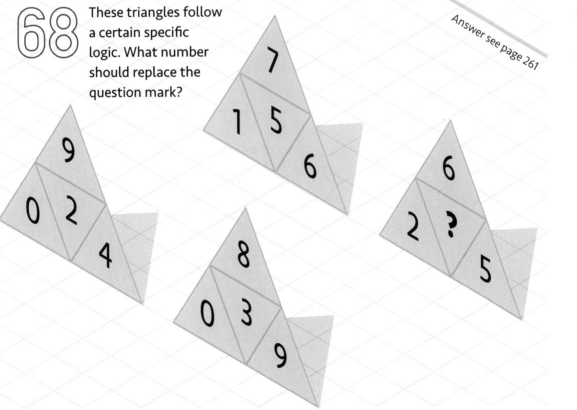

69 Which two cubes show three identical faces to each other?

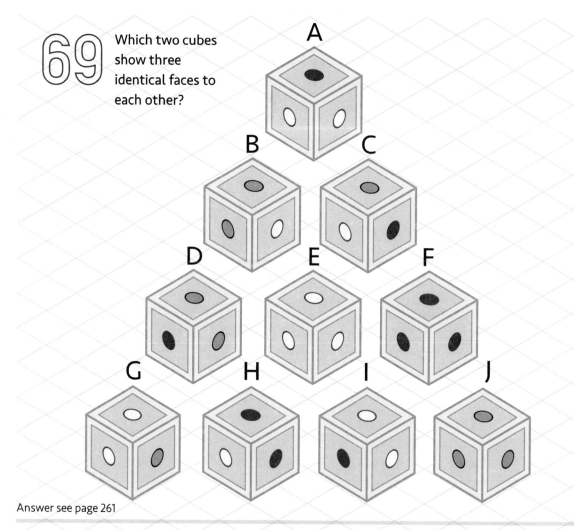

A

B   C

D   E   F

G   H   I   J

Answer see page 261

Answer see page 261

70 Fill in the missing plus, minus, multiplication, division, and/or factorial signs to make the equation below correct, performing all calculations strictly in the order they appear on the page.

21 11 18 5 15 21 4 = 59

71

What number should replace the question mark?

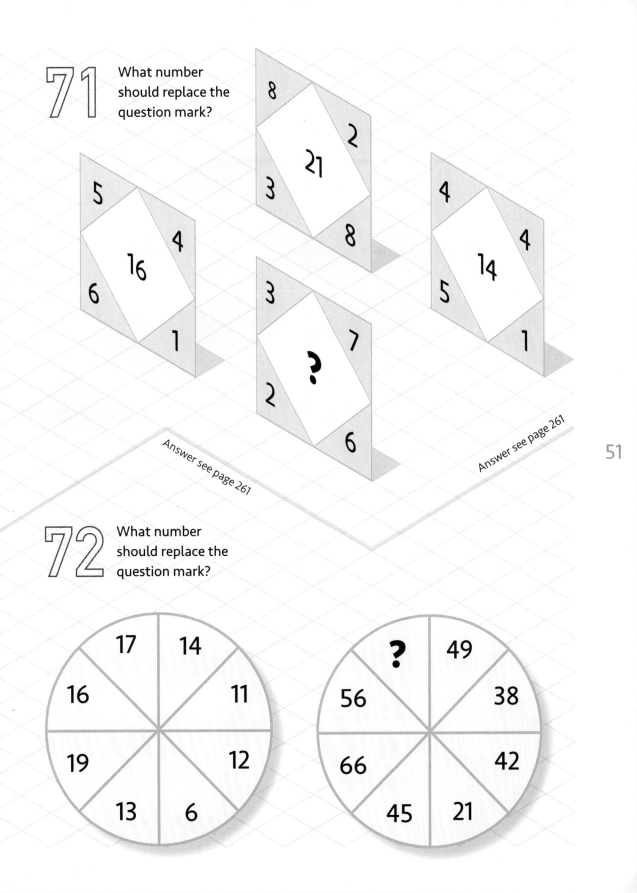

8 2 21 3 8

5 4 16 6 1

3 7 ? 2 6

4 4 14 5 1

Answer see page 261

Answer see page 261

72

What number should replace the question mark?

17 14 16 11 19 12 13 6

? 49 56 38 66 42 45 21

73 In the grid below, how much is each symbol worth?

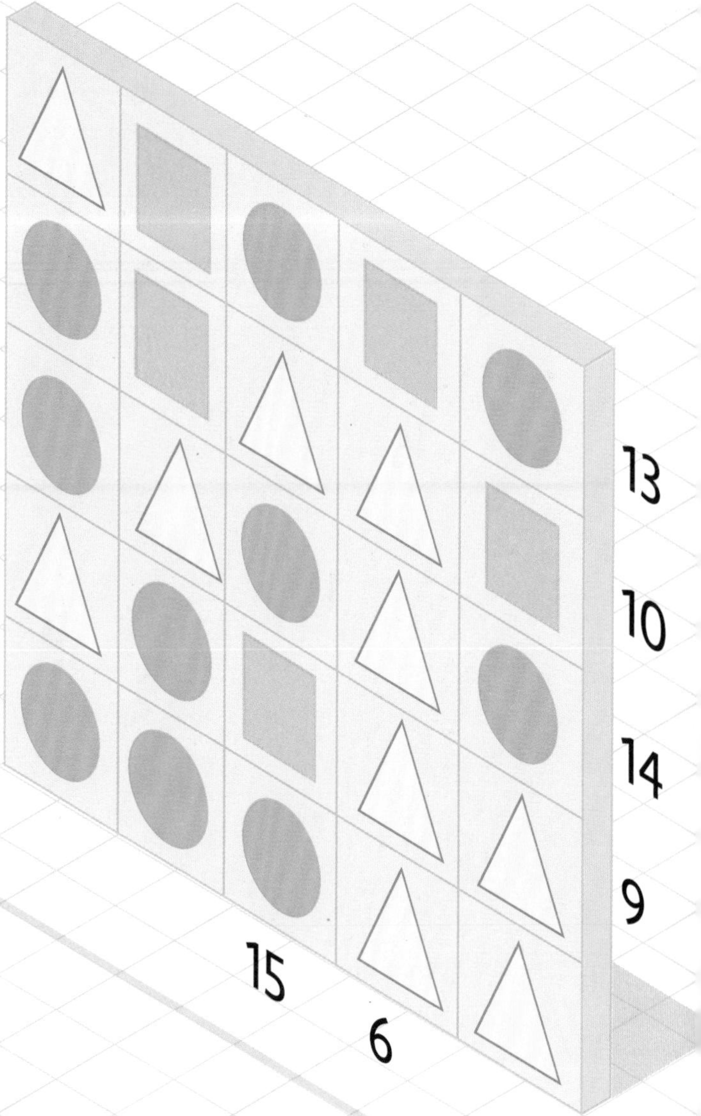

13

10

14

9

15

6

Answer see page 261

52

74 The pieces can be assembled into a regular geometric shape. What is it?

Answer see page 261

Decipher the names of several celebrities using the telephone dial as a guide.

326435723254333

62825437678626

268664622633727

2723539266737

4255323779

5623279268

Answer see page 261

Assemble the pieces shown below into a square grid which reads the same across as it does downwards.

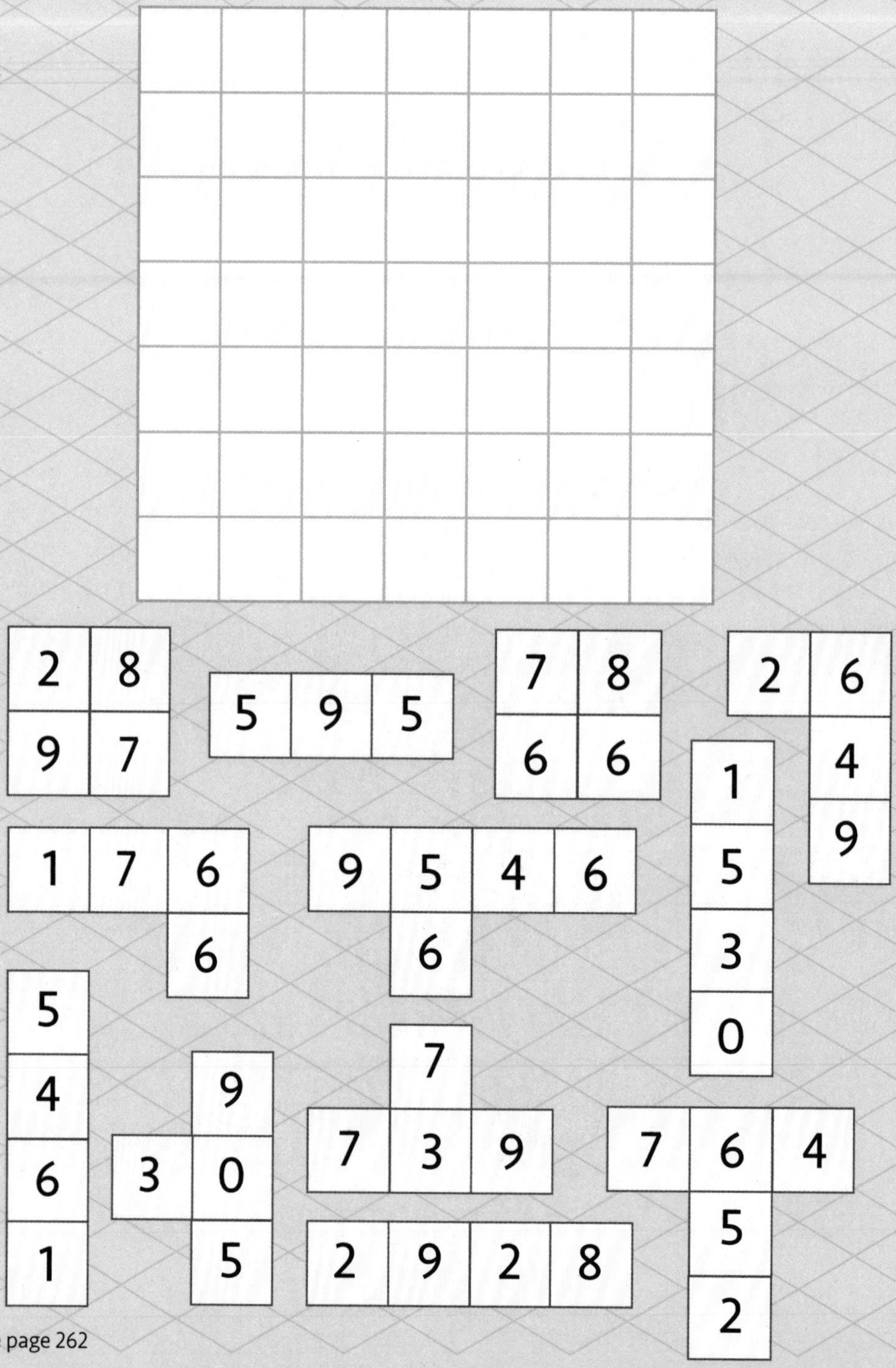

54

| 2 | 8 |
| 9 | 7 |

| 5 | 9 | 5 |

| 7 | 8 |
| 6 | 6 |

2	6
	4
	9

| 1 |
| 5 |
| 3 |
| 0 |

| 1 | 7 | 6 |
| | | 6 |

| 9 | 5 | 4 | 6 |
| | 6 | | |

| 5 |
| 4 |
| 6 |
| 1 |

| 9 |
| 3 | 0 |
| | 5 |

| 7 |
| 7 | 3 | 9 |
| 2 | 9 | 2 | 8 |

7	6	4
	5	
	2	

Answer see page 262

77 Fill in the missing plus, minus, multiplication, division, and/or factorial signs to make the equation below correct, performing all calculations strictly in the order they appear on the page.

(3) (14) (22) (11) (3) (24) (17) = (24)

Answer see page 262

78 In each square, the arrow shows the direction you must move in. The numbers in some squares show that square's position in the correct sequence of moves. Move from top left to bottom right, visiting each square in the grid exactly once.

Answer see page 262

Answer see page 262

79 James likes iris but not peony. Nicole likes rose but not aster. Heather likes sunflower but not lily. Which of the following does Steven like?

LILAC   HYDRANGEA

CARNATION   TULIP

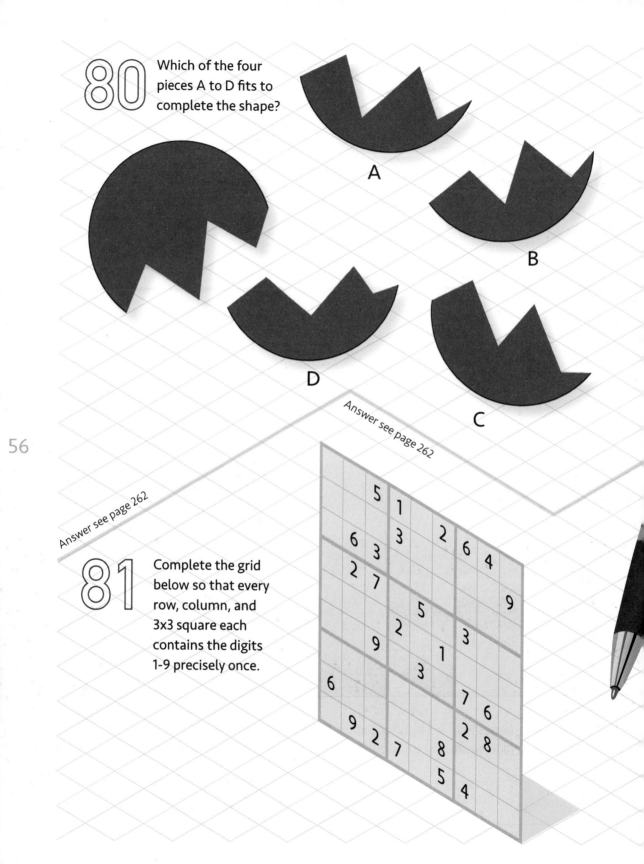

80 Which of the four pieces A to D fits to complete the shape?

A

B

C

D

Answer see page 262

56

Answer see page 262

81 Complete the grid below so that every row, column, and 3x3 square each contains the digits 1-9 precisely once.

		5	1					
	6	3		2	6	4		
	2	7						9
			5		3			
		9	2	1				
6			3			7		
	9	2			2	6		
			7	8			8	
				5	4			

82

Connect each pair of identical numbers with a single continuous path running horizontally and/or vertically through the cells of the grid below. Paths may switch direction at the centre of a cell, but may not branch, loop back on themselves, or cross. When the grid is complete, each cell will contain a single path section.

Answer see page 262

83

Are the following statements true or false?

Answer see page 262

i. The blue-ringed octopus is one of only two octopus species deadly to mankind.
ii. Playing cards were invented around 1200 years ago in China.
iii. Arcturus is the brightest star in the constellation of Boötes.
iv. Helium is the most common substance in the universe.
v. Antwerp is a city in Belgium.
vi. Pansies used to be known as "Love in Idleness".
vii. Jan Tyssowski was a former dictator of Yugoslavia.
viii. Swords were invented in South America more than 3000 years ago.
ix. 1000 is a square number.
x. Phoenix is the capital of Arizona.

84 The grid below shows the numbers on a full set of dominoes, from 0-0 to 9-9 inclusive, that have been pushed together horizontally and vertically to make a solid rectangle. Complete the grid to show where each domino lies.

Answer see page 262

2	4	9	5	5	0	6	7	6	6	9
7	5	1	2	7	3	3	0	8	8	9
4	4	9	1	4	4	1	2	4	2	3
5	9	8	9	6	5	2	3	5	3	8
5	0	1	6	5	0	4	0	2	7	8
0	7	1	4	0	4	3	5	6	2	1
9	7	5	9	2	2	0	9	0	2	6
6	5	7	7	6	4	0	3	7	3	3
9	2	8	3	5	5	2	6	0	1	1
6	8	3	3	2	0	0	7	1	4	4

Answer see page 262

85 The pieces can be assembled into a regular geometric shape. What is it?

86 Shade the cells in the grid below so that each row and column holds continuous lines of shaded cells of the lengths indicated by the numbers shown at the start of that row or column. Blocks are separated from others in the same row or column by at least one empty cell. A picture will emerge when the cells are shaded correctly.

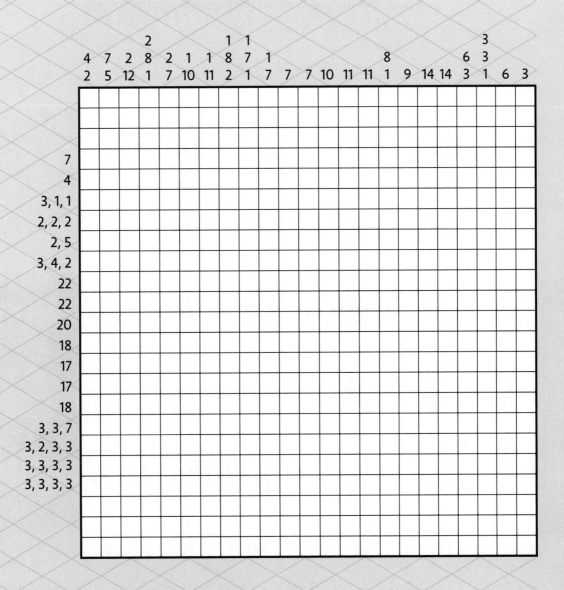

59

Answer see page 262

87

Ten vessels are hidden in the grid below, four one-cell ships, three two-cell ships, two three-cell ships, and one four-cell ship. Ships are positioned horizontally or vertically. No two ships are immediately adjacent to each other, including diagonally. The numbers next to each row and column show the total number of ship segments in that line. Identify the exact locations of all ten vessels. Some ship segments and/or spaces of empty ocean are shown to assist you.

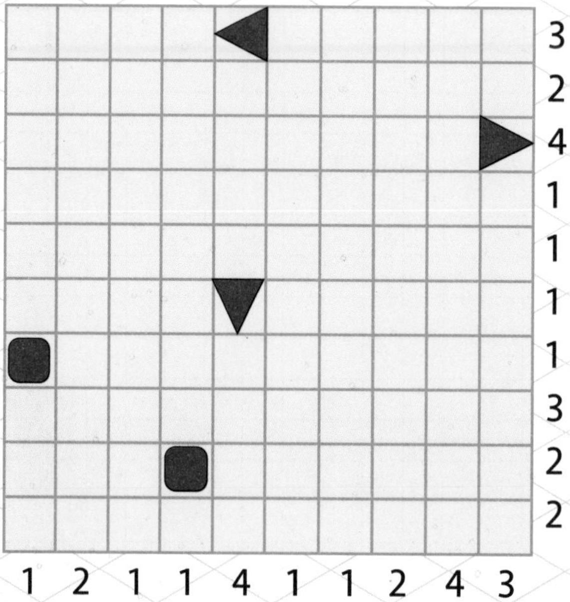
3
2
4
1
1
1
1
3
2
2
1 2 1 1 4 1 1 2 4 3

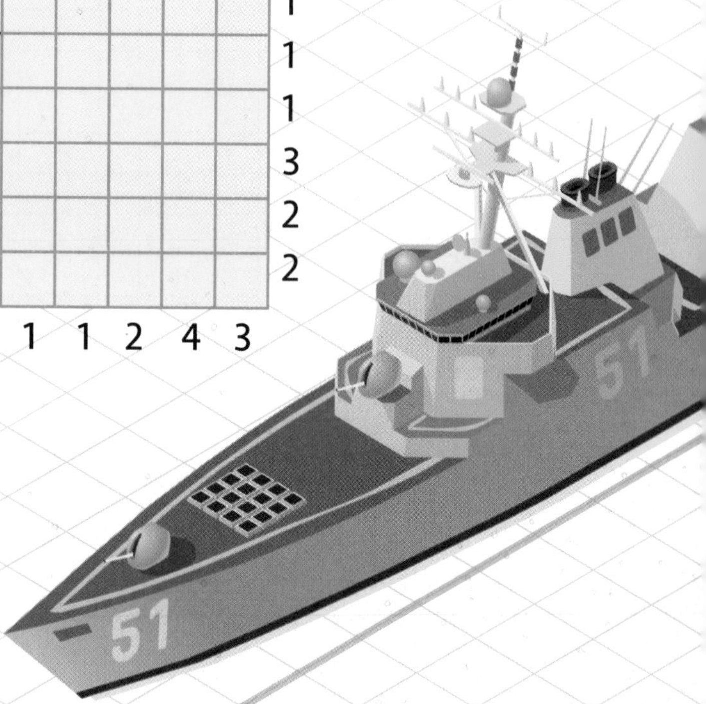
51
51

Answer see page 262

88 Complete the grid below so that every row and column each contains the digits 1-6 precisely once. A cell with a chevron pointing into it is smaller than the cell on the other side of the chevron.

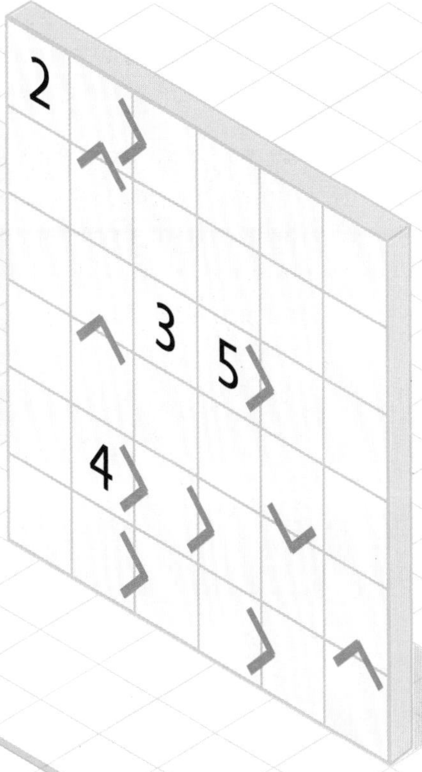

2

3 5

4

Answer see page 263

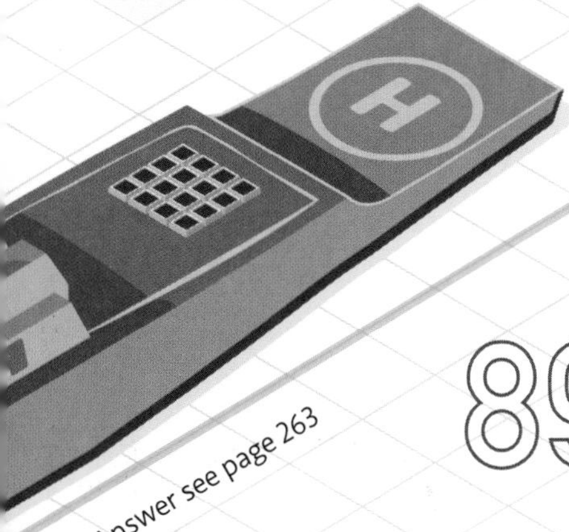

61

89 What number should replace the question mark?

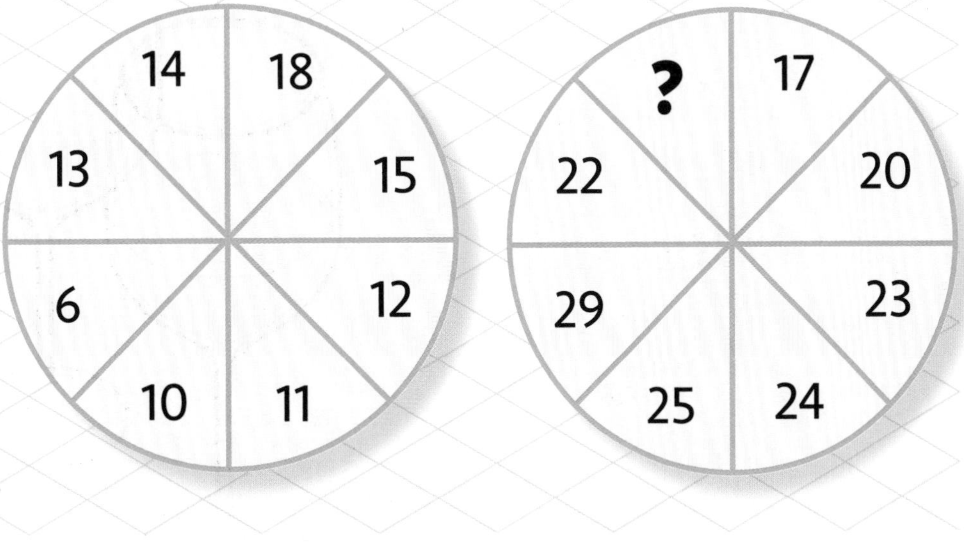

Answer see page 263

14 18
13   15
6   12
10 11

?   17
22   20
29   23
25 24

90

From the information below, what is the name of the merchant who likes Bordeaux?

The merchant from Paris liked wines from Alsace, but was not the blacksmith, who was named Georges. Michel, a goldsmith, was not a fan of Alsace wine. The merchant from Reims enjoyed Bordeaux wine. One of the merchants preferred to drink Burgundy. The whitesmith from Rouen was neither Jacques nor Veronique. The merchant who preferred Champagne was not named Iva or Michel. Jacques liked Beaujolais, and was not a tinsmith. The merchant from Bagnol was not a greensmith. One of the merchants was from Aix.

62

Answer see page 263

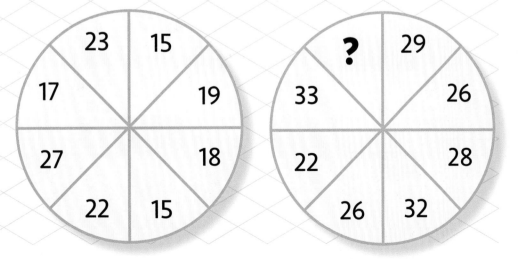

9 1 Using six straight lines, which must each touch at least one edge of the box, divide the design below into seven sections, each containing precisely nine circles.

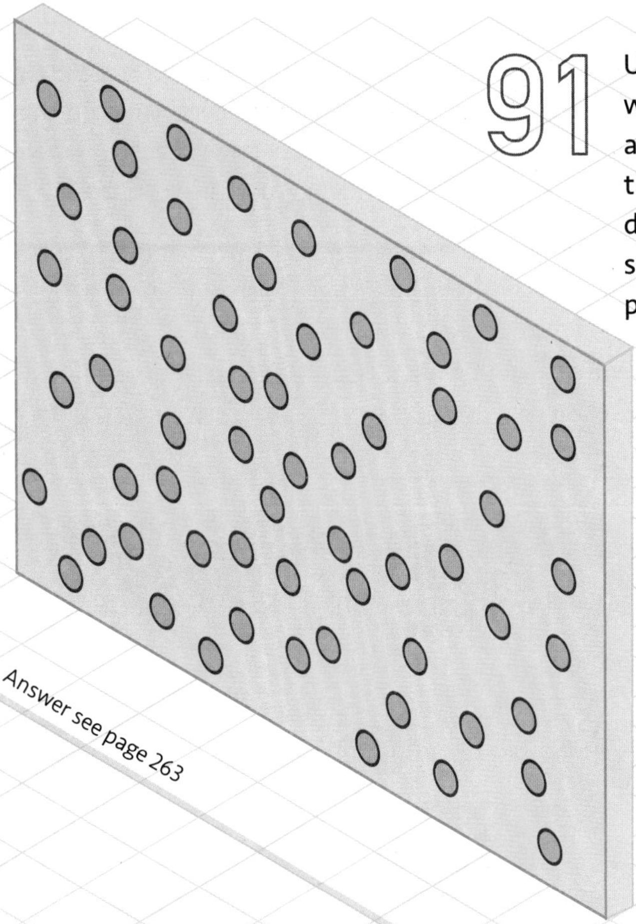

Answer see page 263

Answer see page 263

63

9 2 What number should replace the question mark?

Left circle: 23, 15, 17, 19, 27, 18, 22, 15

Right circle: ?, 29, 33, 26, 22, 28, 26, 32

93

Complete the grid below so that each unbroken horizontal and vertical stretch of light cells sums to the total indicated in the cell to the left or above the stretch respectively. Each cell may contain only the digits 1 – 9, and no digit may be repeated in any given stretch of cells.

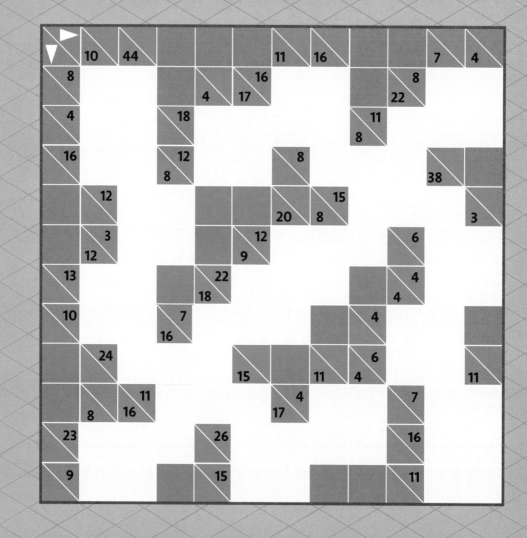

64

Answer see page 263

Which of the four pieces A to D fits to complete the shape?

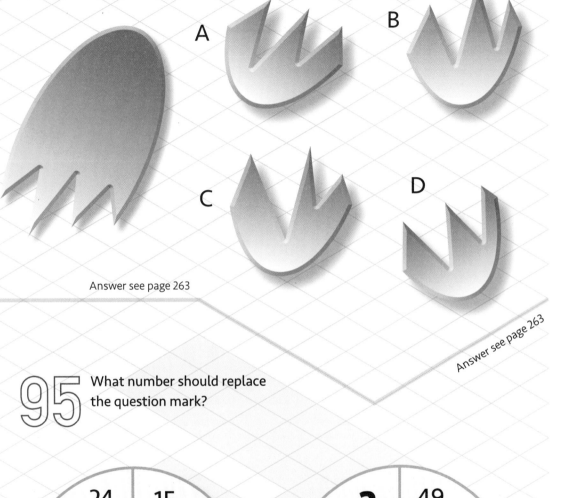

A

B

C

D

Answer see page 263

Answer see page 263

What number should replace the question mark?

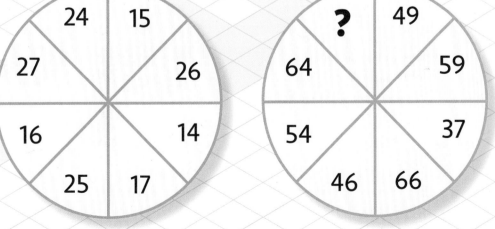

24	15
27	26
16	14
25	17

?	49
64	59
54	37
46	66

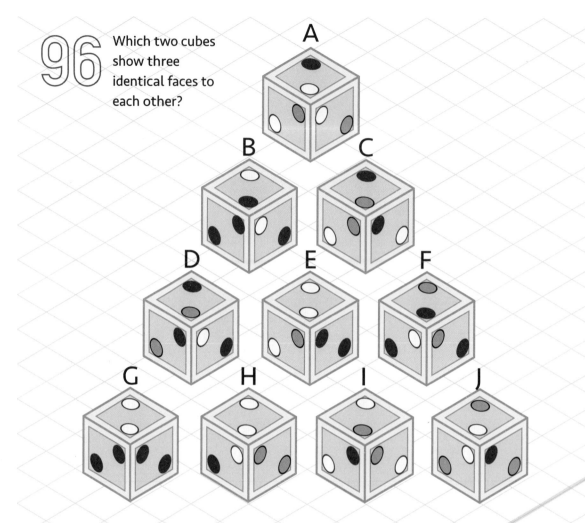

96 Which two cubes show three identical faces to each other?

A

B C

D E F

G H I J

Answer see page 263

Answer see page 263

97 Andrew likes amethyst but not sapphire. Tina likes turquoise but not onyx. Peter likes pearl but not topaz. Which of the following does Diana like?

RUBY
EMERALD

DIAMOND
AQUAMARINE

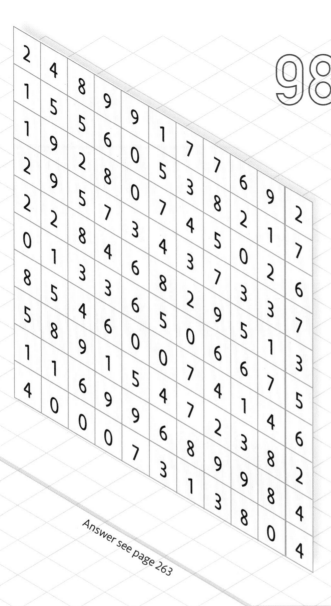

The grid below shows the numbers on a full set of dominoes, from 0-0 to 9-9 inclusive, that have been pushed together horizontally and vertically to make a solid rectangle. Complete the grid to show where each domino lies.

The grid contents:

2	4	8	9	9	1	7	7	6	9	2
1	5	5	6	0	5	3	8	2	1	7
1	9	2	8	0	7	4	5	0	2	6
2	9	5	7	3	4	3	7	3	3	7
2	2	8	4	6	3	2	9	5	1	3
0	1	3	6	8	2	7	5	6	7	5
8	5	3	6	5	0	9	6	6	4	6
5	8	4	0	0	6	5	1	1	2	2
1	1	9	1	7	7	6	3	4	3	4
4	0	6	5	4	4	6	7	8	8	0
	0	0	9	6	7	1	3	9		
		0	7	8	2	4	8	8		
			3	1	9	3	0			

Answer see page 263

67

Answer see page 263

Fill in the missing plus, minus, multiplication, division, and/or factorial signs to make the equation below correct, performing all calculations strictly in the order they appear on the page.

$$17 \quad 25 \quad 19 \quad 15 \quad 4 \quad 23 \quad 8 = 72$$

100 Connect each pair of identical numbers with a single continuous path running horizontally and/or vertically through the cells of the grid below. Paths may switch direction at the centre of a cell, but may not branch, loop back on themselves, or cross. When the grid is complete, each cell will contain a single path section.

Answer see page 263

Answer see page 263

101 Which of the four pieces A to D fits to complete the shape?

A

B

C

D

68

102 Tracey likes aquamarine but not beige. Jeffrey likes firebrick but not gold. Susan likes sienna but not khaki. Which of the following does William like?

PURPLE   IVORY

LAVENDER   OLIVE

Answer see page 263

103

Complete the grid below so that each unbroken horizontal and vertical stretch of light cells sums to the total indicated in the cell to the left or above the stretch respectively. Each cell may contain only the digits 1 – 9, and no digit may be repeated in any given stretch of cells.

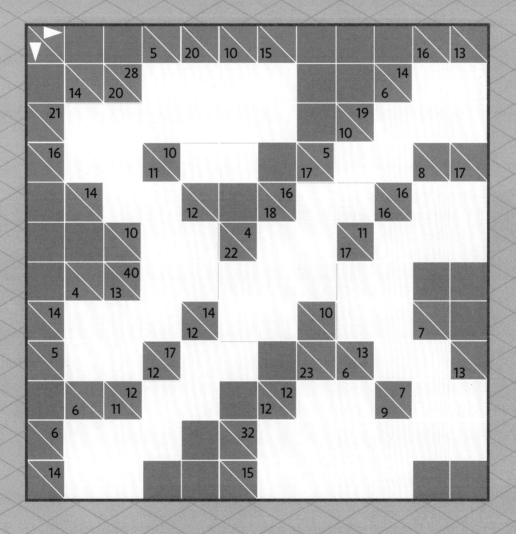

69

Answer see page 264

What number should replace the question mark?

8

4

10

7

5

7

5

9

2

6

6

4

3

8

4

9

5

?

4

5

5

Answer see page 264

Answer see page 264

70

Are the following statements true or false?

i. 46 is a hexagonal number.
ii. Capella is the brightest star in the constellation of Auriga.
iii. Colonel Saye Zerbo was a former ruler of Oman.
iv. Dallas is the capital of Texas.
v. Donetsk is a city in the Ukraine.
vi. Magnesium is named after an area in Greece.
vii. Negative numbers were invented in Arabia 1200 years ago.
viii. Solo is a card game for four players.
ix. The floral genus Aquilegia is better known as the foxgloves.
x. There are five species of mammal that lay eggs.

106 Decipher the names of several celebrities using the telephone dial as a guide.

25722466

52534955364225

94553377355

63426369

72683555225766

86642657

Answer see page 264

107

Shade the cells in the grid below so that each row and column holds continuous lines of shaded cells of the lengths indicated by the numbers shown at the start of that row or column. Blocks are separated from others in the same row or column by at least one empty cell. A picture will emerge when the cells are shaded correctly.

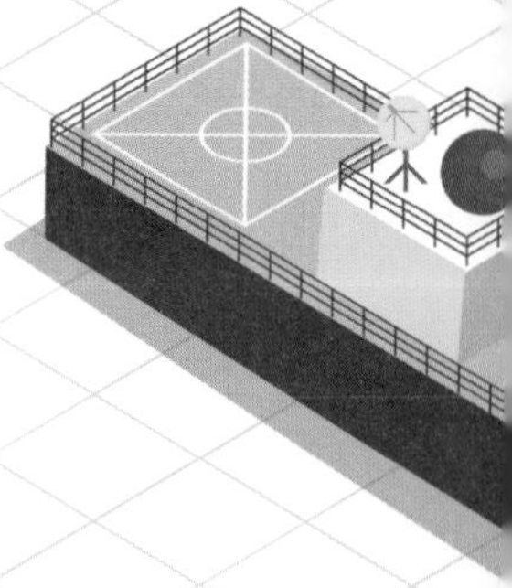

Answer see page 264

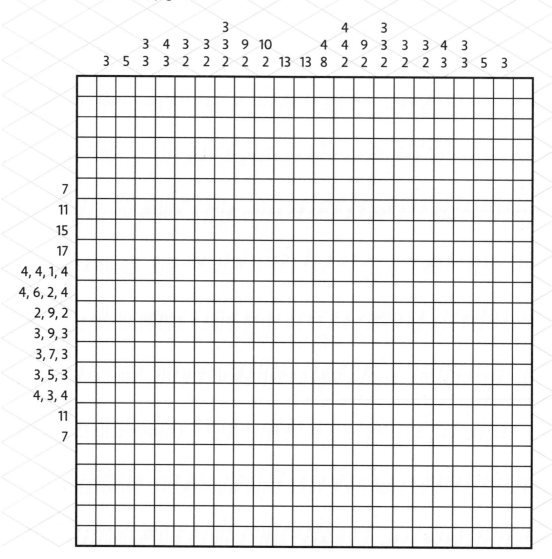

Column clues (left to right):

						3						4		3						
		3	4	3	3	3	9	10			4	4	9	3	3	3	4	3		
3	5	3	3	2	2	2	2	2	13	13	8	2	2	2	2	2	3	3	5	3

Row clues (top to bottom):

7
11
15
17
4, 4, 1, 4
4, 6, 2, 4
2, 9, 2
3, 9, 3
3, 7, 3
3, 5, 3
4, 3, 4
11
7

108

Ten vessels are hidden in the grid below, four one-cell ships, three two-cell ships, two three-cell ships, and one four-cell ship. Ships are positioned horizontally or vertically. No two ships are immediately adjacent to each other, including diagonally. The numbers next to each row and column show the total number of ship segments in that line. Identify the exact locations of all ten vessels. Some ship segments and/or spaces of empty ocean are shown to assist you.

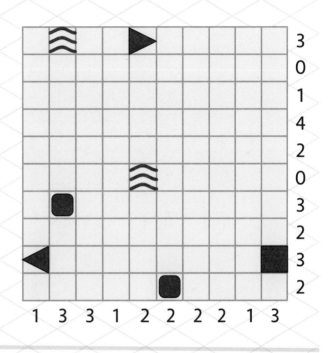

Answer see page 264

73

Answer see page 264

109

The pieces can be assembled into a regular geometric shape. What is it?

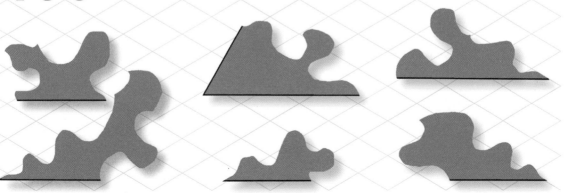

110

The grid below shows the numbers on a full set of dominoes, from 0-0 to 9-9 inclusive, that have been pushed together horizontally and vertically to make a solid rectangle. Complete the grid to show where each domino lies.

Answer see page 264

9	9	1	2	0	8	2	1	1	8	6
3	7	4	3	3	7	1	2	0	8	6
6	9	5	6	3	9	4	7	4	8	6
0	1	9	7	7	3	2	9	0	4	8
5	6	3	2	8	4	9	0	1	4	1
6	0	5	5	0	2	0	3	1	9	5
5	5	2	7	8	6	4	2	9	1	8
3	8	2	7	3	2	0	1	3	0	9
6	4	4	2	2	0	8	9	7	7	
0	0	7	5	1	6	8	3	8	6	4	3

111

Caroline likes penguins but not finches. Philip likes cranes but not owls. Harmony likes parrots but not hummingbirds. Which of the following does Mellissa like?

Answer see page 264

SWALLOWS

SWIFTS

CUCKOOS

WOODPECKERS

112

What number should replace the question mark?

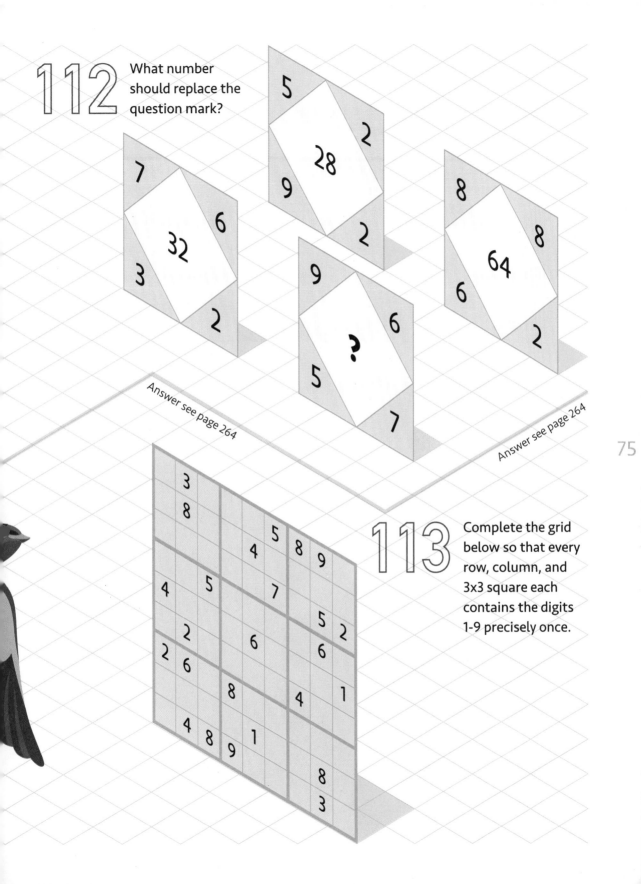

5
2
28
9
2

7
6
32
3
2

9
6
?
5
7

8
8
64
6
2

Answer see page 264

Answer see page 264

113

Complete the grid below so that every row, column, and 3x3 square each contains the digits 1-9 precisely once.

	3							
	8			5	8	9		
			4					
4		5		7				
	2		6			5	2	
2	6					6		
		8		4			1	
	4	8	9	1				
						8	3	

114

Complete the grid below so that every row, column, and 3x3 square each contains the digits 1-9 precisely once. The sum of the digits in each group of cells with a dotted outline must total the number in the group's top left corner.

12	11		6		12		11	
	9	9		18	12		8	
9		13				14		17
			11			14		
12	6		16	4	14		8	
	17					3		11
7		14	10		25	7		
17			9			10		21
		8						

Answer see page 265

Answer see page 264

115

In the grid below, how much is each symbol worth?

116

Complete the grid below so that each unbroken horizontal and vertical stretch of light cells sums to the total indicated in the cell to the left or above the stretch respectively. Each cell may contain only the digits 1 – 9, and no digit may be repeated in any given stretch of cells.

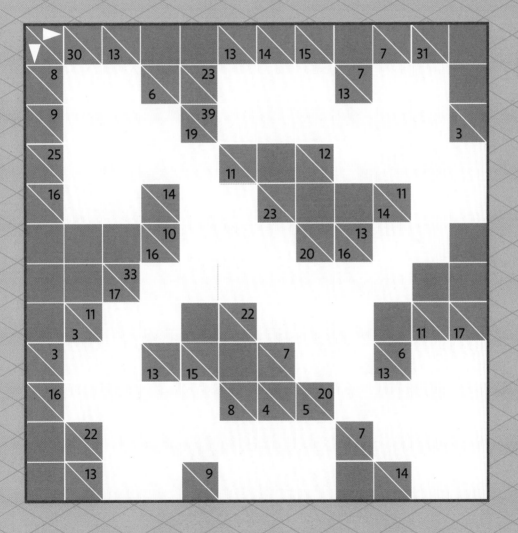

Answer see page 265

Decipher the names of several celebrities using the telephone dial as a guide.

7437232767626
62228529285546
675263625666
53472564448539
366278663
787735527693

Answer see page 265

118 Using four straight lines, divide the design below into seven sections, each containing precisely eight circles.

Answer see page 265

Answer see page 265

119 Are the following statements true or false?

i. Deneb is the brightest star in the constellation of Crux.
ii. Jorge Montt was a former ruler of Algeria.
iii. Match-sticks were invented in China 1400 years ago.
iv. Minsk is a city in Lithuania.
v. Promethium is the only element with no stable isotope.
vi. Providence is the capital of Rhode Island.
vii. Rummy is a trick-taking card game.
viii. The Aztec people called armadillos 'Turtle-Rabbits'.
ix. The English daisy, Bellis perennis, does not close up at night.
x. The numbers (20, 99, 101) form a Pythagorean triple.

120 From the information below, what was the favourite food of the person who was born in California?

The person who said tofu was their favourite food was a teacher, and was not the auburn-haired person, who was born in Wales. The person from Cyprus loved cherries, and was neither blonde nor grey-haired. One of the group was a therapist, and another had fresh bread as their favourite food. The person who loved lamb was a counsellor. The nurse was neither bald nor black-haired. The person who was born in Provence did not love chocolate. The bald person, who was born in Tuscany, was not a teacher. The blonde person was a trainer, and was not born in California.

80

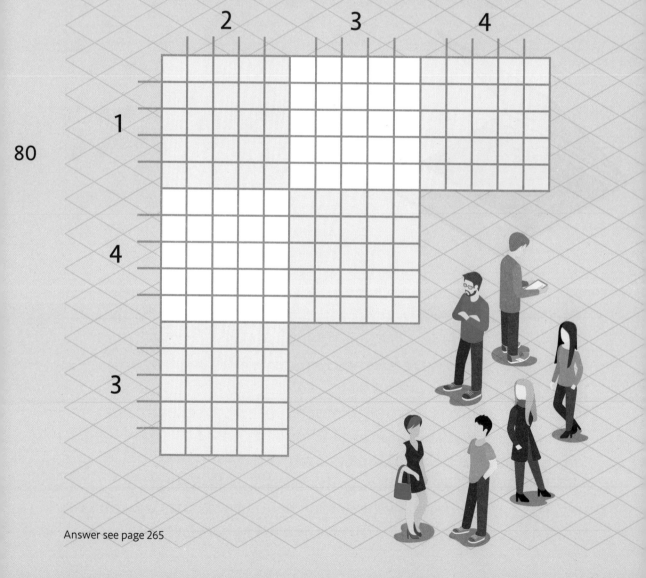

Answer see page 265

121

Simon Barker likes Everest but not Denali. Debi Jenkins likes Kilimanjaro but not Elbrus. Anthony Richardson likes Damavand but not Mont Blanc. Which of the following does Tristan Kennedy like?

SEREBUS   KANGCHENJUNGA
TEIDE   YUSHAN

Answer see page 265

Answer see page 265

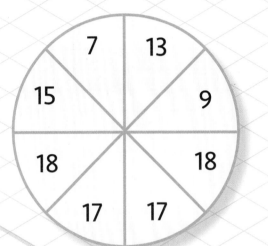

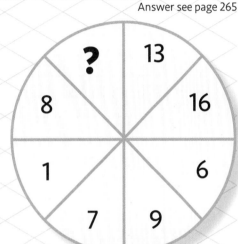

81

122

What number should replace the question mark?

Answer see page 265

123

In each square, the arrow shows the direction you must move in. The numbers in some squares show that square's position in the correct sequence of moves. Move from top left to bottom right, visiting each square in the grid exactly once.

Shade the cells in the grid below so that each row and column holds continuous lines of shaded cells of the lengths indicated by the numbers shown at the start of that row or column. Blocks are separated from others in the same row or column by at least one empty cell. A picture will emerge when the cells are shaded correctly.

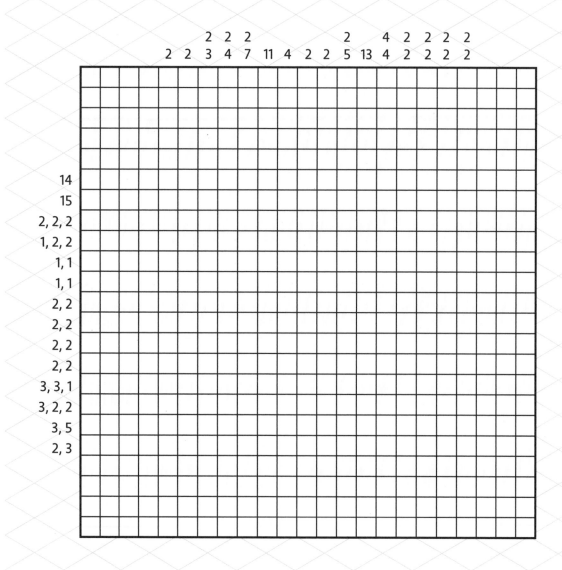

Answer see page 265

Which symbols are missing from the grid below?

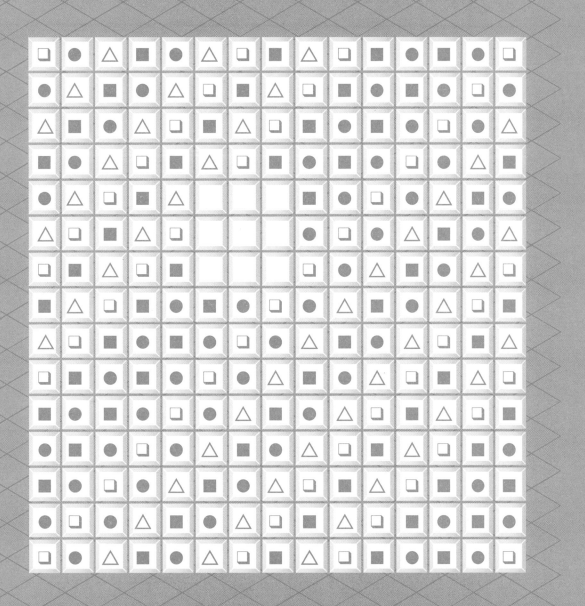

Answer see page 265

Decipher the names of several celebrities using the telephone dial as a guide.

2455687729
2474784262253
42662535536
738377355377
64265272243
8664433537866

Answer see page 265

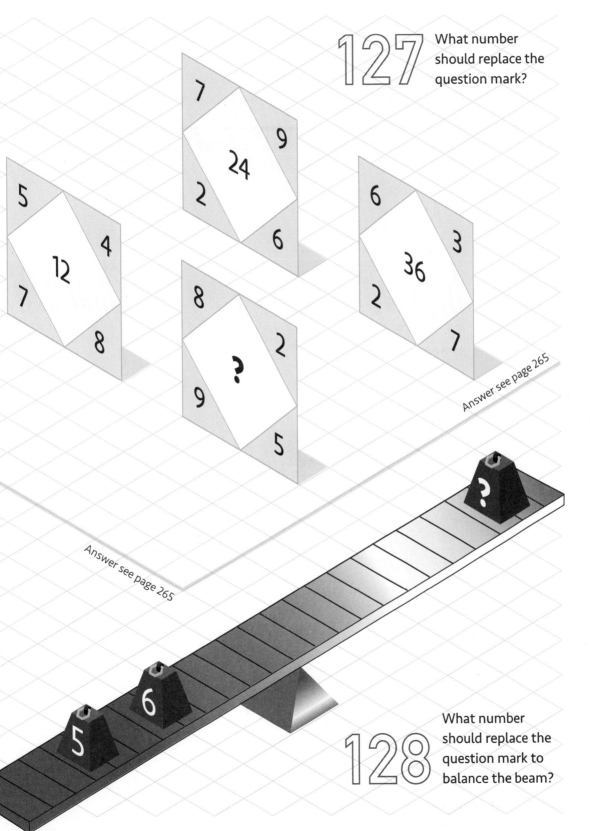

127 What number should replace the question mark?

7
9
24
2
6

5
4
12
7
8

8
2
?
9
5

6
3
36
2
7

Answer see page 265

Answer see page 265

128 What number should replace the question mark to balance the beam?

?
5
6

129 Complete the grid below so that each unbroken horizontal and vertical stretch of light cells sums to the total indicated in the cell to the left or above the stretch respectively. Each cell may contain only the digits 1 – 9, and no digit may be repeated in any given stretch of cells.

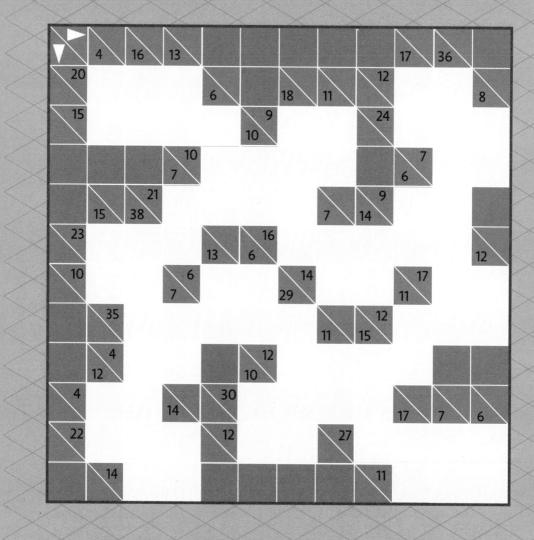

130

The grid below shows the numbers on a full set of dominoes, from 0-0 to 9-9 inclusive, that have been pushed together horizontally and vertically to make a solid rectangle. Complete the grid to show where each domino lies.

Answer see page 266

5	4	8	2	2	0	3	7	1	3	8
5	4	1	2	0	3	7	1	3	8	7
7	7	7	4	6	4	9	4	5	8	6
7	7	6	4	3	6	4	0	9	6	5
8	8	6	1	4	9	1	2	6	5	9
7	6	9	1	5	7	0	9	6	0	0
0	9	2	9	9	5	1	2	6	8	0
7	8	3	2	3	5	5	4	6	0	0
6	2	0	1	0	8	5	0	3	3	5
1	1	3	5	7	9	6	8	9	3	3

131

Which of the four objects A to D fits to complete the shape?

Answer see page 266

A

B

C

D

132

The grid below shows the numbers on a full set of dominoes, from 0-0 to 9-9 inclusive, that have been pushed together horizontally and vertically to make a solid rectangle. Complete the grid to show where each domino lies.

Answer see page 266

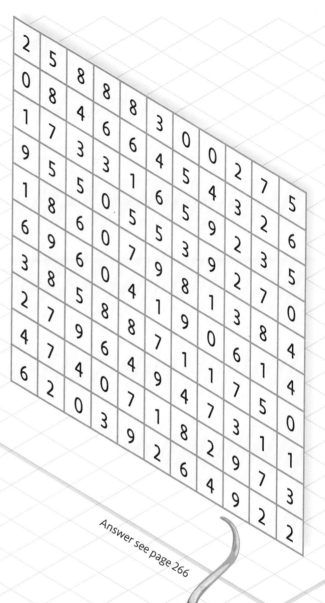

2	5	8	8	8	3	0	0	2	7	5
0	8	4	6	6	4	5	2	3	2	6
1	7	3	3	1	5	4	9	2	3	5
9	5	5	0	6	5	9	2	2	7	0
1	8	6	0	5	5	3	9	3	8	4
6	9	6	0	7	9	8	9	2	1	4
3	8	0	4	9	8	1	2	7	5	0
2	7	5	8	1	1	9	3	8	1	1
4	7	9	8	7	9	0	6	1	7	3
6	2	4	6	4	1	1	1	7	5	2

Answer see page 266

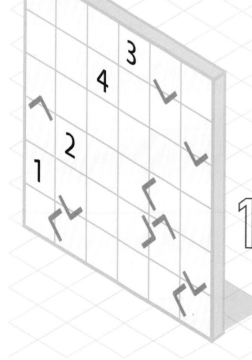

133

Complete the grid below so that every row and column each contains the digits 1-6 precisely once. A cell with a chevron pointing into it is smaller than the cell on the other side of the chevron.

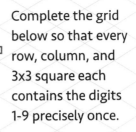

134 Complete the grid below so that every row, column, and 3x3 square each contains the digits 1-9 precisely once.

Answer see page 266

Answer see page 266

135 Are the following statements true or false?

i. 28 is a perfect number.
ii. Castor is the brightest star in the constellation of Gemini.
iii. Klondike is a card game for three players.
iv. Lithium is the lightest of all metals in the periodic table.
v. Madison is the capital of Wisconsin.
vi. Manuel Quezon was a former ruler of the Philippines.
vii. Native tulips can be found around the globe.
viii. The dinosaurs went completely extinct.
ix. The oldest existing university is in Morocco.
x. Wrexham is a town in England.

90

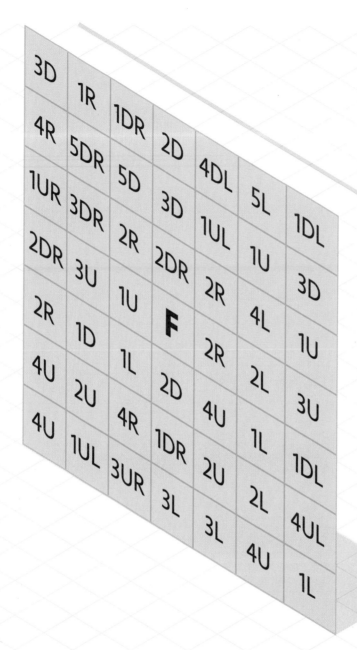

Answer see page 268

01 Each square on this grid shows you the move you must make to arrive at the next square in the sequence, Left, Right, Up, and/or Down. So 3R would be three squares right, and 4UL would be 4 squares diagonally up and left. Your goal is to end up on the finish square, F, having visited every square exactly once. Can you find the starting square?

02

These rings obey a certain logic. What letter should replace the question mark?

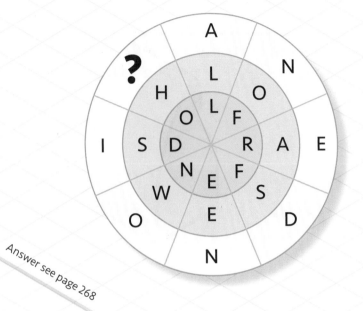

Answer see page 268

03

This set of diagrams follows a certain logic. What should replace the question mark?

Answer see page 268

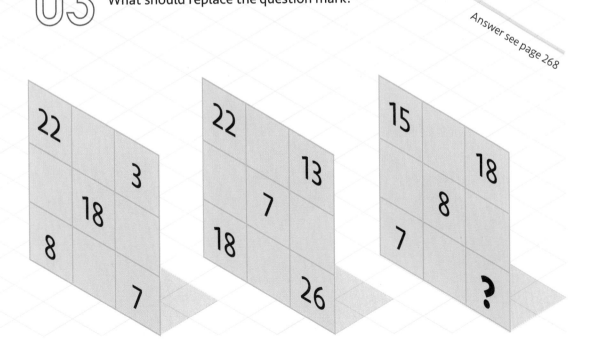

04   A bag holds four counters. One of them is white. Each of the others is either black or white at equal chance. You randomly draw out two counters, and discover they are both white. If you then randomly draw a third counter, what is the chance that it is white?

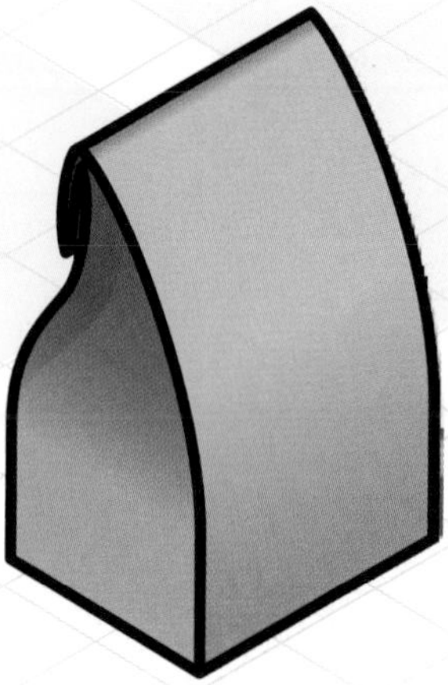

Answer see page 268

Answer see page 268

94

05   What weight will balance the beam?

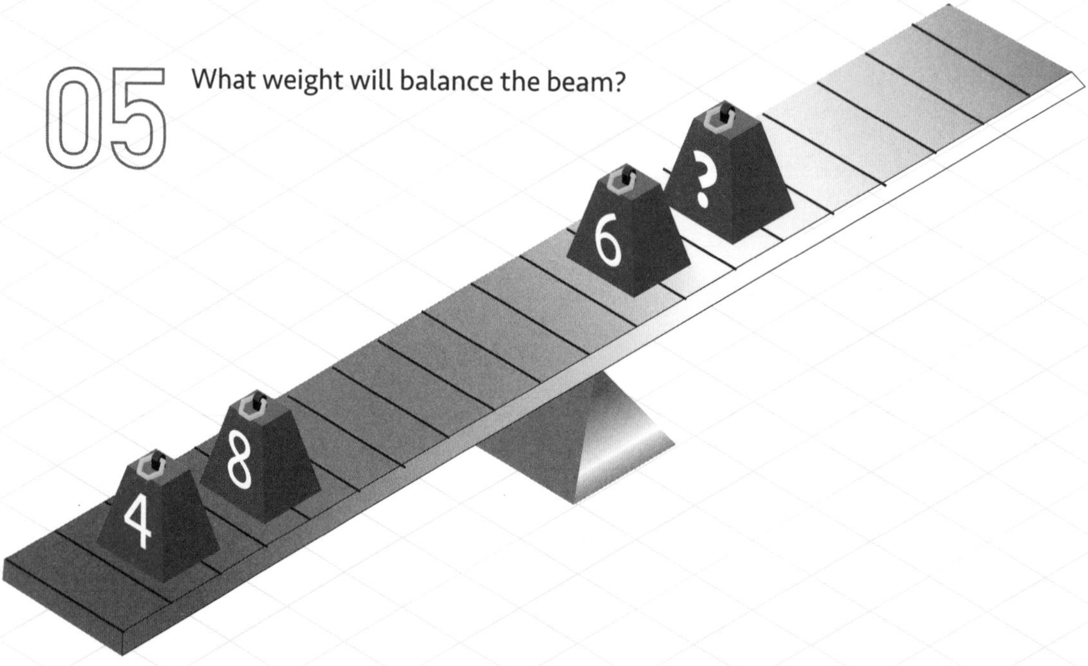

06

Can you divide up this board to correctly show the 28 dominoes listed below?

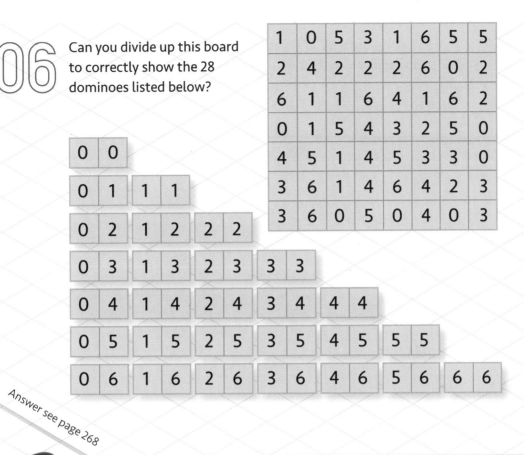

1	0	5	3	1	6	5	5
2	4	2	2	2	6	0	2
6	1	1	6	4	1	6	2
0	1	5	4	3	2	5	0
4	5	1	4	5	3	3	0
3	6	1	4	6	4	2	3
3	6	0	5	0	4	0	3

0	0

0	1	1	1

0	2	1	2	2	2

0	3	1	3	2	3	3	3

0	4	1	4	2	4	3	4	4	4

0	5	1	5	2	5	3	5	4	5	5	5

0	6	1	6	2	6	3	6	4	6	5	6	6	6

Answer see page 268

95

Answer see page 268

07

Anna's mother has four children that she is equally proud of. All of them are daughters, and have inherited her green eyes and red hair. The eldest was born in June, so has Rose as her birth flower, and is named Rose. The second eldest was born in July, so has Lily as her birth flower, and is named Lily. The second youngest was born in August, so has Poppy as her birth flower, and is named Poppy. The youngest was born in September, and has Aster as her birth flower. What is her name?

Following the logic of this diagram, what symbols should the triangle at the top contain?

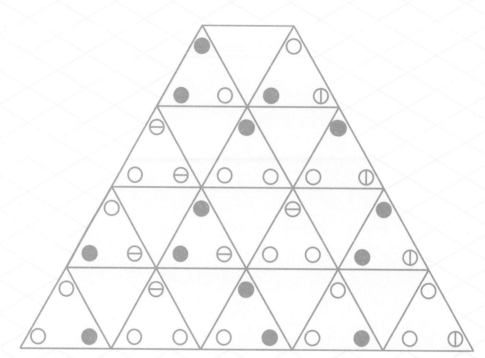

Answer see page 268

 Can you uncover the logic of this grid of letters and replace the question mark with the right letter?

Answer see page 268

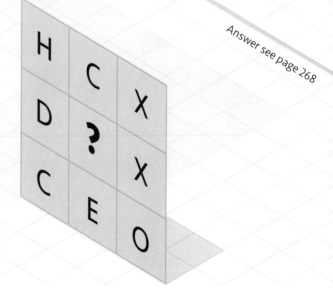

10

The following grid operates according to a specific pattern. Can you fill in the blank section?

Answer see page 268

11

The following numbers obey a certain logic. What should replace the question mark?

12 14 24 32 42

13 21 31 41 ?

Answer see page 268

Answer see page 268

12

The following items are all famous drinks. Can you decrypt them?

GUB PDUWLQL

PDQKDWWDQ

ROG-IDVKLRQHG

PDUJDULWD

GDLTXLUL

JLQ ILCC

PLQW MXOHS

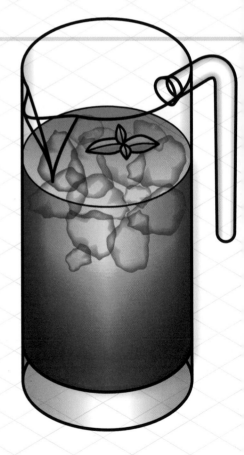

13 If you were to walk a mile at 5mph, how quickly would you have to walk on the return journey to make your average speed there and back 10mph?

Answer see page 268

14 You have two different medicines that you take one pill of each day. The pills are indistinguishable. One morning, you realise that you have absent-mindedly taken out one pill from the first bottle, but two from the second. You have no idea which is which.

Is it possible to get the correct dose without throwing the three pills away?

Answer see page 268

The following tiles have been taken from a five by five square of numbers. When they have been reassembled accurately, the square will show the same five numbers reading both across and down.

Can you rebuild it?

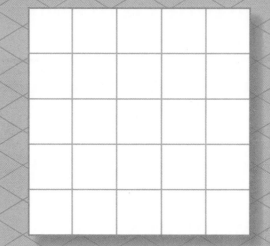

| 2 | 8 | 5 |
| 6 | 1 | 9 |
| 7 |

| 4 |
| 1 |
| 1 |

| 6 |
| 2 |
| 1 |

| 4 |
| 2 |

| 8 |
| 6 |

| 8 | 3 | | 9 | 6 | | 1 | 5 | | 4 | 8 |

Answer see page 268

Which of these shapes is the odd one out?

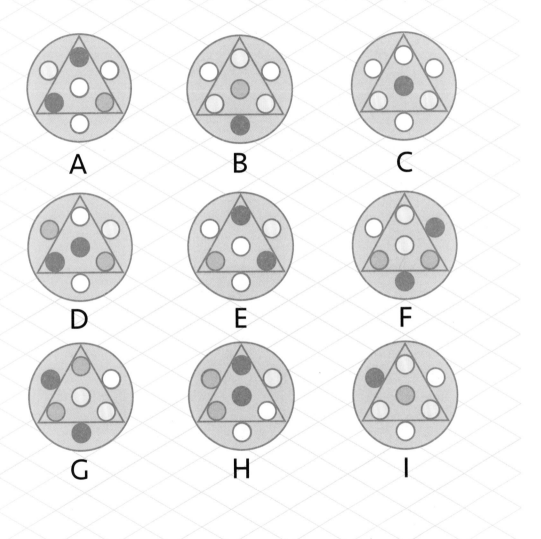

Answer see page 268

17 The following list of numbers represents items of furniture whose letters have been encoded into the numbers needed to reproduce them on a typical phone dial. Can you decode them?

268 683 786 7

752 973 6

268 462 227 727

273 336 92

743 326 273

825 526 9

Answer see page 268

A is to B as C is to V, W, X, Y or Z?

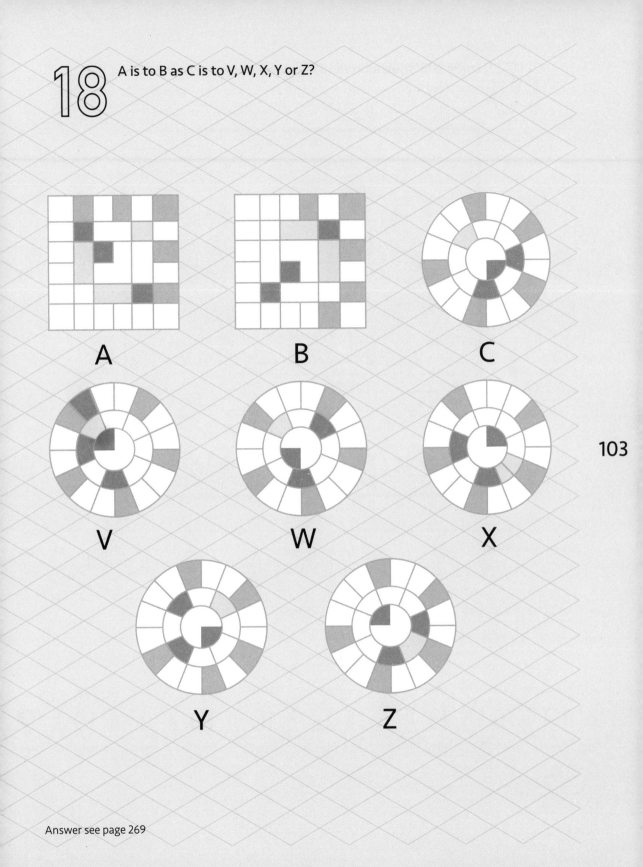

A

B

C

V

W

X

Y

Z

Answer see page 269

One of the squares in the 3x3 grid is incorrect. Which one?

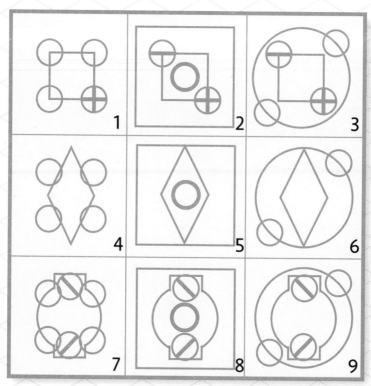

1 2 3

4 5 6

7 8 9

Answer see page 269

Answer see page 269

20

Can you tell what number comes next in this sequence?

10 6 13 1 13 10 10 1 19 ?

To which of the lower shapes, A-E, could a single ball be added so that both balls matched the conditions of the balls in the upper shape?

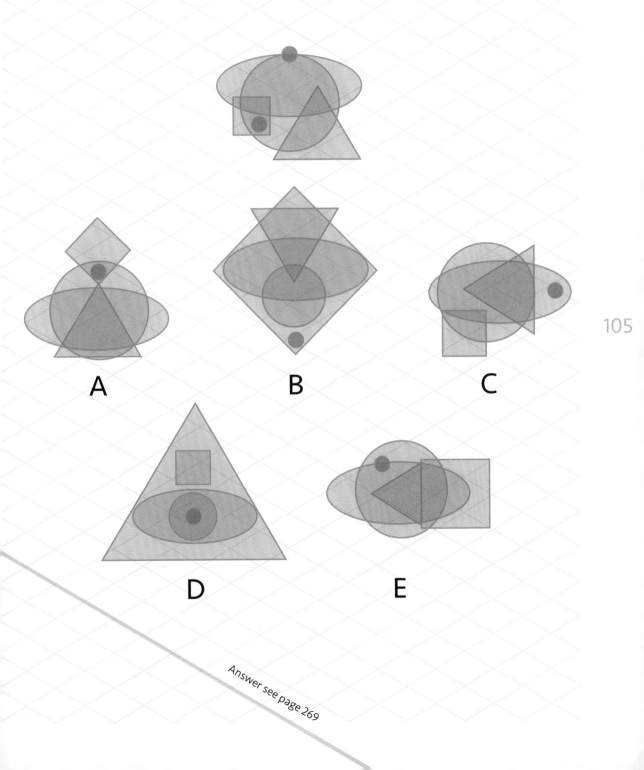

A

B

C

D

E

105

Answer see page 269

22 Can you divide this square into four identical shapes, each one containing just one of each of the five symbols?

Answer see page 269

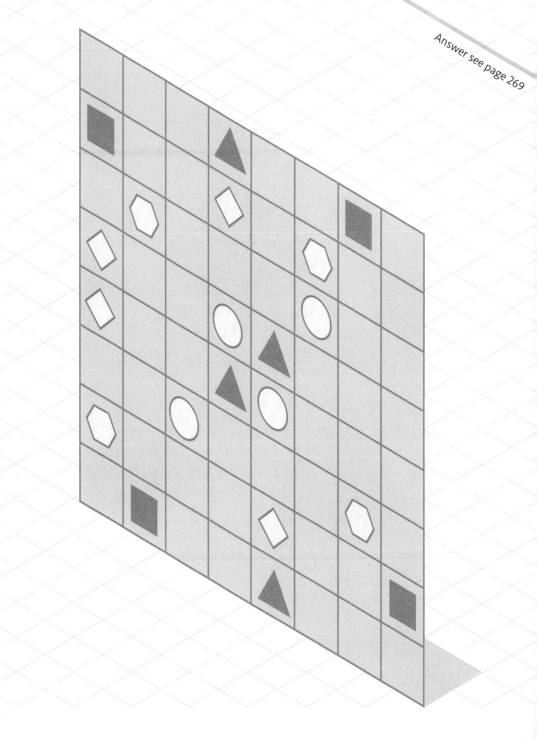

23 Each of the circles below contains the name of a work of literature and its author. Can you unscramble them?

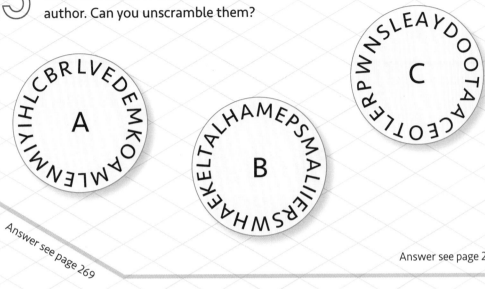

A

B

C

Answer see page 269

Answer see page 269

24 In this long division calculation, each digit has been consistently replaced with a symbol chosen at random. Can you discover the original calculation?

25

These columns observe a certain logic. What should the next column look like?

8
4 2
9 3 4
1 7 9
7 1 1
3 9 7
2 4 3 **?**

108

Answer see page 269

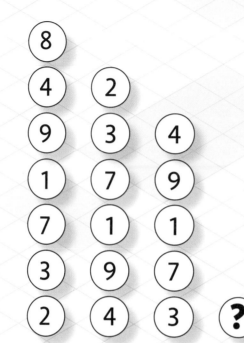

Answer see page 269

26

If Richmond likes Montreal but not Ottawa, Adrienne likes El Paso but not Naperville, Bartholomew likes Haboro but not Osaka, and Romaine likes Ioannina but not Naxos, which location does Mathilda dislike?

A. Fife
B. Glasgow
C. Leuchars
D. Dundrennan
E. Inverness

This set of diagrams follows a certain logic. What should replace the question mark?

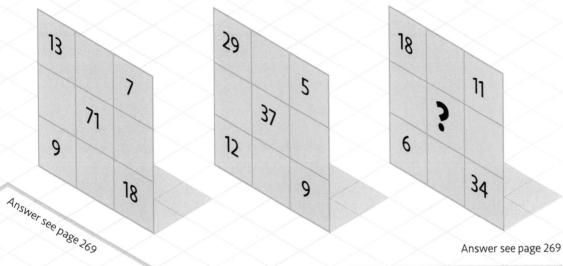

Answer see page 269

Answer see page 269

The following design works according to a certain logic. What number should replace the question mark?

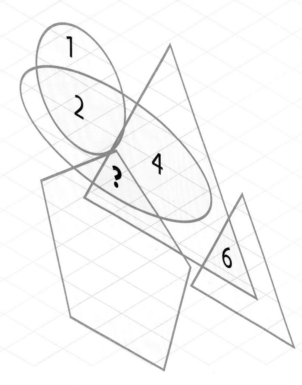

Five keen gardeners meet at a flower show, and compare their preferences. Which of the five had brought cheese sandwiches?

Hayden had brought ham sandwiches – but was not the person who was there to look at geraniums, who preferred red flowers. The person with chicken sandwiches preferred blue flowers, and was not there to look at pansies or at camellias. One person preferred pink flowers. Magdalena did not bring egg sandwiches. Thad did not bring egg sandwiches either, and wasn't there to look at geraniums. The person who'd brought tuna sandwiches was there to look at azaleas, and did not prefer white flowers. Liza was there to investigate delphiniums. Matt, finally, preferred purple flowers, and was not there to look at azaleas.

Which of the five had brought cheese sandwiches?

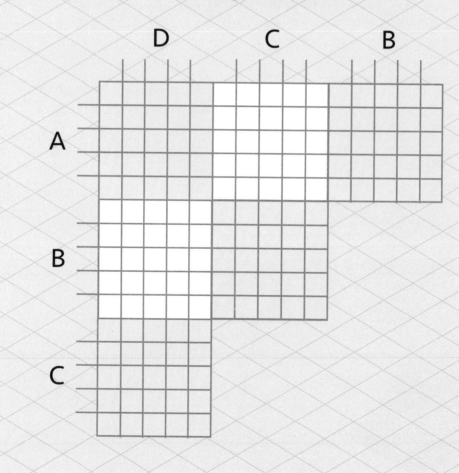

Answer see page 269

30 Each square on this grid shows you the move you must make to arrive at the next square in the sequence, Left, Right, Up, and/or Down. So 3R would be three squares right, and 4UL would be 4 squares diagonally up and left. Your goal is to end up on the finish square, F, having visited every square exactly once. Can you find the starting square?

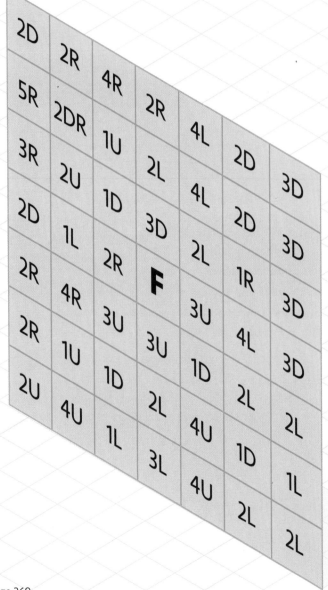

31 Using six straight lines that each touch at least one side of the box, can you divide the box into sections containing 1, 2, 3, 4, 5, 6, and 7 shapes?

Answer see page 269

112

32 These triangles follow a specific logic. What should replace the question mark?

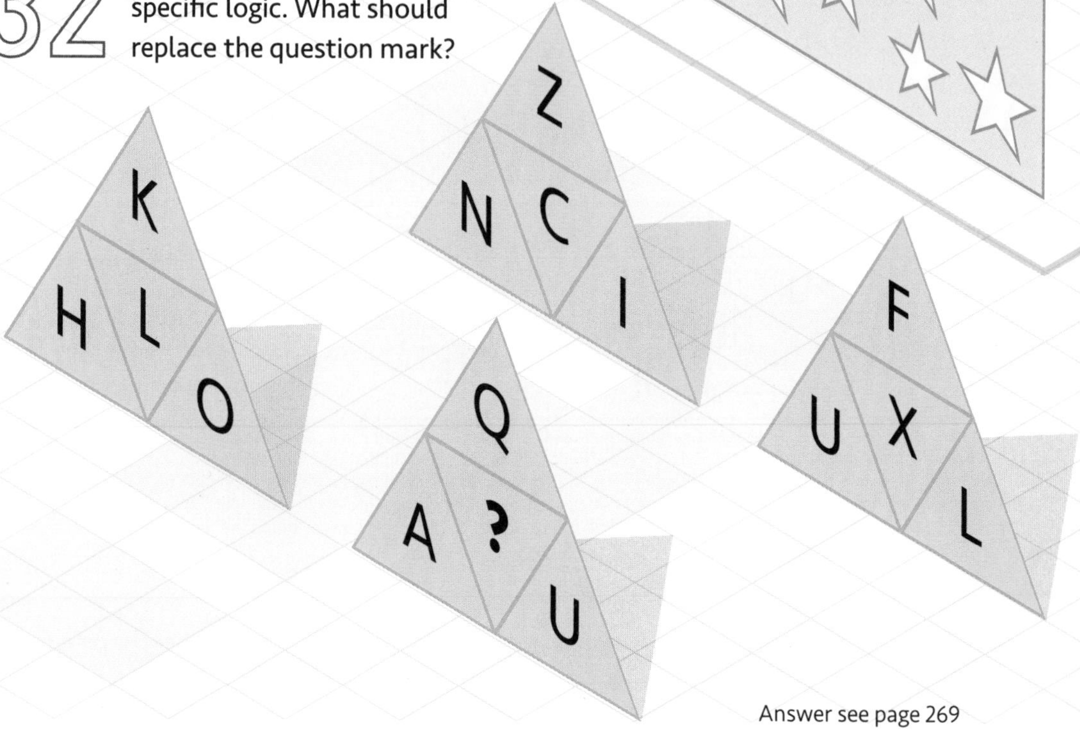

K
H L O

Z
N C I

Q
A ? U

F
U X L

Answer see page 269

33

These clocks obey a specific sequence. What should the time on the fourth clock be?

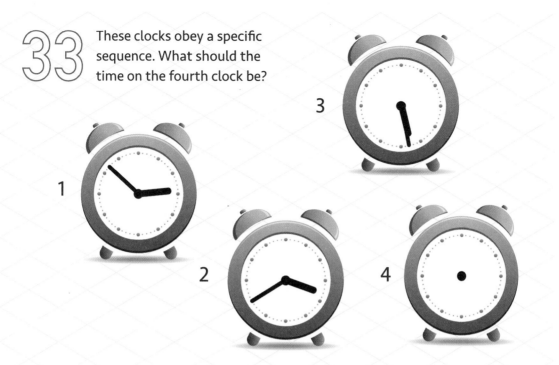

1

2

3

4

Answer see page 269

nswer see page 269

34

The letters and numbers in this square obey a certain logic. What number should replace the question mark?

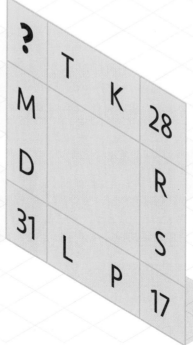

?	T	K	28
M		R	
D		S	
31	L	P	17

35 These columns observe a certain logic. What should the next column look like?

Answer see page 269

114

Answer see page 269

36 Five crooks are accused of a robbery. Each gives a statement, but two of the statements are false. This is enough to give a decisive answer. Who is guilty?

A: It was B.

B: A is lying.

C: D is innocent.

D: E is innocent.

E: D is telling the truth.

37

A race was run in four legs. Given the distances in kilometres of each leg, and the average speed in meters per second for that leg for the top five contestants, can you work out who won, and in what total time?

	Leg:	A-B	B-C	C-D	D-E
Runner	Distance:	5.8km	4.6km	7.3km	0.9km
V		4.8	4.3	3.4	5.2
W		4.6	4.2	3.7	5.1
X		4.7	4.4	3.5	5.0
Y		4.9	4.25	3.1	5.4
Z		4.7	4.6	3.3	5.2

Answer see page 270

Answer see page 270

38

The diagram below operates according to a specific logic. What should the missing square look like?

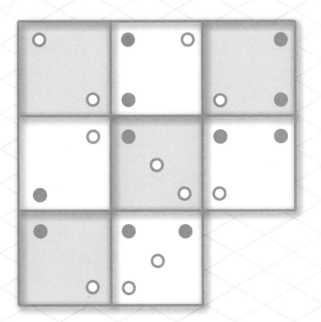

39 Each symbol in the grid has a consistent value. What number should replace the question mark?

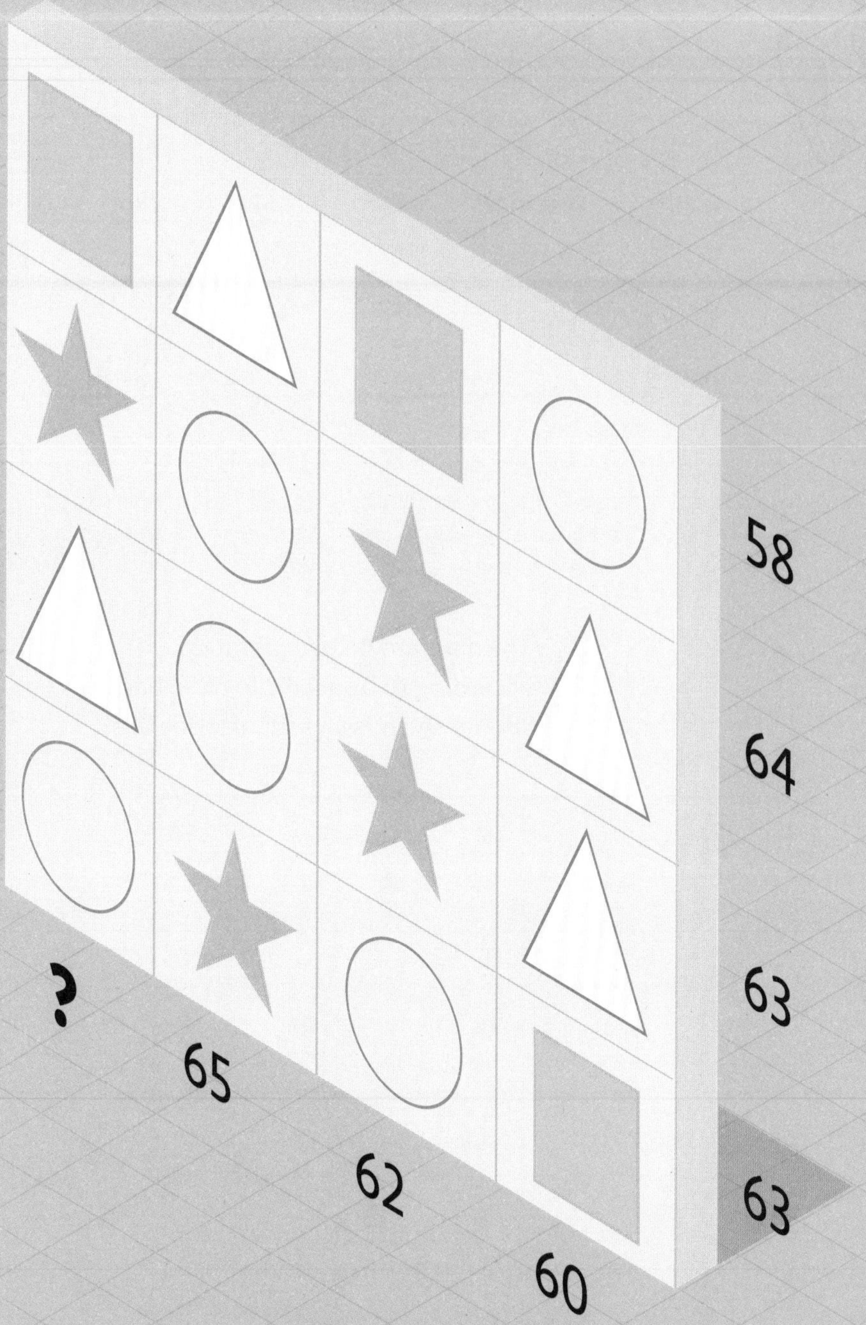

116

58

64

63

?

65

62

63

60

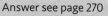

Answer see page 270

40

Can you place the segments below the triangular grid over the grid itself in such a way as to ensure that every node is covered by an identical symbol? Not all connecting lines will be covered.

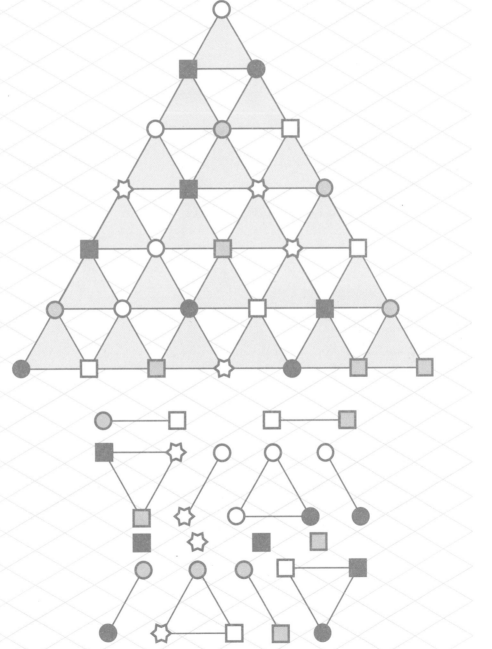

117

Answer see page 270

Four of these five pieces fit together to make a regular geometric shape. Which one is left over?

Answer see page 270

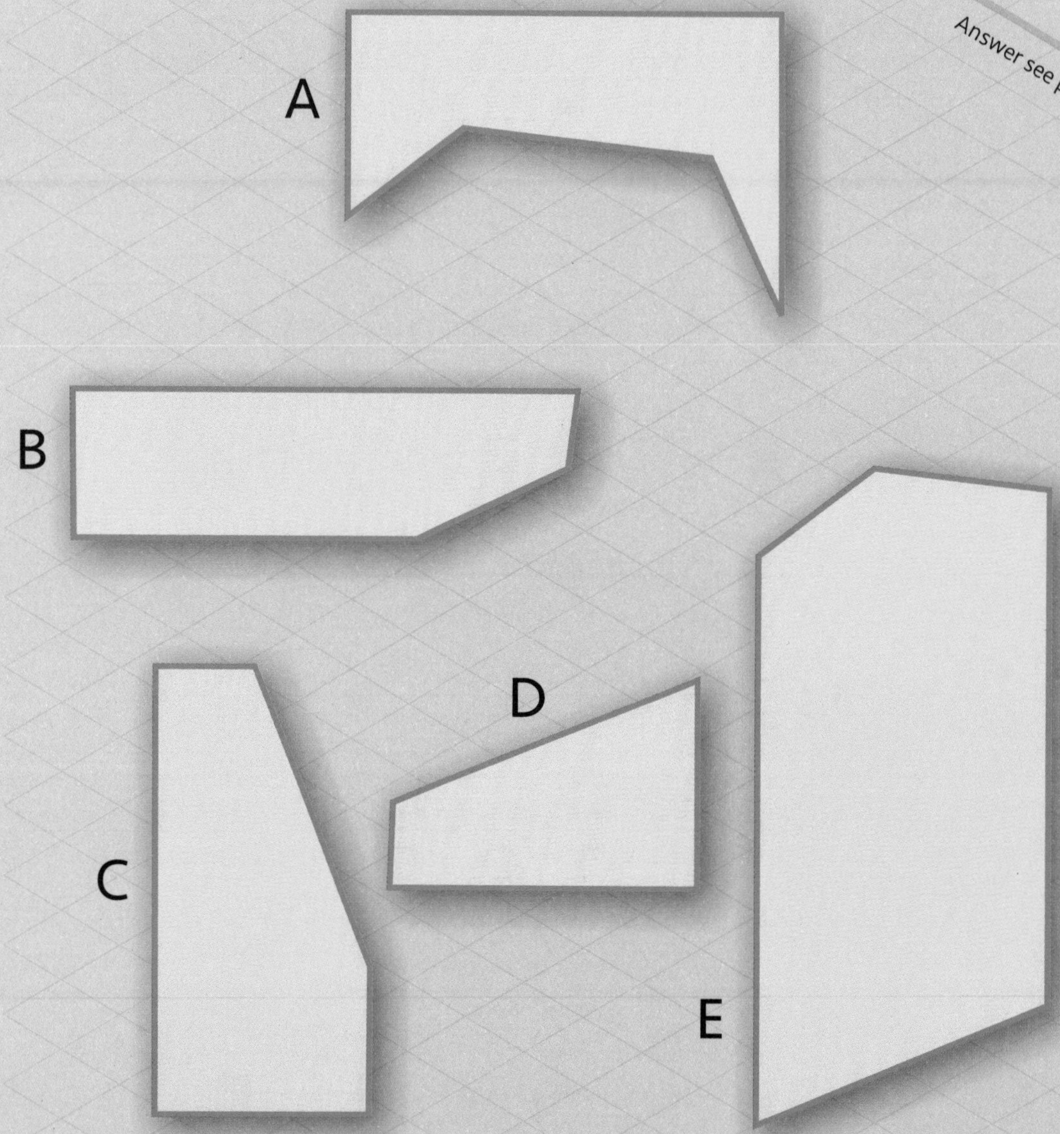

A

B

118

C

D

E

42 You are faced with two doors, either of which might be wired to kill you as soon as you open it. Each door bears a sign. The sign on door A is true if its door is safe, whilst the sign on door B is false if its door is safe. However, the signs have been removed from the doors, and you don't know which fits which.

Which door should you open?

Sign 1: This door is deadly.

Sign 2: Both doors are deadly.

Answer see page 270

Answer see page 270

43 This diagram obeys a certain logic. What is the missing number?

20 · 42 · ? · 24 · 17 · 29 · 15

Can you fill in the numbers provided to correctly complete the grid?

Answer see page 270

120

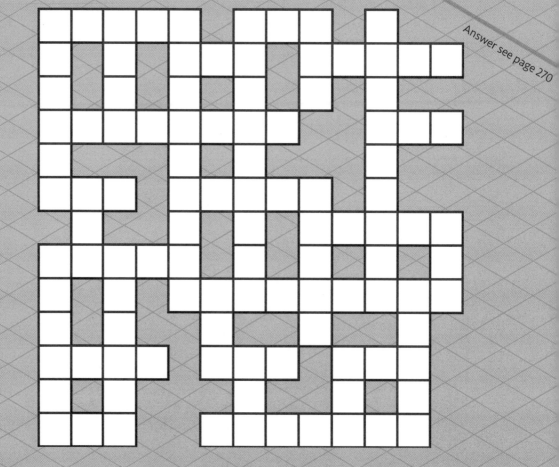

3 digit numbers		4 digit numbers	5 digit numbers	6 digit numbers	7 digit numbers	9 digit numbers
142	639	3089	10985	187127	7347385	215628072
178	673	9112	11624	277892		326602260
232	678		18291	364382	**8 digit numbers**	524755252
253	749		37255			937660985
293	834		51200		11217966	
393	942		56071			
477			73985			

45

Can you match the fragments to reassemble the names of several Hollywood celebrities?

NI	EY	BE	TON	JEN
LAW	BA	PET	KIN	DEN
HAL	ZEL	SON	HER	CY
CO	STOR	CAT	FER	RO
SHI	DEN	HEN	RRY	MIL
WA	EUVE	ER	INE	CHA
MARE	SA	RUS	AT	REN
CE	WAN	LE	RON	NG

Answer see page 270

Answer see page 270

121

46

You are faced with three women, A, B, and C, who know each other. One of the three always lies, one always tells the truth, and one either tells the truth or lies randomly. Each makes one statement to you.

Which is the one who always tells the truth?

A: B always tells the truth.

B: A is not the liar.

C: If you asked me, I'd say that B is random.

47 Examine the top three shapes.
Which of the five options A-E
continues the sequence?

Answer see page 270

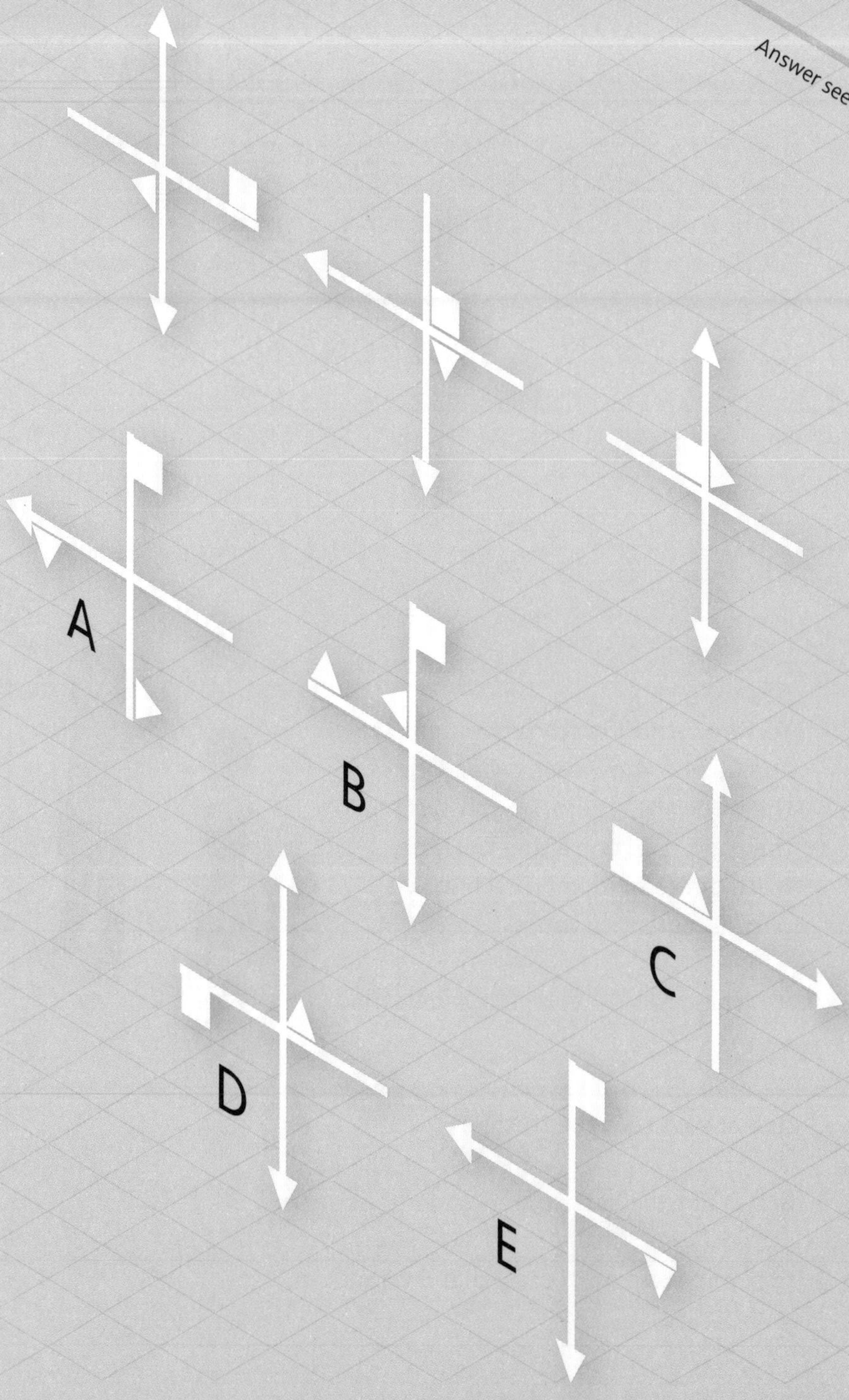

A

B

C

D

E

How many of the following statements are true?

- At least one of these statements is false.
- At least two of these statements are false.
- At least three of these statements are false.
- At least four of these statements are false.
- At least five of these statements are false.
- At least six of these statements are false.
- At least seven of these statements are false.
- At least eight of these statements are false.
- At least nine of these statements are false.
- All ten of these statements are false.

Answer see page 270

Which group of shapes, A-D, most closely corresponds with the conditions of the large group of shapes above?

Answer see page 270

A

B

C

D

These 12-hour digital clocks follow a specific logic. Can you work out the time of the fifth clock?

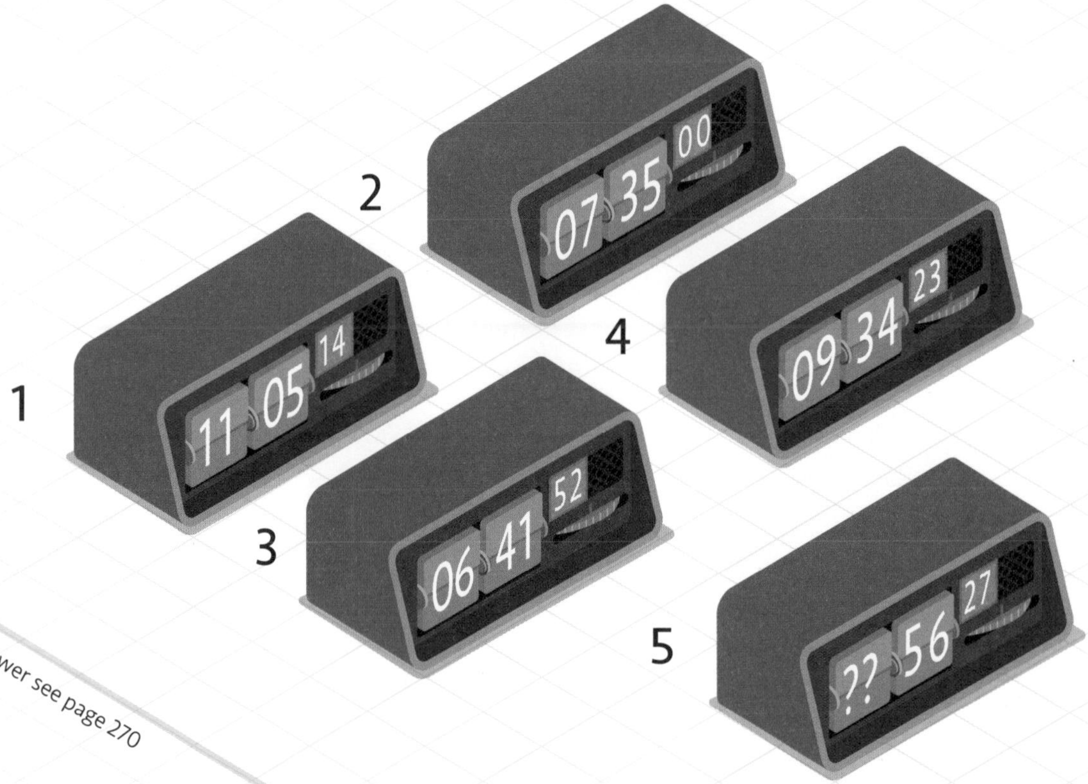

2

07 35 00

4

09 34 23

1

11 05 14

3

06 41 52

5

?? 56 27

Answer see page 270

Answer see page 270

Can you rearrange the digits in this equation to make it correct, without adding any mathematical operators?

$$4\ 4\ =\ 6\ 3$$

Can you tell what number comes next in this sequence?

(3) (13) (1113) (3113) (132113)

Answer see page 270

Answer see page 270

53 Three archers were practising their skills on the same boss. After each had fired five shots, they paused to compare scores, and discovered that they had each scored 78 points. During evaluation, they noted that A had scored thirteen with the first two shots, whilst C had scored 8 with the final two. Who did not get a bulls-eye?

1
3
4
5
10
15
25
50

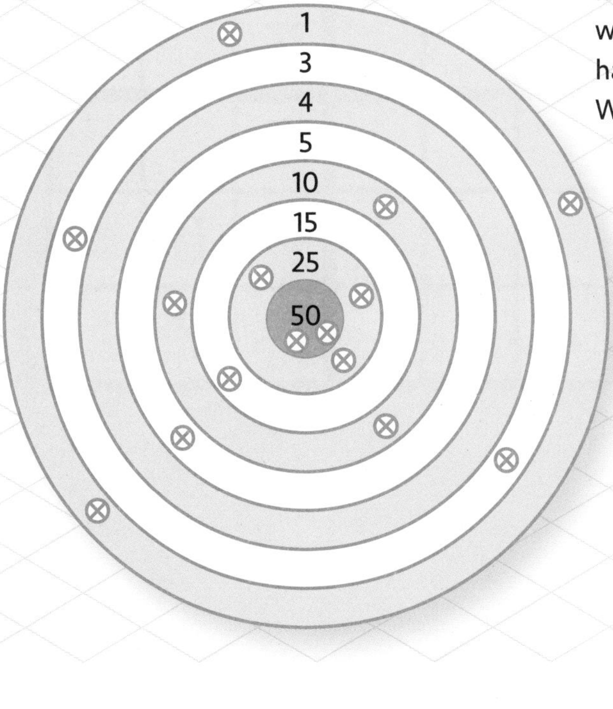

Answer see page 271

Complete the grid so that:
- Each 9x9 row and column contains each digit from 1 to 9 once only
- Each 3x3 box contains each digit from 1 to 9 once only.

126

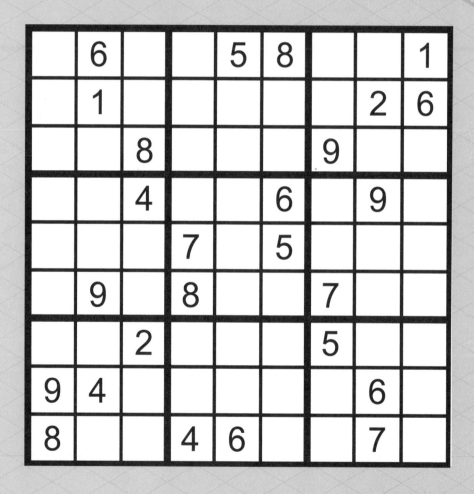

Follow this set of simple instructions. What is the result?

1. Write down the number 7.
2. Subtract 3 from the last number you wrote down, and remember the result.
3. Write down the number you are remembering next to the last number you wrote down.
4. Add 2 to the last number you wrote down, and remember the result.
5. Write down the number you are remembering next to the last number you wrote down.
6. Add 2 to the last number you wrote down, and remember the result.
7. Have you written down at least nine digits? If no, go back to 2, else proceed.
8. Write down the number 1 next to the last number you wrote down.
9. Stop.

Answer see page 271

Answer see page 271

Examine the following sets of scales, which are in perfect balance. How many balls are needed to balance the final scale?

57 Examine the following sets of scales, which are in perfect balance. How many balls are needed to balance the final scale?

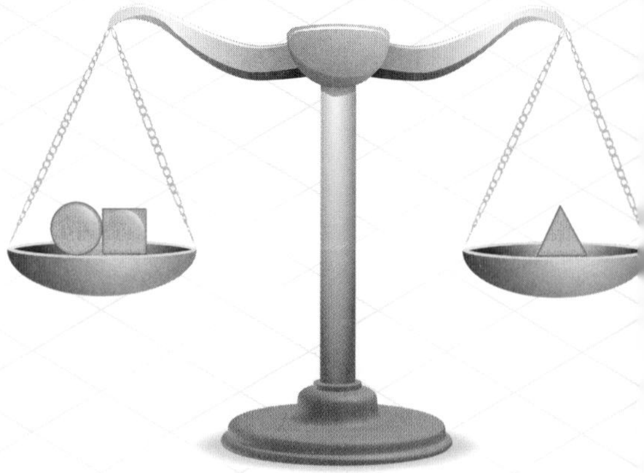

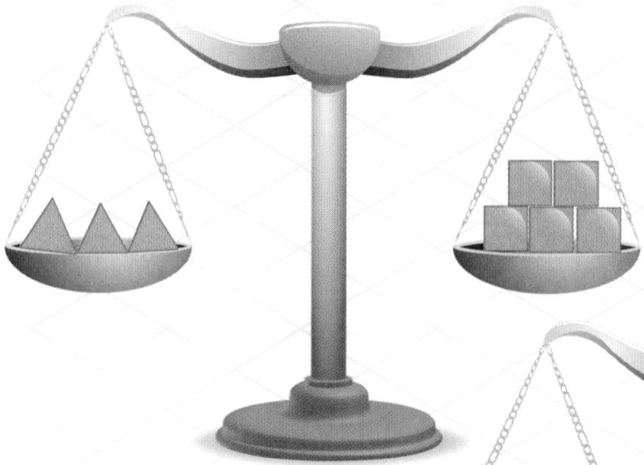

Answer see page 271

Answer see page 271

58 The following playwrights have had the vowels and spaces removed from their names. Can you untangle them?

HNRKBSN	TMSTPPRD
LXNDRSTRVSK	THRNTNWLDR
MKHLBLGKV	PRRCRNLL
HRLDPNTR	JHNSBRN
MGLDCRVNTS	JNRZDLRCN

59 Look at the diagram. What is the largest version of the same shape that can be drawn within the box so that none of its edges touch any other edges, or stray outside the box?

Answer see page 271

Answer see page 271

60 Amongst a group of thirty-eight mountaineers, twelve have successfully climbed Everest, seven have successfully climbed K2, two have successfully climbed the Dawn Wall, and all but six have successfully climbed Annapurna. What is the least possible number of people who have successfully climbed just one of the four?

61 The word THROAT is located exactly once in the grid below, but could be horizontally, vertically or diagonally forwards or backwards. Can you locate it?

Answer see page 271

130

H T T O T T R T T A T R A H R
O A A R H T O T R O A O R T R
T T H A T A T T H A H T H A T
O R R T R T A T R O H R T H O
T T O T T O A T O R T T H O T
H A A R T A O A R T R T O O R
T R T R O T T R T T H H R A O
T H T R H T R H O H T R O H O
T O R H R R R A T O H O O T O
R O H T T A O A H H T H O R T
R T T R A T O O R H O T T R H
R A T T T T O R O T T O T O
R T T T R H R O T T H A O T A
R T T A O A A H T A T A R T H
A H O A H T T T O A H T R R T

62

Fill in the underlined spaces below using only the digits 0-9, so that the following statement is truthful:

In the five lines below, there are

__ instance/s of the number 1; __ instance/s of the number 2; __ instance/s of the number 3; __ instance/s of the number 4; and __ instance/s of the number 5.

Answer see page 271

Answer see page 271

63

Signs – symbols in a specific position – which appear in the outer circles are transferred to the inner circle as follows: If it appears once, it is definitely transferred. If it appears twice, it is transferred if no other symbol will be transferred from that position. If it appears three times, it will be transferred if there is no sign appearing once in that position. If it appears four times, it is not transferred. In instances where signs with the same count are competing, then from high to low, priority runs top left – top right – bottom left – bottom right. What does the inner circle look like?

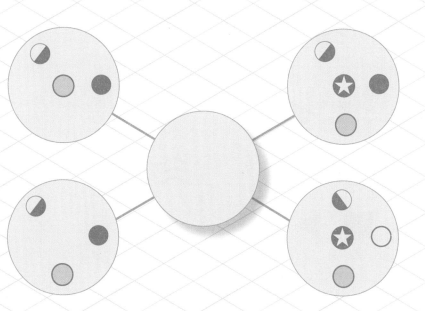

64 Ten vessels are hidden in the grid below, four one-cell ships, three two-cell ships, two three-cell ships, and one four-cell ship. Ships are positioned horizontally or vertically. No two ships are immediately adjacent to each other, including diagonally. The numbers next to each row and column show the total number of ship segments in that line. Identify the exact locations of all ten vessels. Some ship segments and/or spaces of empty ocean are shown to assist you.

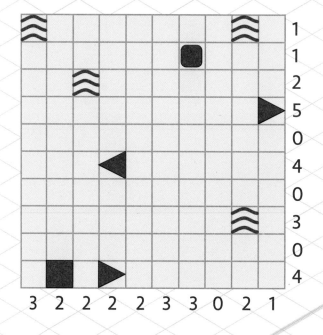

Answer see page 271

65 In the grid below, how much is each symbol worth?

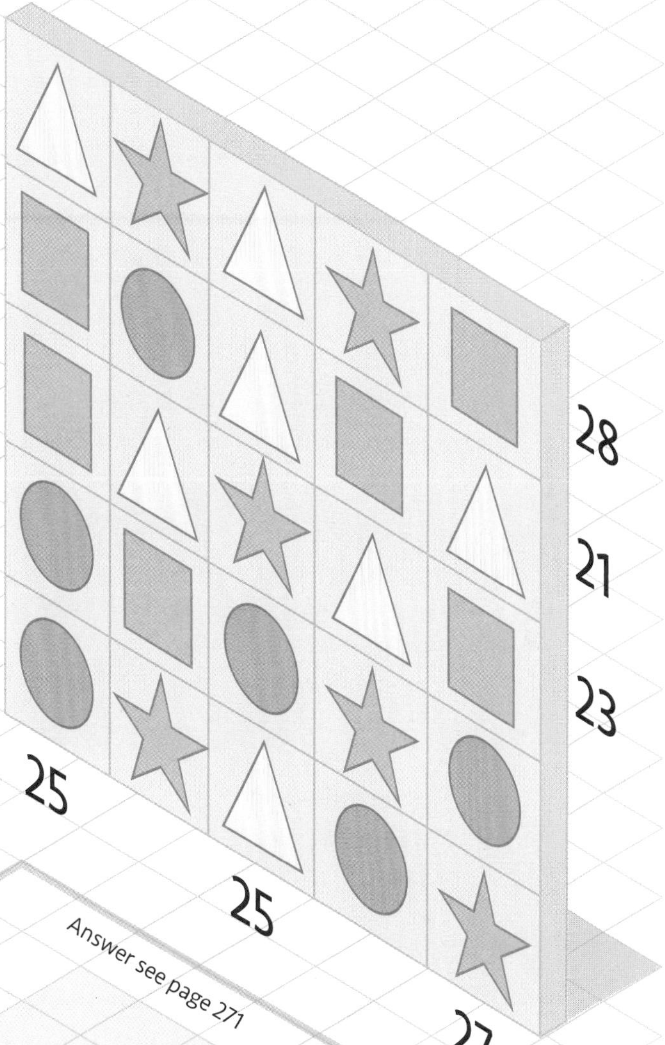

28

21

23

25

25

27

Answer see page 271

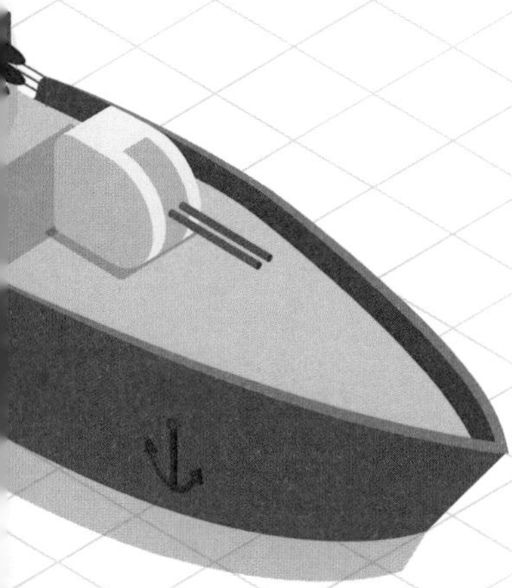

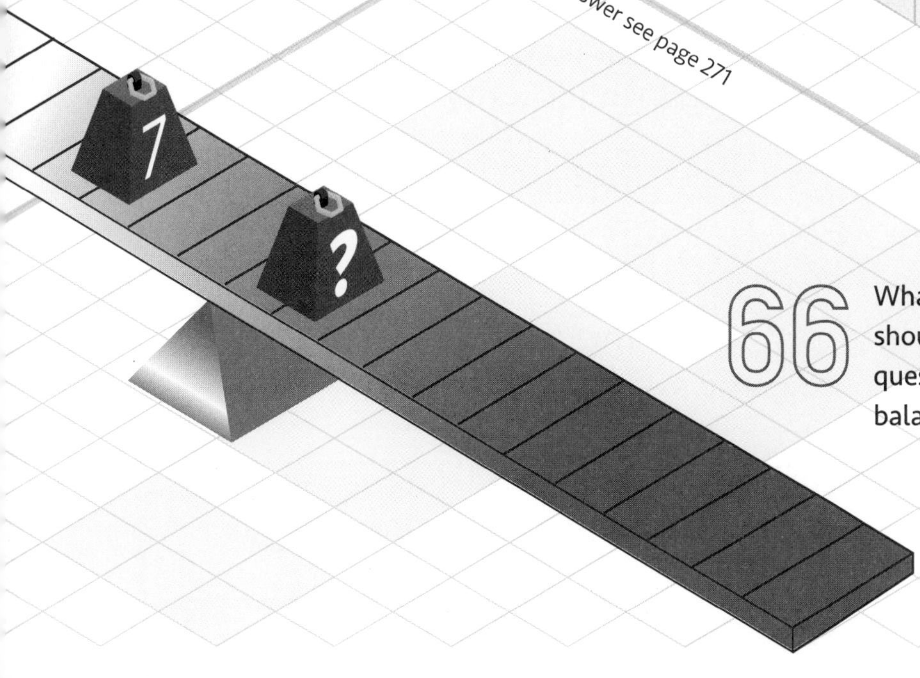

7

?

Answer see page 271

66 What number should replace the question mark to balance the beam?

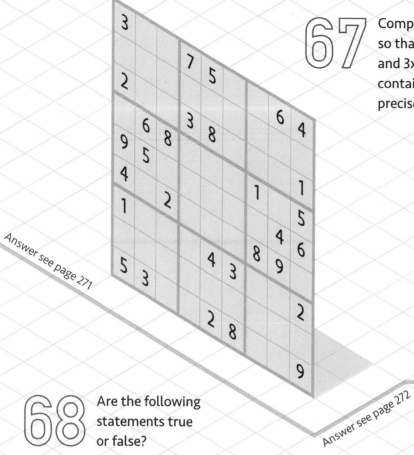

Complete the grid below so that every row, column, and 3x3 square each contains the digits 1-9 precisely once.

Answer see page 271

Answer see page 272

68 Are the following statements true or false?

i.   537 is a prime number.
ii. Fluorine will react with almost all other elements.
iii. Gunpowder was invented in India in the 9th century AD.
iv. Nabis was a former tyrant of Sicily.
v.   New York City is the capital of New York state.
vi. Pazin is a city in Serbia.
vii. Rigel is the brightest star in the constellation of Orion.
viii. Senet was a board game played in ancient Egypt 5,000 years ago.
ix. Some parrots have been shown to understand, and correctly use, hundreds of words of human language.
x.   The daffodil is part of the floral genus Narcissus.

69 Are the following statements true or false?

i.   78 is a triangular number.
ii. In a 52-card deck, there are ~10^25 possible orderings of the cards.
iii. Jerry Rawlings was a former ruler of Ghana.
iv. Kazan is a city in Estonia.
v.   Los Angeles is the capital of California.
vi. Mirrors were invented 2500 years ago in the Lebanon.
vii. Silicon is a non-metallic element.
viii. Sirius is the brightest star in the constellation of Canis Minor.
ix. There are no wild alpacas we know of.
x.   There is a type of rose named after British trade unionist Arthur Scargill.

Answer see page 272

70 In each square, the arrow shows the direction you must move in. The numbers in some squares show that square's position in the correct sequence of moves. Move from top left to bottom right, visiting each square in the grid exactly once.

Answer see page 272

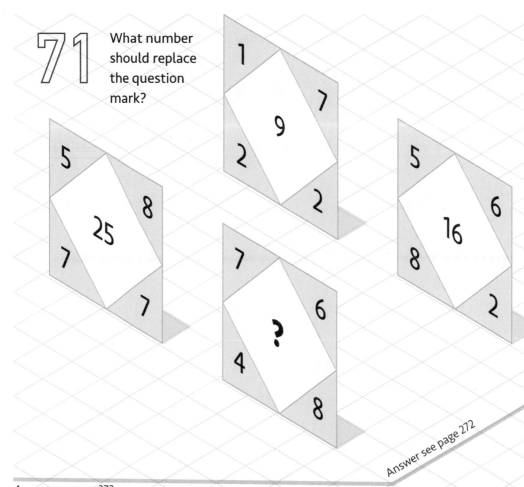

71 What number should replace the question mark?

1 7 9 2 2

5 8 25 7 7

5 6 16 8 2

7 6 ? 4 8

Answer see page 272

136

Answer see page 272

72 Complete the grid below so that every row, column, and 3x3 square each contains the digits 1-9 precisely once. The sum of the digits in each group of cells with a dotted outline must total the number in the group's top/left corner.

17	13	11		10	10	11		17
		13	9			7		
				11		10		
10	15	12	11	11		11	4	
					10		19	
8			9	11		11		
12		17			12	9	11	25
9			8					
6			15					

Decipher the names of several celebrities using the telephone dial as a guide.

52637372626

5646693377

52832325467253

846343735

328438366268

2643546256543

Answer see page 272

74 Ten vessels are hidden in the grid below, four one-cell ships, three two-cell ships, two three-cell ships, and one four-cell ship. Ships are positioned horizontally or vertically. No two ships are immediately adjacent to each other, including diagonally. The numbers next to each row and column show the total number of ship segments in that line. Identify the exact locations of all ten vessels. Some ship segments and/or spaces of empty ocean are shown to assist you.

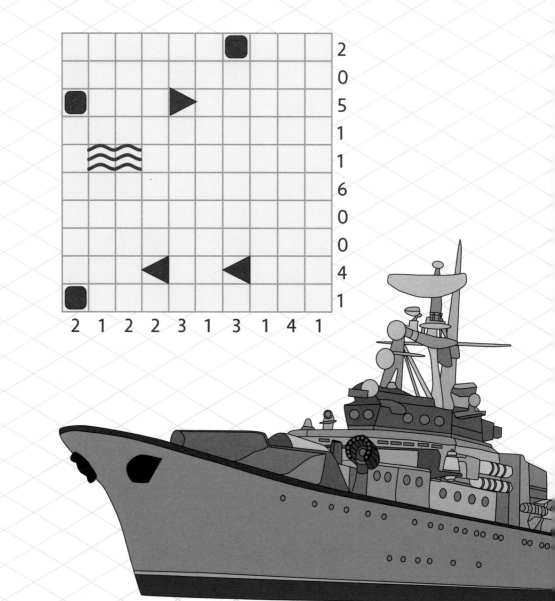

Answer see page 272

75 Assemble the pieces shown below into a square grid which reads the same across as it does downwards.

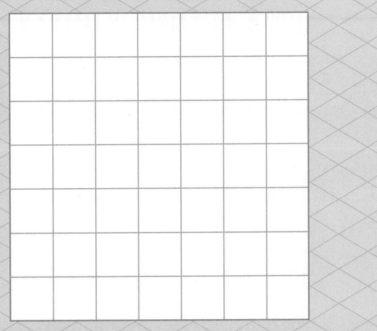

6

5	6	1

8	5	7
3	4	

5	8	3	1
8			

0

1	9	2

6	4
4	3

9	3	5

2
5
3

9
4	9	3
5

0	3
3	9
5	8

5
2	7	0
9

2
2	5	3
5

Answer see page 272

Fill in the missing plus, minus, multiplication, division, and/or factorial signs to make the equation below correct, performing all calculations strictly in the order they appear on the page.

$$(11) \quad (5) \quad (4) \quad (7) \quad (23) \quad (7) \quad (16) = (19)$$

Answer see page 272

Answer see page 272

 Are the following statements true or false?

i. There are no radioactive isotopes of aluminium.
ii. Lizards can be found on every continent on Earth.
iii. Miami is the capital of Florida.
iv. Pervez Musharraf is a former ruler of Afghanistan.
v. Pi, the ratio of a circle's diameter to its circumference, is a rational number.
vi. Poznan is a city in Poland.
vii. Some dice have twelve sides.
viii Some mimosas can close up quickly when touched.
ix. The constellation of Columba represents a dove.
x. The number zero was invented in Arabia in the 9th century AD.

78 Which two cubes show three identical faces to each other?

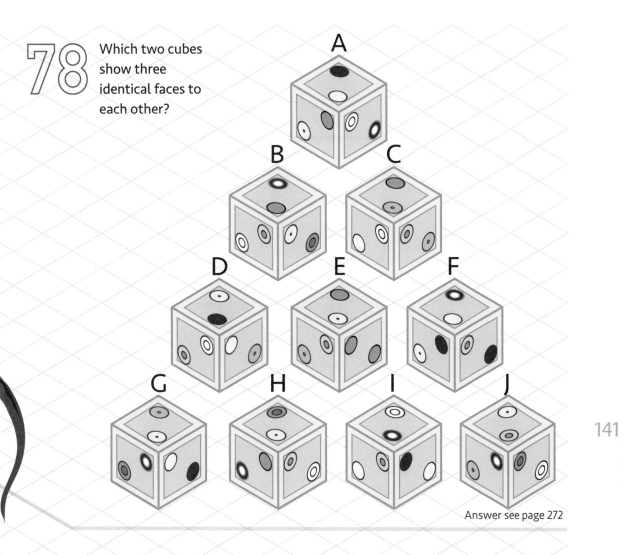

Answer see page 272

79 Using six straight lines, none of which touch an edge of the box, divide the design below into five sections, each containing precisely sixteen circles.

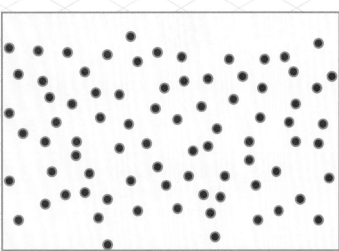

Answer see page 272

80 In the grid below, how much is each symbol worth?

Answer see page 273

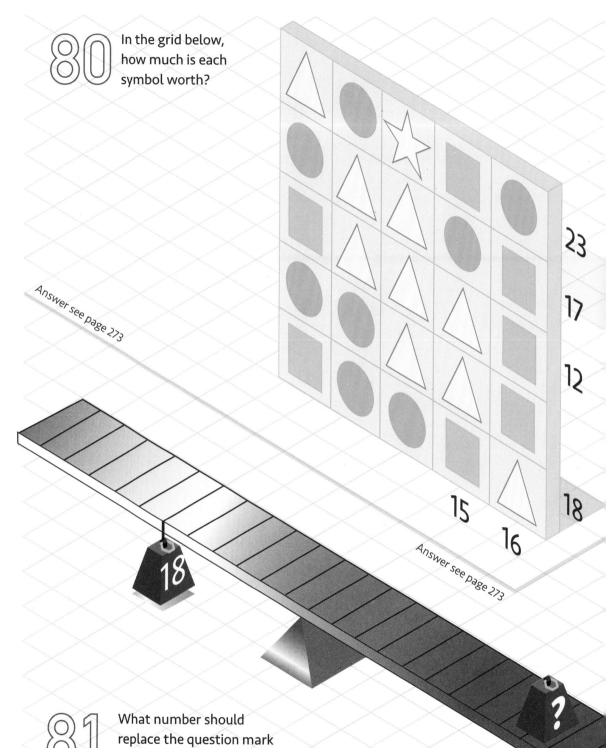

23

17

12

18

15

16

Answer see page 273

81 What number should replace the question mark to balance the beam?

82

Complete the grid below so that each number shown forms part of a group of horizontally and/or vertically connected cells. The number of cells in the group must be the same as the number shown on the grid. So a '2' indicates a group that is a pair of two cells. No group shares a horizontal or vertical boundary with another group of the same size/number. Every group of cells has at least one number shown.

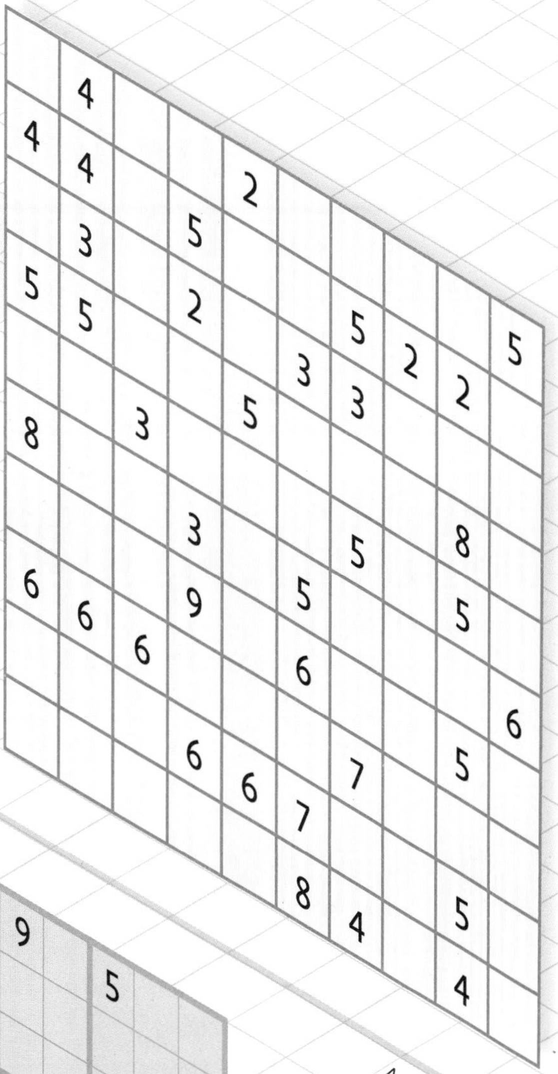

Answer see page 273

Answer see page 273

83

Complete the grid below so that every row, column, and 3x3 square each contains the digits 1-9 precisely once.

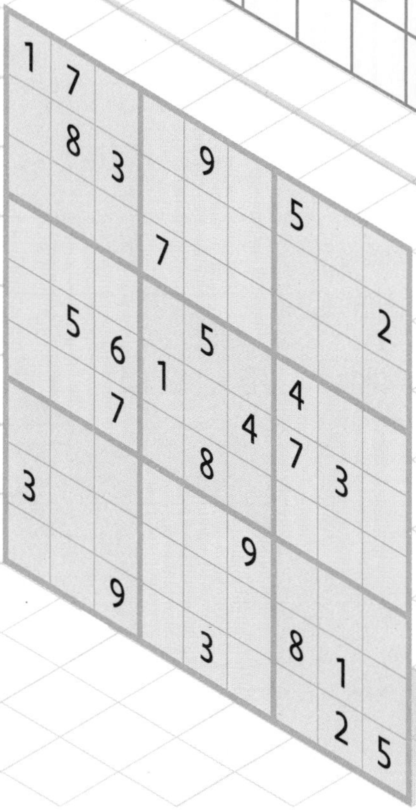

What number should replace the question mark?

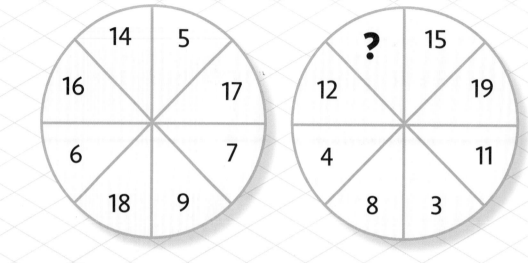

Answer see page 273

Answer see page 273

85 Complete the grid below so that every row, column, and 3x3 square each contains the digits 1-9 precisely once. The sum of the digits in each group of cells with a dotted outline must total the number in the group's top/left corner.

Which symbols are missing from the grid below?

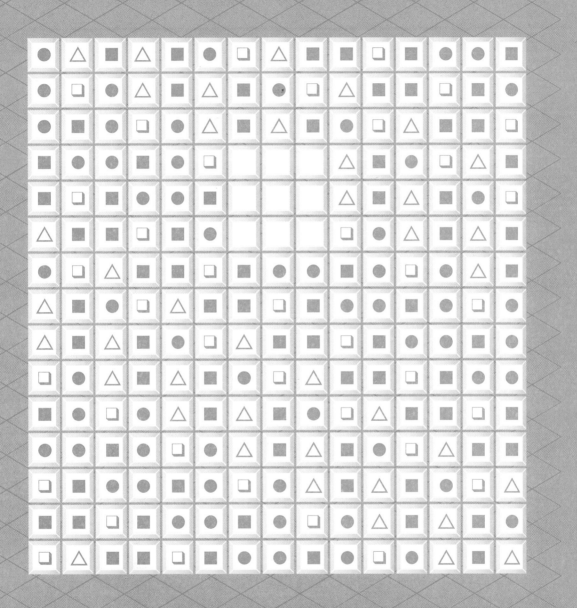

Answer see page 273

87

Ten vessels are hidden in the grid below, four one-cell ships, three two-cell ships, two three-cell ships, and one four-cell ship. Ships are positioned horizontally or vertically. No two ships are immediately adjacent to each other, including diagonally. The numbers next to each row and column show the total number of ship segments in that line. Identify the exact locations of all ten vessels. Some ship segments and/or spaces of empty ocean are shown to assist you.

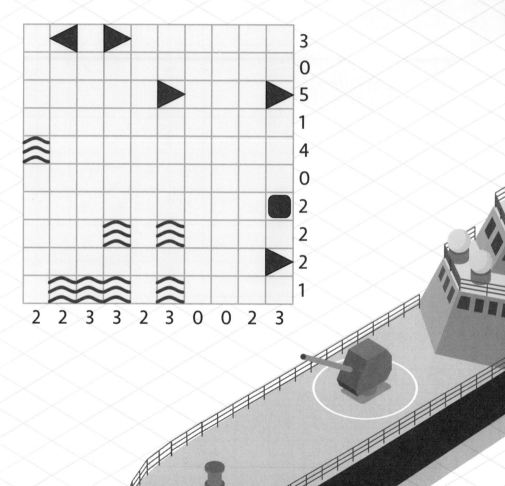

Answer see page 273

88 In each square, the arrow shows the direction you must move in. The numbers in some squares show that square's position in the correct sequence of moves. Move from top left to bottom right, visiting each square in the grid exactly once.

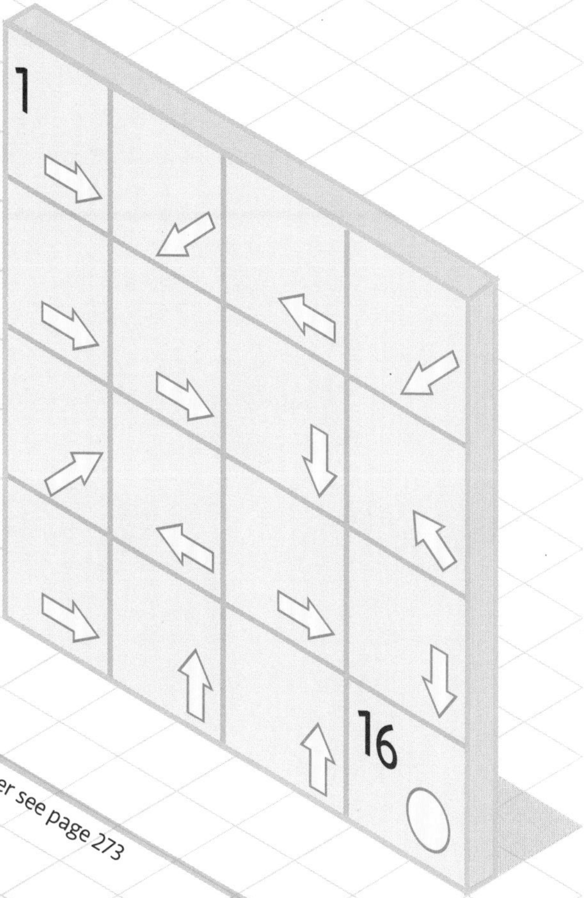

Answer see page 273

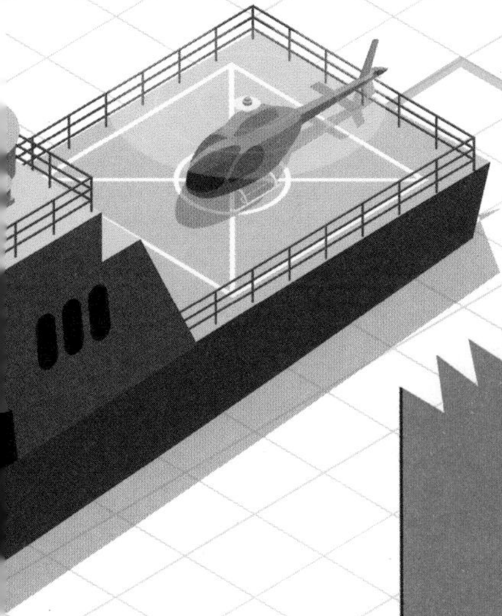

Answer see page 273

89 Which of the four pieces A to D fits to complete the shape?

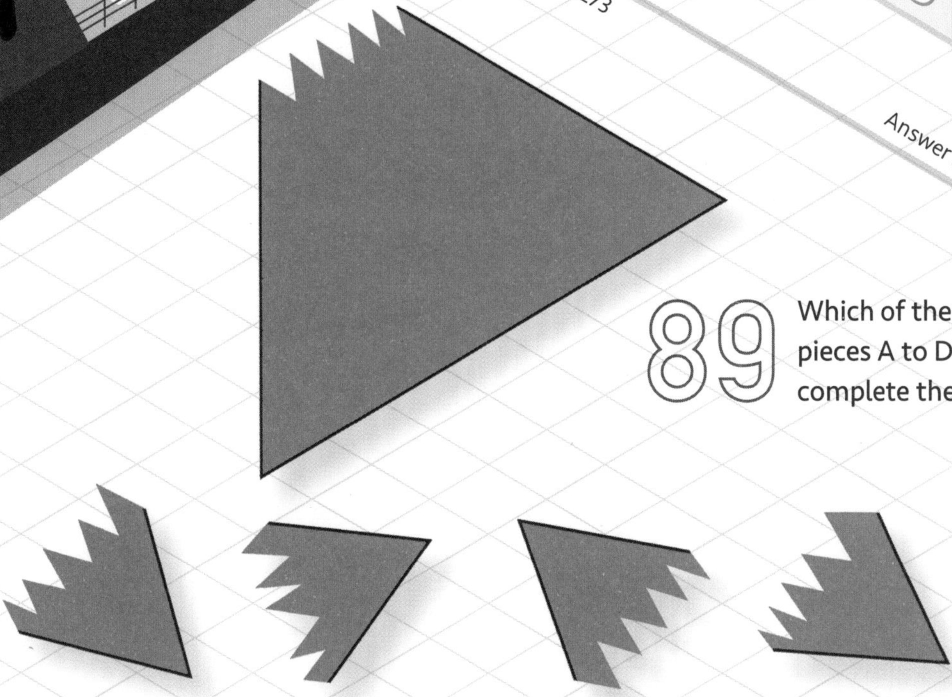

A   B   C   D

Decipher the names of several celebrities using the telephone dial as a guide.

78737847468

339273667866

5225642465766

2426646482886

27823945547

52637622869

Answer see page 273

91 In the grid below, how much is each symbol worth?

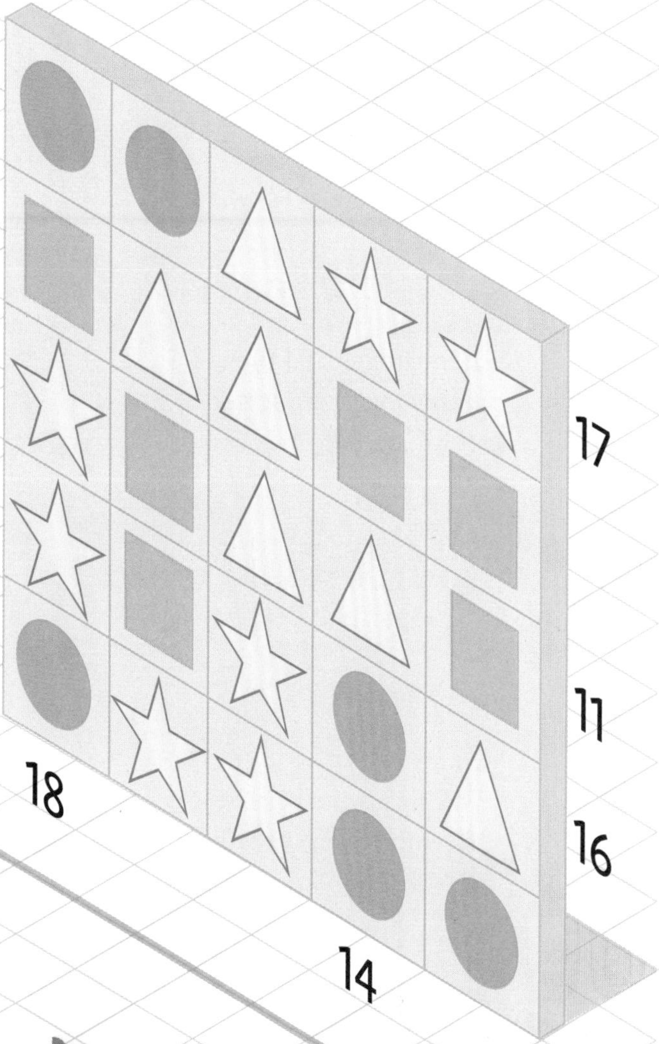

Answer see page 273

17

11

16

18

14

92 The pieces can be assembled into a regular geometric shape. What is it?

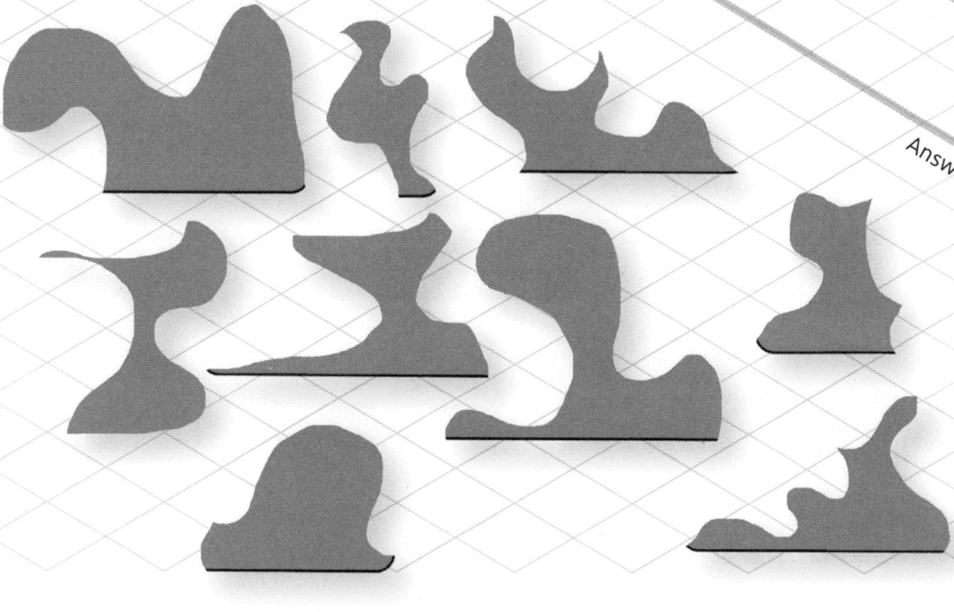

Answer see page 273

93

Complete the grid below so that every row, column, and 3x3 square each contains the digits 1-9 precisely once. The sum of the digits in each group of cells with a dotted outline must total the number in the group's top/left corner.

15
11
7
16
16
11
10
12
7
12
6
12
6
11
12
16
7
8
12
16
9
5
10
11
12
11
15
5
7
12
13
9
11
15
14
5
18

Answer see page 273

Answer see page 274

94

The pieces can be assembled into a regular geometric shape. What is it?

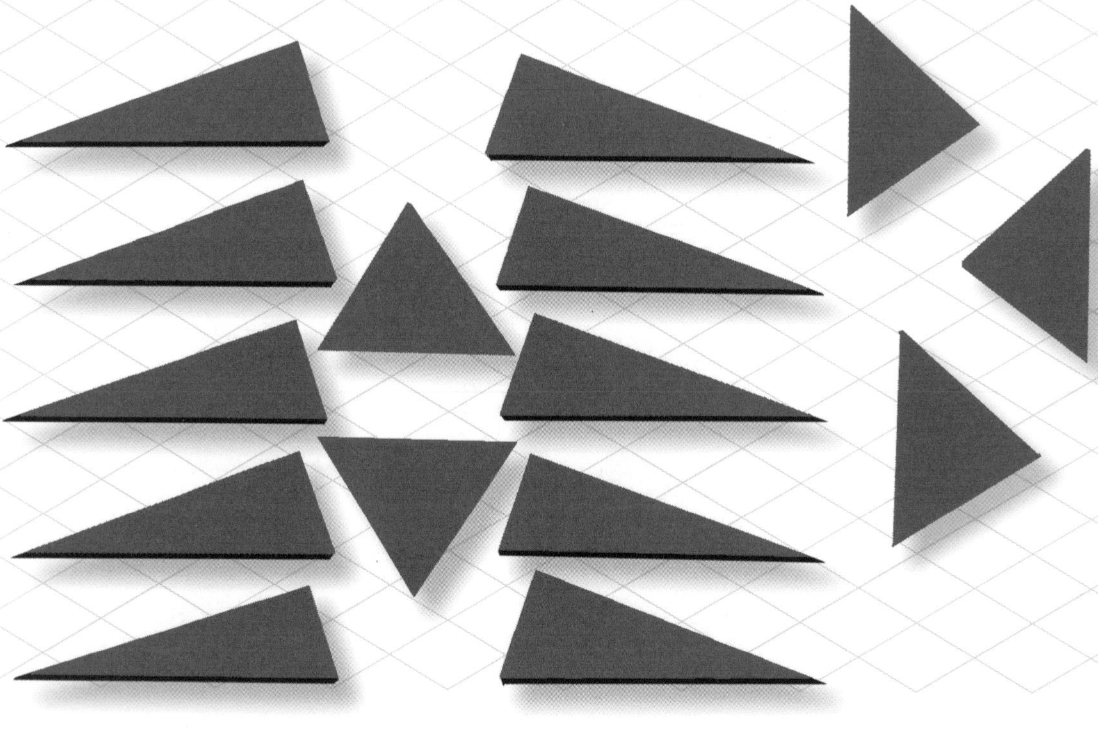

In the grid below, how much is each symbol worth?

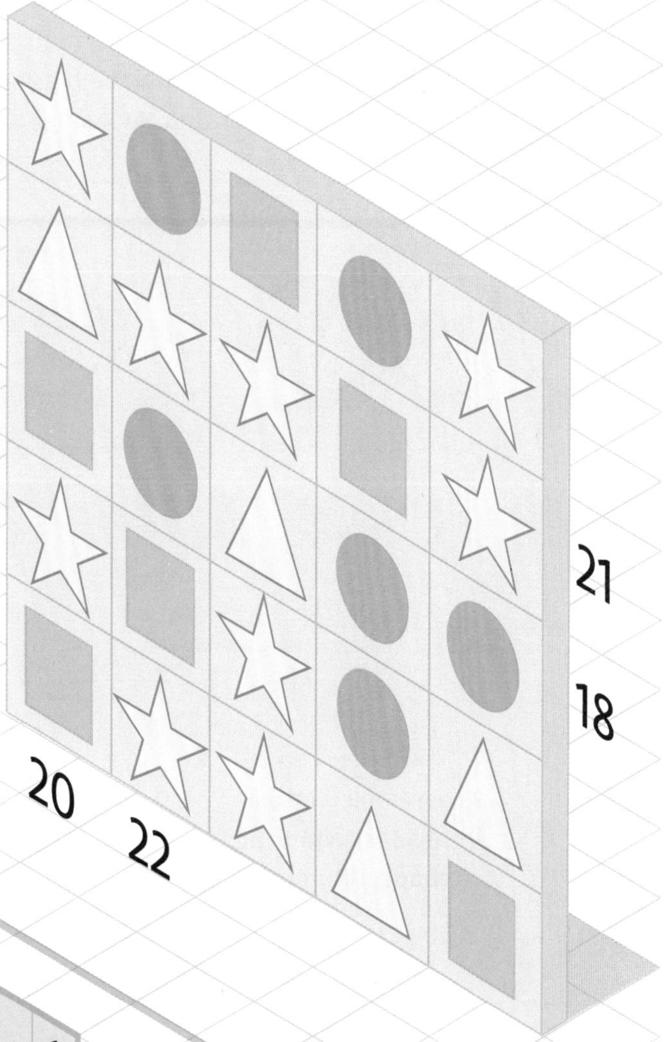

21

18

20

22

Answer see page 274

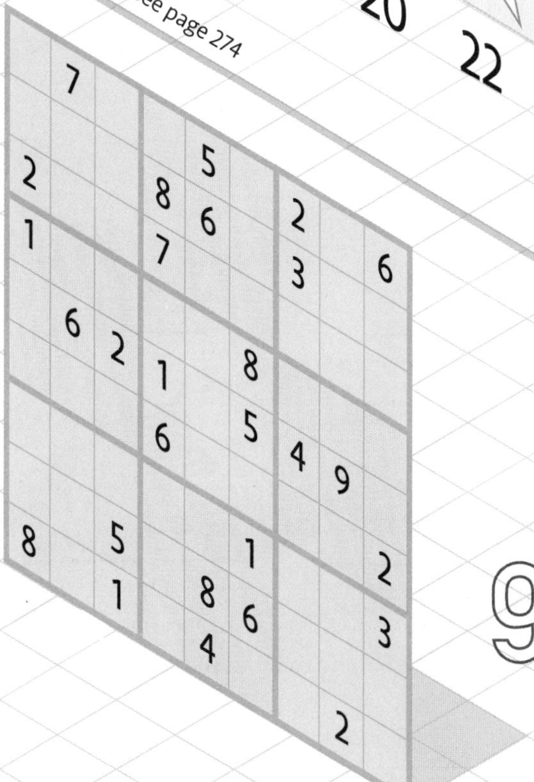

151

	7			5				
2			8	6		2		
1			7			3		6
	6	2	1		8			
			6		5	4	9	
8		5		8	1			2
		1		4	6			3
							2	

Answer see page 274

96 Complete the grid below so that every row, column, and 3x3 square each contains the digits 1-9 precisely once.

Fill in the missing plus, minus, multiplication, division, and/or factorial signs to make the equation below correct, performing all calculations strictly in the order they appear on the page.

$$10 \quad 15 \quad 11 \quad 9 \quad 9 \quad 23 \quad 14 = 83$$

Answer see page 274

The pieces can be assembled into a regular geometric shape. What is it?

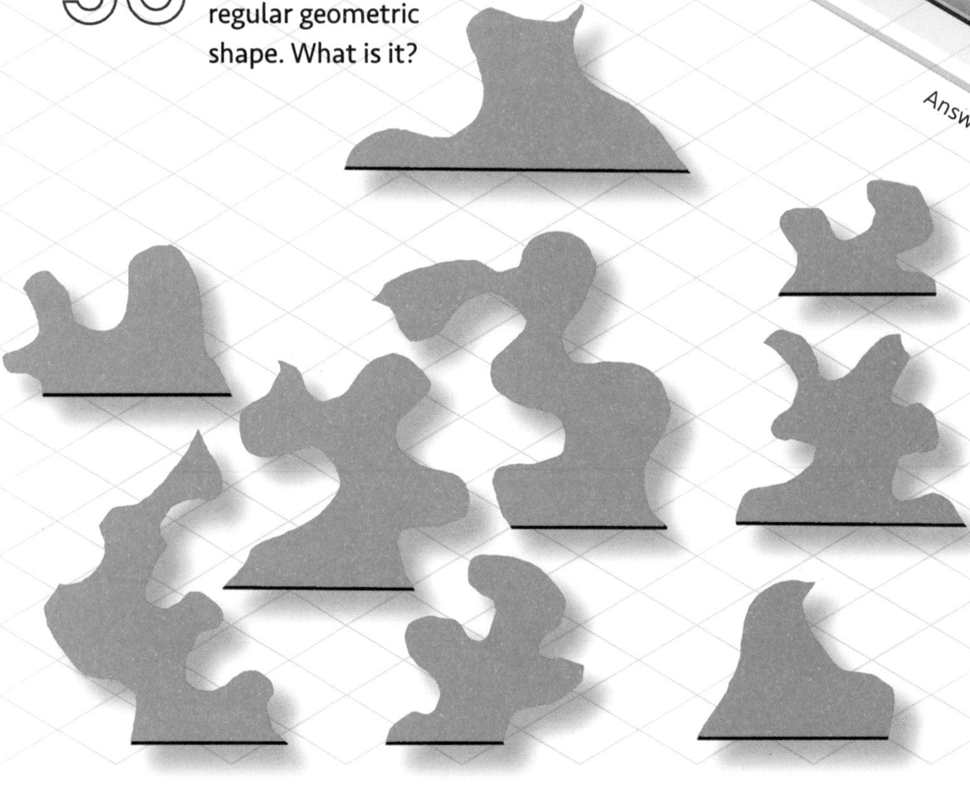

Answer see page 274

In the grid below, how much is each symbol worth?

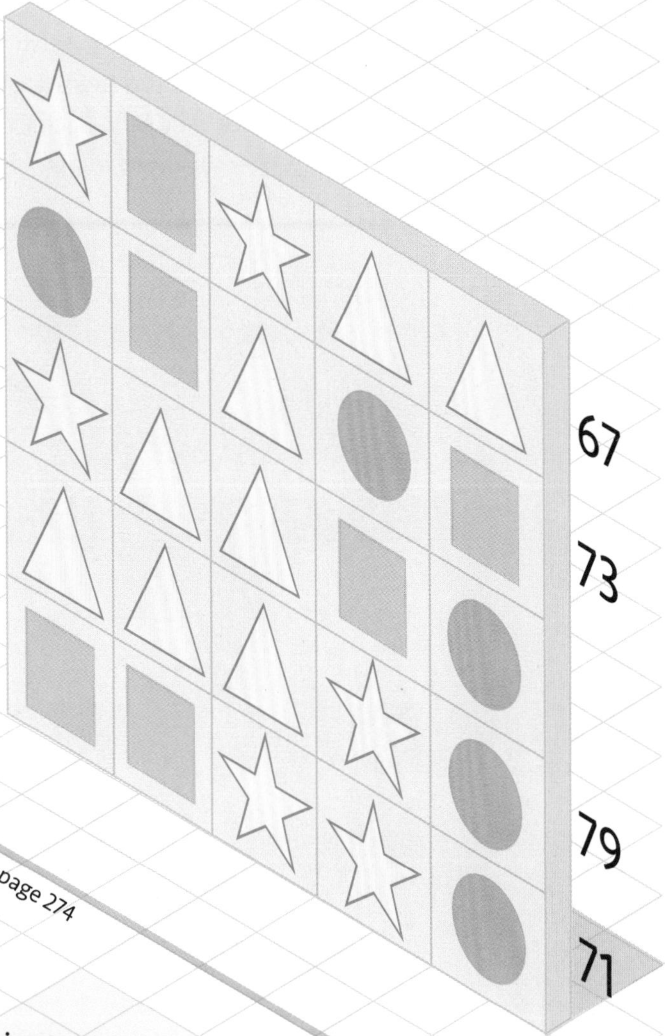

67
73
79
71

Answer see page 274

100

Fill in missing plus, minus, multiplication, division, and/or factorial signs to make the equation below correct, performing all calculations strictly in the order they appear on the page.

Answer see page 274

(20) (1) (23) (7) (16) (20) (4) = (265)

Complete the grid below so that each unbroken horizontal and vertical stretch of light cells sums to the total indicated in the cell to the left or above the stretch respectively. Each cell may contain only the digits 1 – 9, and no digit may be repeated in any given stretch of cells.

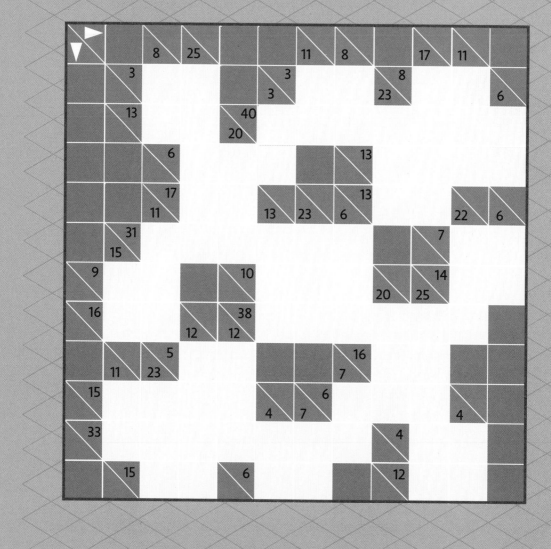

Answer see page 274

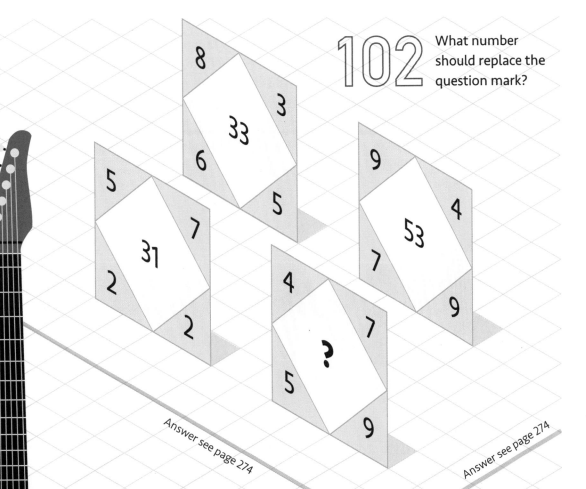

102

What number should replace the question mark?

Answer see page 274

Answer see page 274

103

Jason likes Nirvana but not AC/DC. Sam likes Metallica but not Black Sabbath. Jennifer likes Red Hot Chili Peppers but not Green Day. Which of the following does Thomas like?

SONIC YOUTH   THE BEATLES
LED ZEPPELIN   PINK FLOYD

104 Ten vessels are hidden in the grid below, four one-cell ships, three two-cell ships, two three-cell ships, and one four-cell ship. Ships are positioned horizontally or vertically. No two ships are immediately adjacent to each other, including diagonally. The numbers next to each row and column show the total number of ship segments in that line. Identify the exact locations of all ten vessels. Some ship segments and/or spaces of empty ocean are shown to assist you.

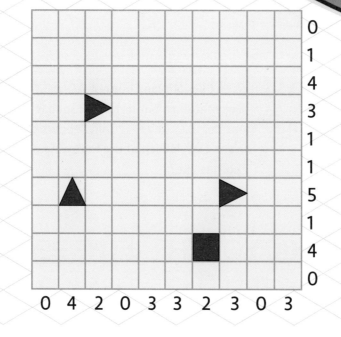

Answer see page 274

Which symbols are missing from the grid below?

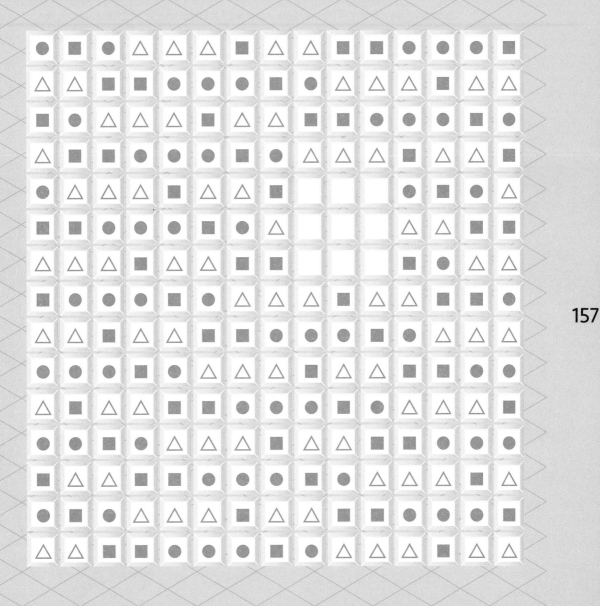

157

Answer see page 274

106

From the information below, what was the school sport of the person with a scarred forearm?

The former gymnast had become a librarian, and was not Rebecca, who had a torn hamstring. The person who had a sprain was a sprinter at school, and was neither Kevin nor Elizabeth. The teacher was not named Daniel or Kelly. The former snowboarder had become a barista. The person with a broken arm did not play football at school. Kelly, who had been in a car crash, was not a librarian. Kevin was a cook, and did not have a forearm scar. The pharmacist was not a former pole vaulter.

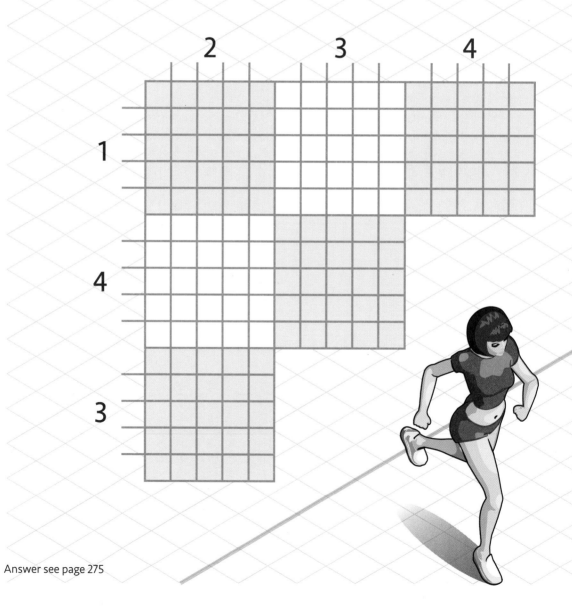

Answer see page 275

107 The grid below shows the numbers on a full set of dominoes, from 0-0 to 9-9 inclusive, that have been pushed together horizontally and vertically to make a solid rectangle. Complete the grid to show where each domino lies.

Answer see page 275

Answer see page 275

108 What number should replace the question mark to balance the beam?

Which symbols are missing from the grid below?

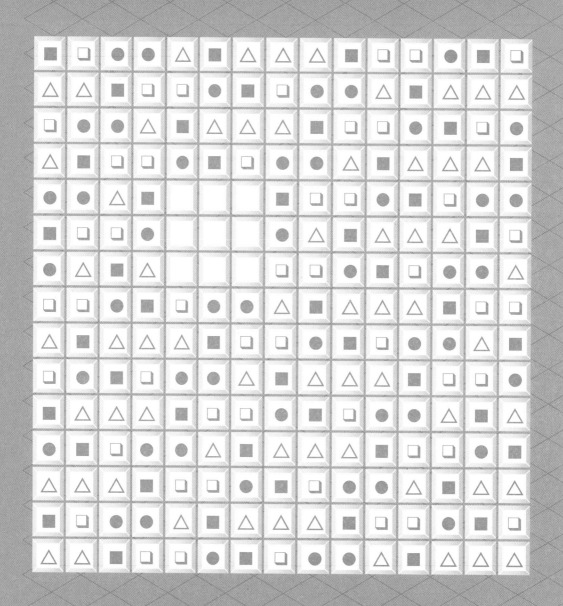

160

Answer see page 275

Assemble the pieces shown below into a square grid which reads the same across as it does downwards.

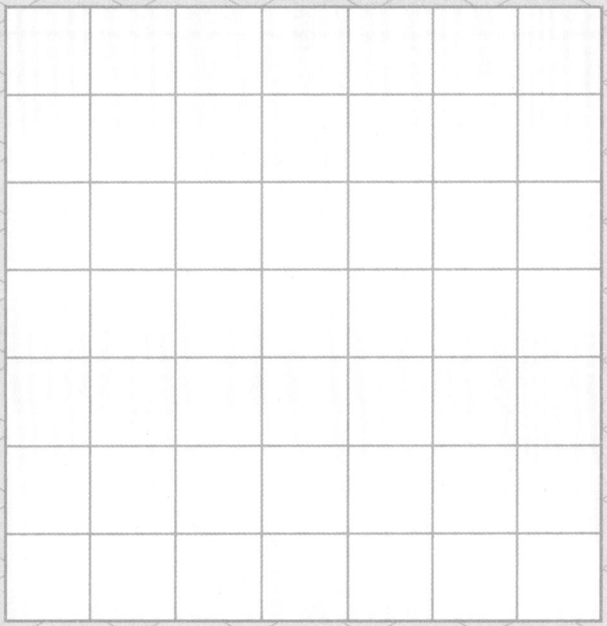

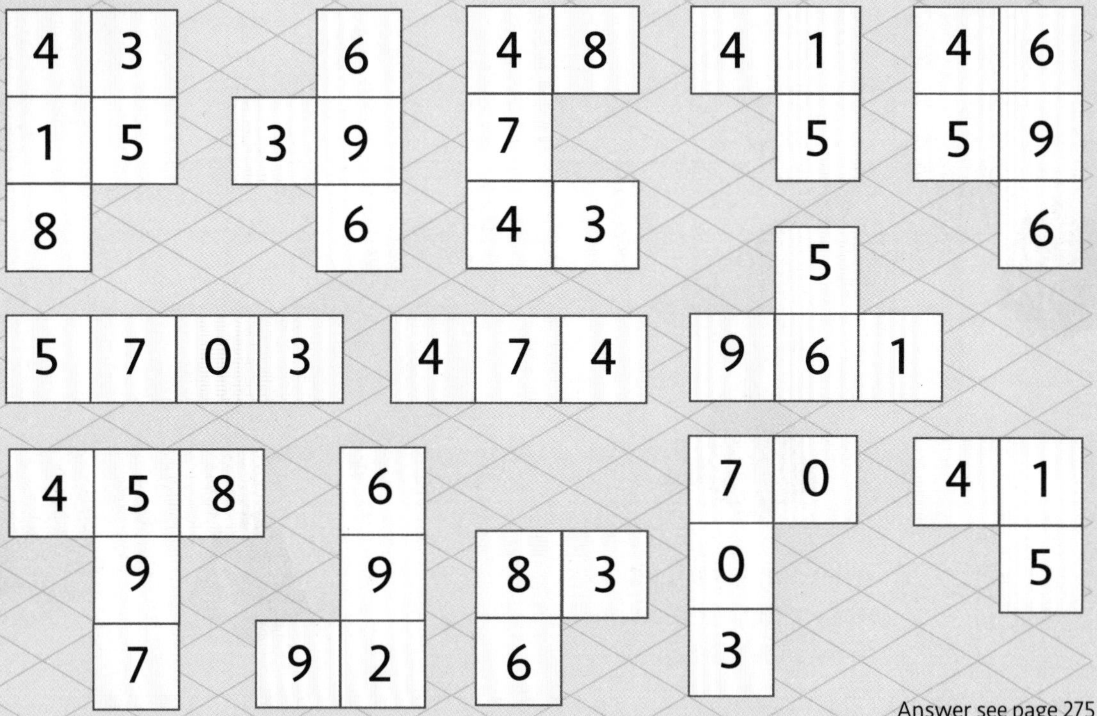

161

4	3
1	5
8	

	6
3	9
	6

4	8
7	
4	3

4	1
	5

4	6
5	9
	6

	5

5	7	0	3

4	7	4

9	6	1

4	5	8
	9	
	7	

6
9
9	2

8	3
6	

7	0
0	
3	

4	1
	5

Answer see page 275

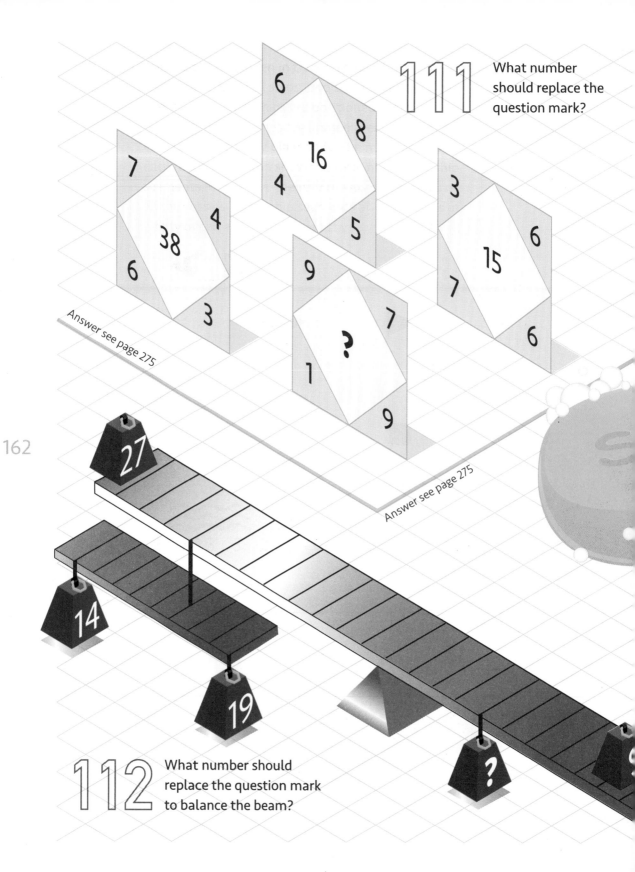

111 What number should replace the question mark?

6
8
16
4
5

7
4
38
6
3

3
6
15
7
6

9
7
?
1
9

Answer see page 275

Answer see page 275

162

27
14
19
?

112 What number should replace the question mark to balance the beam?

113

Using six straight lines, divide the design below into six sections, each containing precisely fifteen circles.

Answer see page 275

Answer see page 275

114

Are the following statements true or false?

i. Chlorine means 'greenish-yellow'.
ii. Crocodile hearts have six chambers.
iii. Hypergammon is a variant of backgammon.
iv. In Italy, asphodel leaves are used to wrap a type of salami.
v. Lugo is a city in Portugal.
vi. Olympia is the capital of Washington.
vii. Soap was invented in roughly 2800BC.
viii. The constellation of Lacerta represents a lizard.
ix. Thomas Klestil was a former president of Austria.
x. Zero is an imaginary number.

Which symbols are missing from the grid below?

164

116 Complete the grid below so that every row, column, and 3x3 square each contains the digits 1-9 precisely once.

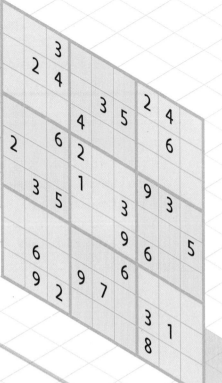

Answer see page 275

117 Which of the four pieces A to D fits to complete the shape?

Answer see page 275

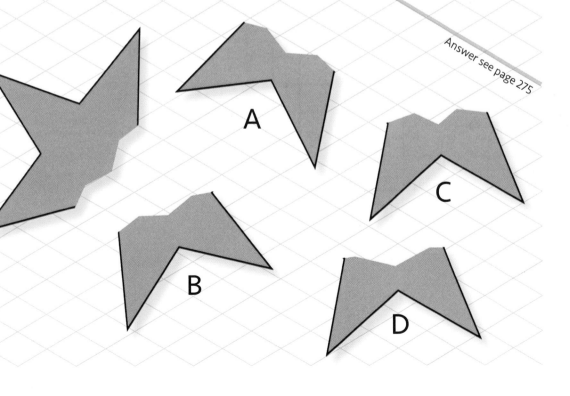

118

From the information below, what was the coffee served with the black forest gateau, and how much did it cost?

Either Scott or Jeffrey paid $5.50 and had an espresso. Jeffrey paid more than the person who had a blueberry muffin. Either Mary ate the black forest gateau and Richard had an americano, or Jeffrey ate the black forest gateau and Mary had the americano. Amanda, who got a ristretto, paid 50¢ more than the person who had a pain au chocolat, who was either Scott or Jeffrey. The person who ordered a latte paid less than the person who didn't have a black forest gateau, but who ordered an espresso. Someone had a cappuccino. The pain au chocolat meal cost more than the croissant meal. The amounts paid were $4.00, $4.50, $5.00, $5.50 and $6.00. Someone ordered a red velvet cake.

166

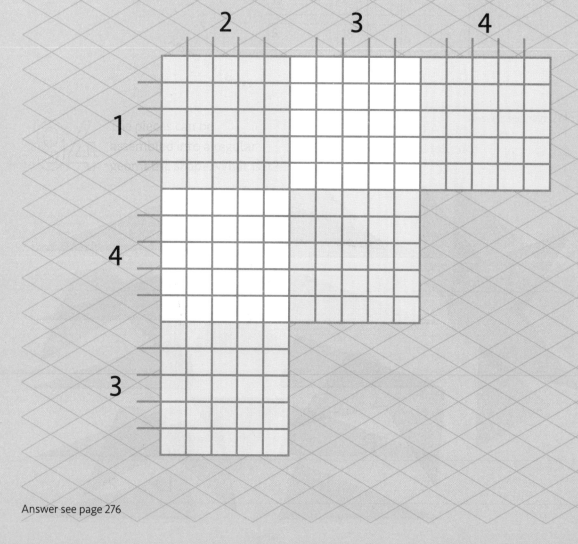

Answer see page 276

119

Using seven straight lines, divide the design below into seven sections, each containing precisely seven triangles.

Answer see page 276

Answer see page 276

120

What number should replace the question mark?

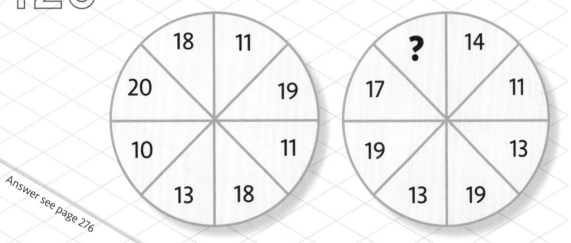

Answer see page 276

121

Which of the four pieces A to D fits to complete the shape?

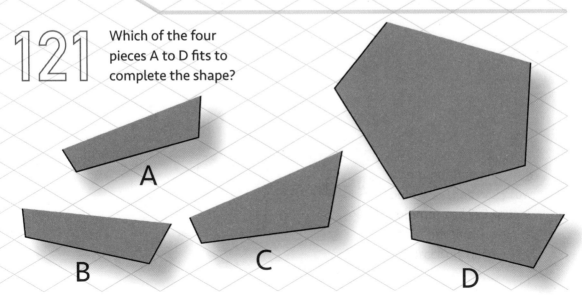

Decipher the names of several celebrities using the telephone dial as a guide.

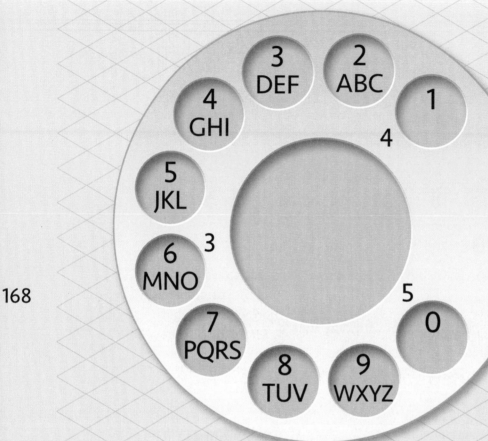

168

2367845537
628832666
6936945766
266342842929
84625536
7624694554267

Answer see page 276

Assemble the pieces shown below into a square grid which reads the same across as it does downwards.

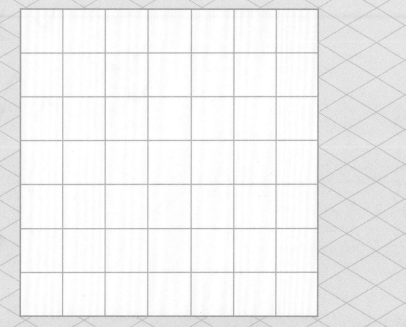

| 9 |
| 4 |
| 2 |

| 2 | 9 |
| 9 | 1 |

| 8 |
| 0 |
| 5 |
| 4 |

| | 4 |
| 1 | 7 | 9 |

| 9 | 4 | 7 |
| | 8 |

1	2
2	
5	

| 5 | 1 | 9 |
| | | 3 |

| 4 | 2 |
| 9 | 3 |

| 5 |
| 8 |
| 1 |
| 2 |

| 1 | 2 |
| 5 | 4 |

| 4 |
| 6 |
| 1 |

| 3 |
| 9 |
| 3 |

| 9 | 4 | 6 | 1 |

Answer see page 276

Complete the grid below so that every row and column each contains the digits 1-6 precisely once. A cell with a chevron pointing into it is smaller than the cell on the other side of the chevron.

Answer see page 276

What number should replace the question mark?

Answer see page 276

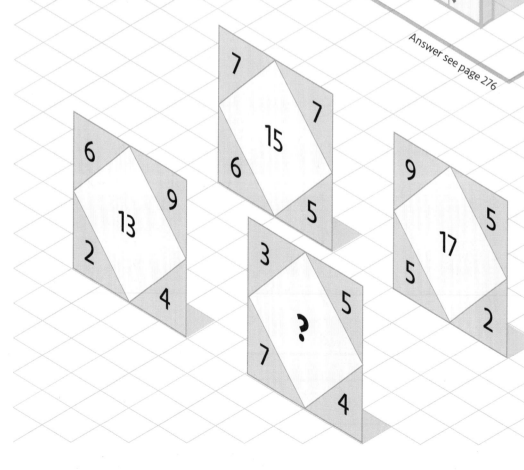

126 The grid below shows the numbers on a full set of dominoes, from 0-0 to 9-9 inclusive, that have been pushed together horizontally and vertically to make a solid rectangle. Complete the grid to show where each domino lies.

Answer see page 276

9	5	2	5	0	7	2	7	9	9	3
1	6	1	8	9	8	8	3	2	5	0
9	6	1	4	3	2	8	9	5	5	2
2	6	8	8	0	8	3	2	7	5	0
4	5	4	1	8	9	0	6	3	5	8
0	1	7	6	8	7	6	9	5	0	1
7	3	0	4	1	5	9	0	5	9	3
6	1	8	6	9	1	9	0	9	4	7
6	4	2	2	4	3	3	4	2	1	7
5	8	5	3	7	4	4	2	6	9	7

Answer see page 276

171

127 Complete the grid below so that every row and column each contains the digits 1-6 precisely once. A cell with a chevron pointing into it is smaller than the cell on the other side of the chevron.

01 Can you draw three circles within the box so that each one completely encloses exactly one triangle, one square, and one pentagon? No two circles may enclose the same three elements.

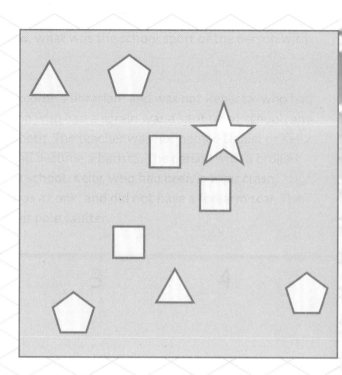

Answer see page 278

174

02 The Roman numeral equation spelled out with matchsticks below is incorrect. Can you add just one matchstick to form a correct equation?

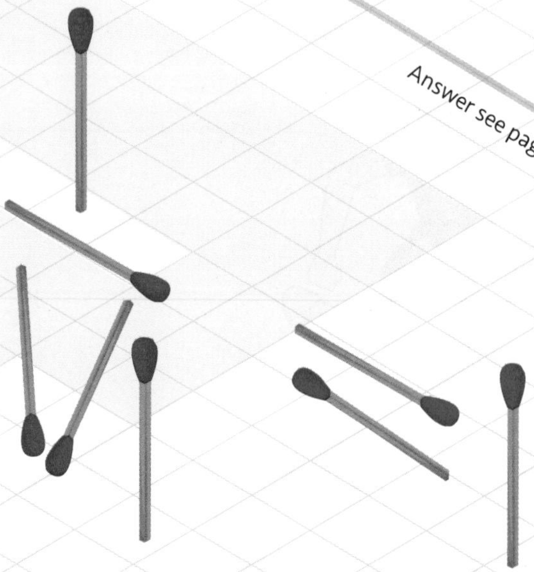

Answer see page 278

03 Ten people are sitting in two rows, facing each other, men on one side, and women on the other. From the information given below, can you say which desk Andy is at?

Either David or Richard are at desk 8. Either Debbie or Caroline are at desk 3. Either Amber or April are at desk 4. Sean is only sitting next to one person. Debbie is three desks away from Amber. Bernard is opposite the woman next to Lisa. Lisa is opposite David. Sean is next to Andy and opposite Amber. Andy is three desks from David, and desk 1 is opposite desk 10.

Answer see page 278

175

Answer see page 278

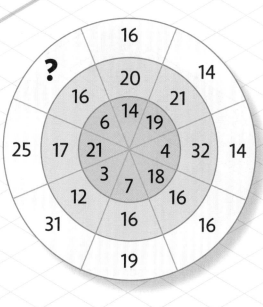

04 These rings obey a certain logic. What number should replace the question mark?

There are two bags. One, A, contains a single counter, either white or black at equal chance. The other, B, contains three counters, two black and one white. A white counter is added to A. A is then shaken, and a counter drawn randomly, which proves to be white. Your goal is to randomly draw a white counter from one of the two bags. Is it better to flip a coin to select a bag to draw from at random, or is it better to pour both A and B into a single third bag, C, and draw a counter from there?

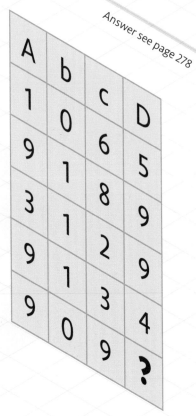

Answer see page 278

Answer see page 278

176

The following numbers obey a certain logic. What number should replace the question mark?

A	b	C	D
1	0	6	5
9	1	8	9
3	1	2	9
9	1	3	4
9	0	9	?

07

Starting in the centre rather than in a corner, follow the paths until you have five numbers, including the one where you started. Do not backtrack. Add the five together. What is the highest number you can obtain?

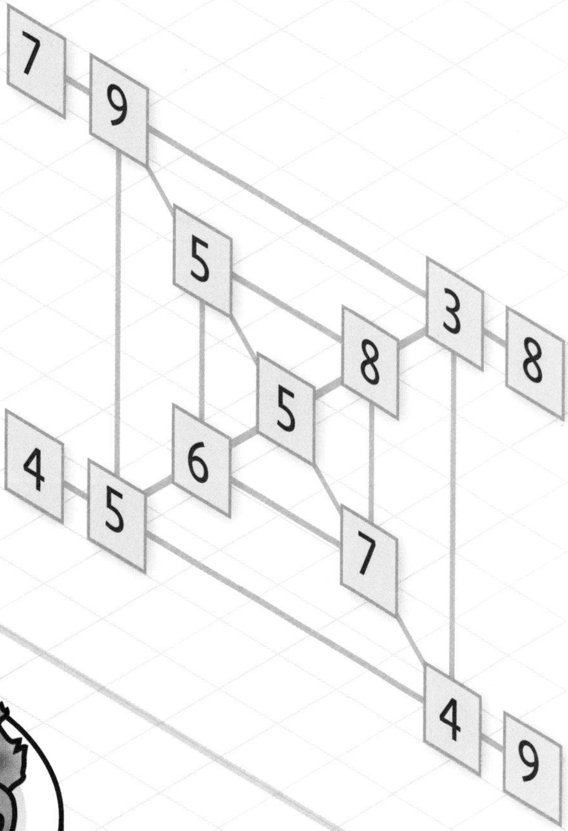

7 9

5

3 8

8

5

4 5 6

7

4 9

Answer see page 278

Answer see page 278

08

The following items are all foods. Can you decrypt them?

QPIITCQTGV RPZT

DPIBTPA

THRPAXKPSP

FJDGC

RDGCTS QTTU

YPBQPAPNP

GPIPIDJXAAT

YTGZN

Which group of shapes, A–D, most closely corresponds with the conditions of the large group of shapes above?

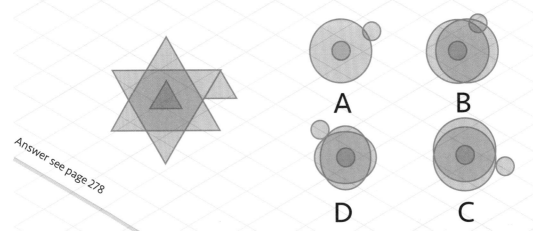

A   B

D   C

Answer see page 278

Answer see page 278

10

Can you place the segments below the triangular grid over the grid itself in such a way as to ensure that every node is covered by an identical symbol? Not all connecting lines will be covered.

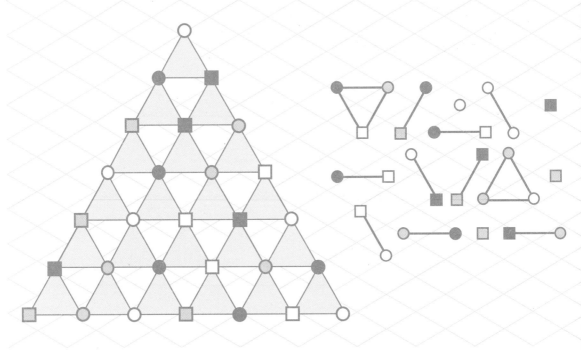

11

Figure #1 is to figure #2 as figure #3 is to which figure?

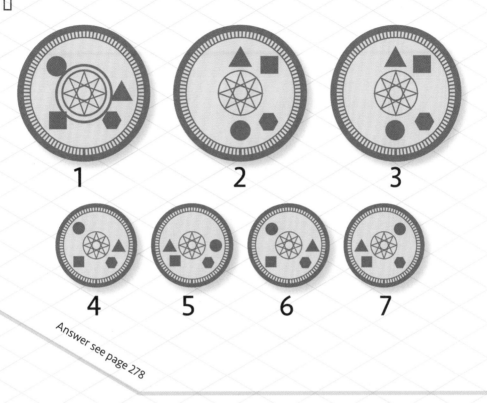

1   2   3

4   5   6   7

Answer see page 278

179

Answer see page 278

12

I find a piece of wood on the ground, one that I have never seen before. I pick it up, heft it thoughtfully, and then throw it. The piece of wood travels a reasonable distance before stopping completely. It then starts heading back towards me, arriving back finally to my hand again. It does not bounce or ricochet in any way, nor did I have anything tied to it. What happened?

13 Look at the diagram below. What is the largest version of the same shape that can be drawn within the box so that none of its edges touch any other edges, or stray outside the box?

Answer see page 278

14 Can you insert the mathematical operators:
+ – * / ^ . √ ! ( )
to make these equations valid?

Answer see page 278

A   4   2   3   4   8   =   4

B   2   5   4   2   4   3   =   1   7

C   5   5   5   5   5   5   5   5   =   5   5

15 Using six straight lines that each touch at least one side of the box below, can you divide the box into sections containing 1, 2, 3, 4, 5, 6, and 7 shapes?

Answer see page 278

16 This diagram obeys a certain logic. What could be the missing number?

Answer see page 278

? | 11

1224 | 619

1111 | 74

1012

17 These circles function according to a certain logic. What number should replace the question mark?

Answer see page 279

A

B

C

18 These triangles follow a certain specific logic. What number should replace the question mark?

Answer see page 279

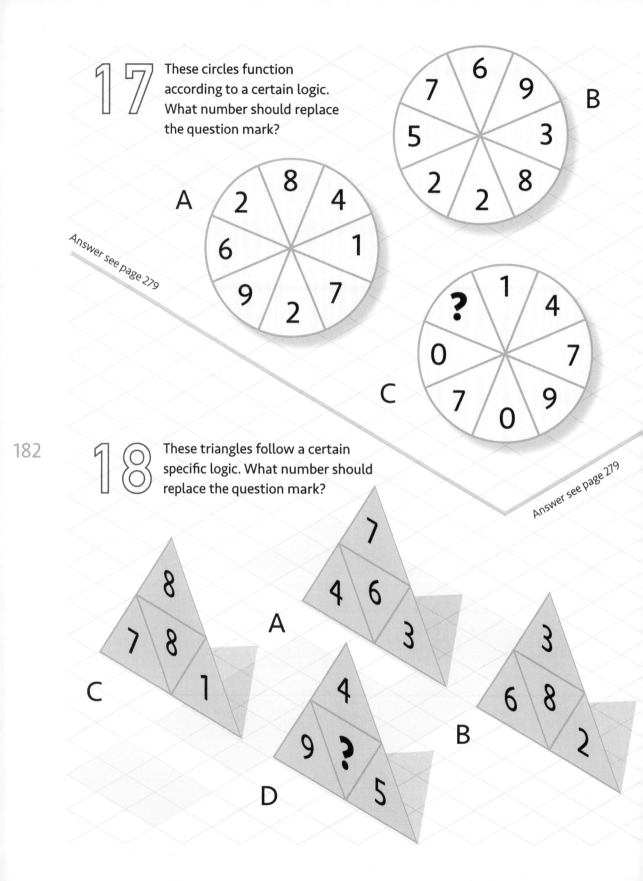

Can you fill in the numbers provided to correctly complete the grid?

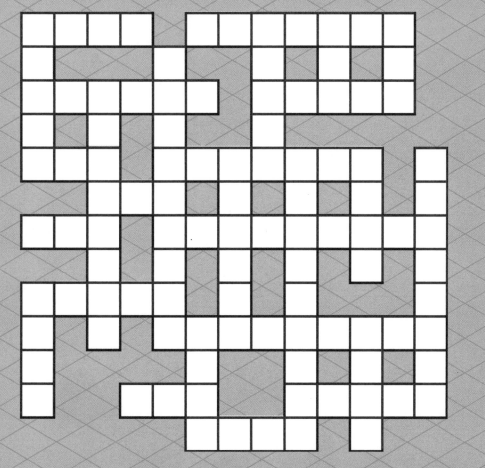

183

3 digit numbers	4 digit numbers	5 digit numbers	6 digit numbers	7 digit numbers	8 digit numbers	9 digit numbers
310	3410	12870	637251	5037593	36534897	148028558
417	4476	32570	854708	9581646	78783756	154331455
537	5536	34131				456941301
548	6414	36397				693352634
874	6848	98604				
963	9590					

Answer see page 279

20 Can you divide this square into four identical shapes, each one containing just one of each of the five symbols?

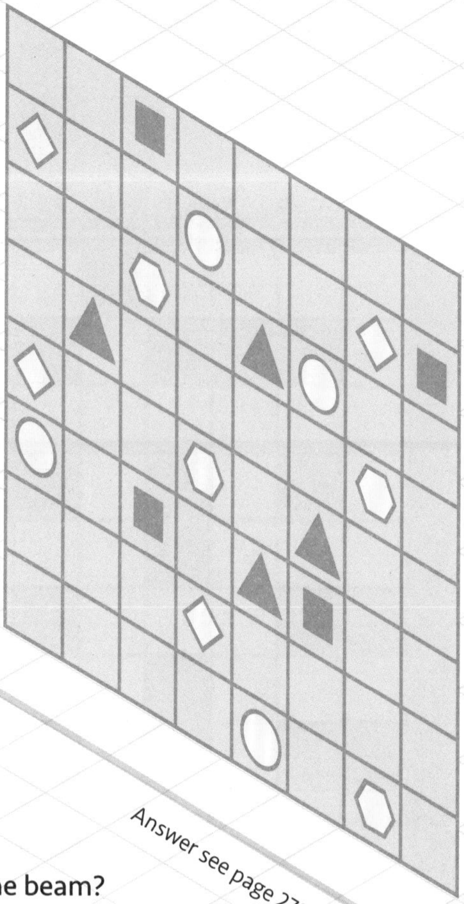

Answer see page 279

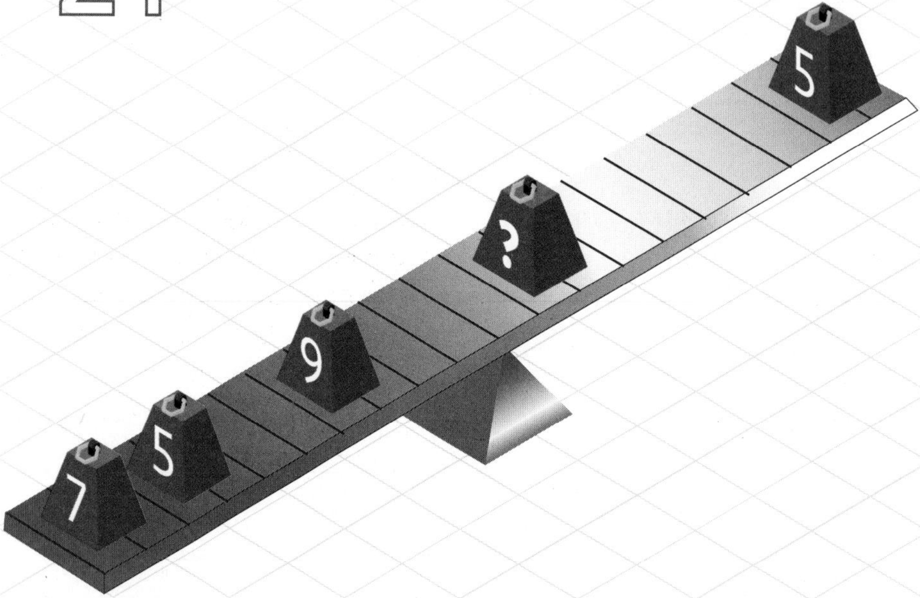

Answer see page 279

21 What weight will balance the beam?

22 Starting at any corner, follow the paths until you have five numbers, including the one where you started. Do not backtrack. Add the five together. What is the highest number you can obtain?

7 9 4 5 6 7 8 4 5 6 8 7 7 8 7

Answer see page 279

185

Answer see page 279

23 Ten people are in different locations in the city centre, and want to meet up. Which street corner should they pick to minimise their total combined journey?

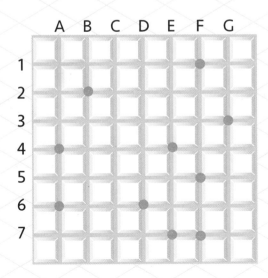

24

A group of friends decided to spend a day practising some survival skills. They persuaded their most competent friend, Wolfgang, to put them through their paces in a number of situations. He declared himself the General for the day, tested them all, and after each hour, assigned them promotions or demotions according to the table below.

Answer see page 279

Wolfgang's scoring was as follows. Hour 0: Everyone starts at private. Hour 1: Lito promoted by one, Riley by twice Lito's promotion, Nomi by twice Riley's promotion, and Capheus by twice Nomi's promotion. Hour 2: Kala promoted to First Sergeant, Sun promoted to two above Kala, Will placed four below Sun. Hour 3: Sun and Capheus both promoted by 2, Will by 1. Kala demoted by 1. Hour 4: Riley demoted by 1. Kala busted down to private. Nomi made a Captain. Hour 5: Everyone who was promoted after the first hour is again promoted by 1. Hour 6: Sun promoted by 2, Will by 4, and Kala by 1. Hour 7: Capheus demoted by 4. Riley promoted by 3, Kala by 2, and Nomi by 1.

Who did best, and what rank are they?

1. General
2. Brigadier
3. Colonel
4. Lieutenant-Colonel
5. Major
6. Captain
7. First Lieutenant
8. Lieutenant
9. First Sergeant
10. Sergeant
11. Corporal
12. Private

Figure #1 is to figure #2 as figure #3 is to which figure?

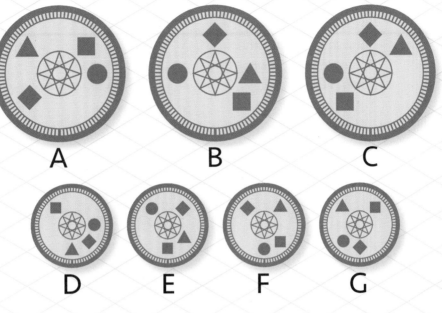

A

B

C

D

E

F

G

Answer see page 279

Answer see page 279

Three students are each taking four out of six subjects, so that each of the six subjects has two of the three students in it. From the information below, can you say which two study physics?

If Anna is studying mathematics, then she is also studying engineering. If she is studying engineering, then she is not studying programming. If she is studying programming, then she is not studying Japanese.

If Flora is studying programming, then she is also studying Japanese. If she is studying Japanese, then she is not studying mathematics. If she is studying mathematics then she is not studying micro-electronics.

If Susie is studying micro-electronics then she is not studying mathematics. If she is not studying mathematics, then she is studying Japanese. If she is studying Japanese, then she is not studying programming.

Can you draw three circles within the box so that each one completely encloses exactly one triangle, one square, and either one pentagon or one oval? No two circles may enclose the same three elements.

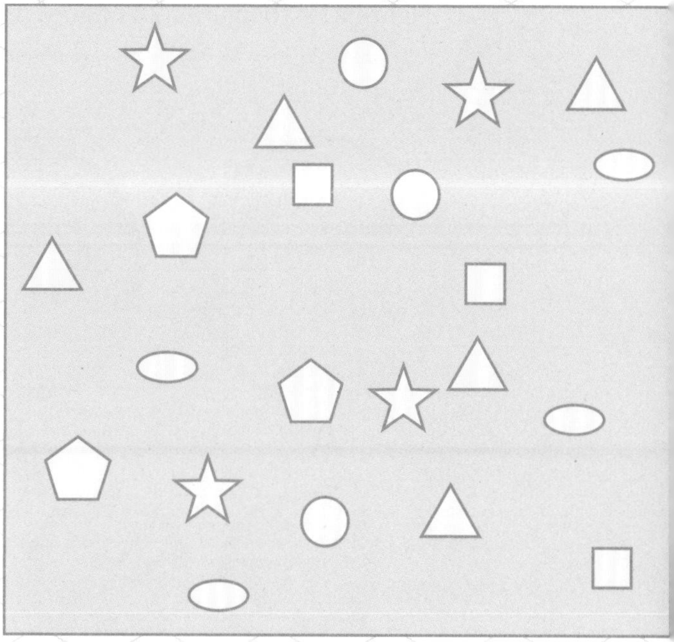

Answer see page 279

These 12-hour digital clocks follow a specific logic. Can you work out the time of the fifth clock?

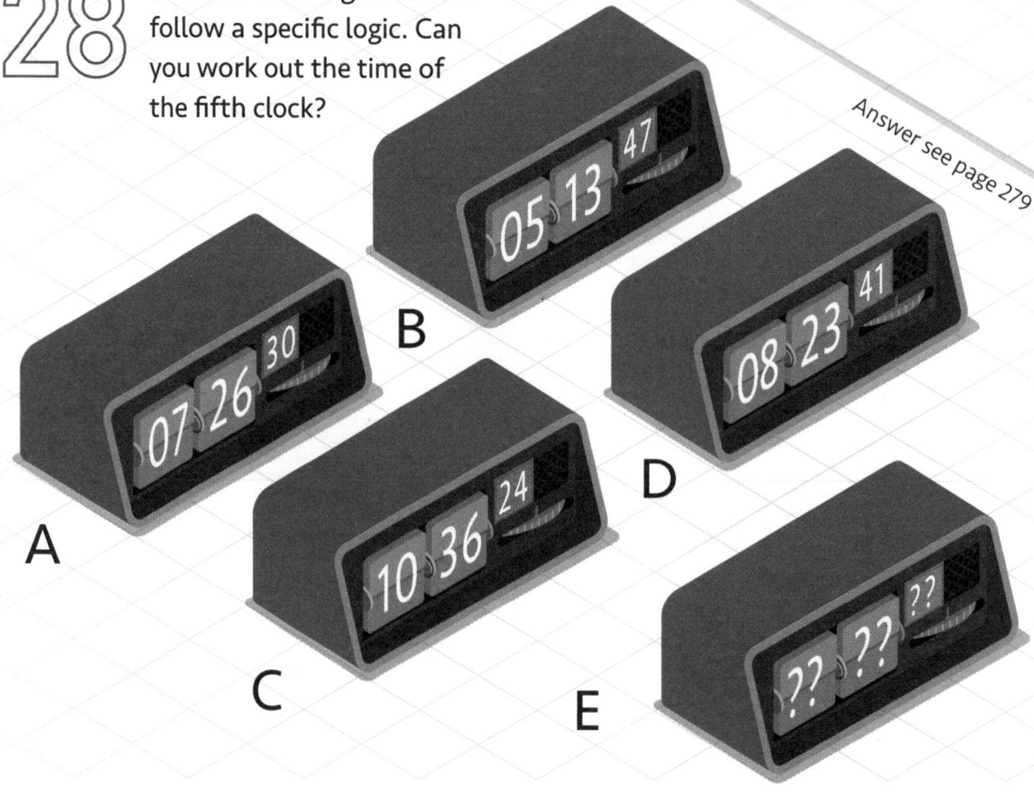

Answer see page 279

05:13 47

B

07:26 30

A

08:23 41

D

10:36 24

C

??:?? ??

E

To which of the lower shapes, A-E, could a single ball be added so that both balls matched the conditions of the balls in the upper shape?

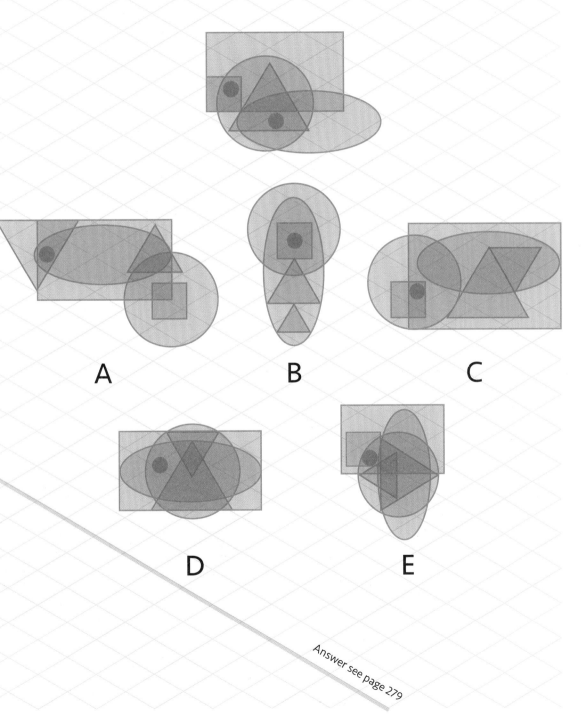

A

B

C

D

E

Answer see page 279

30 The following numbers obey a certain logic. What number should replace the question mark?

A	B	C	D	E
5	4	0	6	9
4	5	1	5	3
8	0	5	6	5
7	4	1	7	2
3	9	3	3	?

Answer see page 279

190

31 Amongst a group of 114 highly-dedicated bird watchers, 86 have seen an ivory-billed kingfisher, 77 have seen a kirtland's warbler, 92 have seen a whooping crane, 26 have seen a nene, and 57 have seen a piping plover. What is the least possible number of people who have seen just two of the five?

Answer see page 279

32 Each symbol in the grid has a consistent value. What number should replace the question mark?

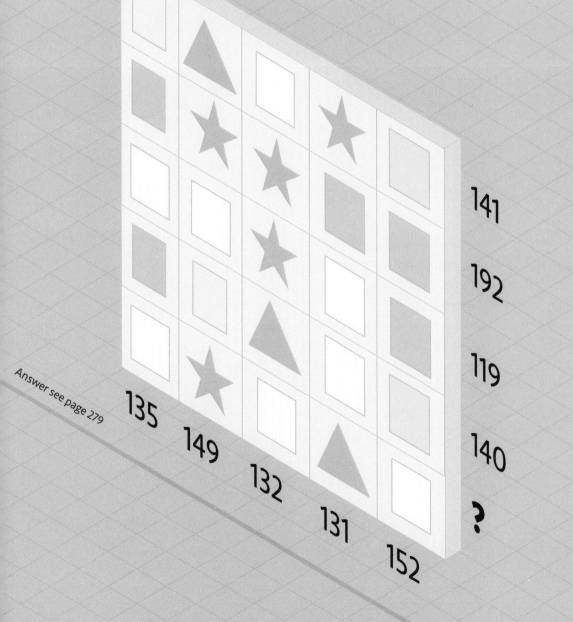

191

141

192

119

140

?

135

149

132

131

152

Answer see page 279

33 Which of these shapes is incorrect?

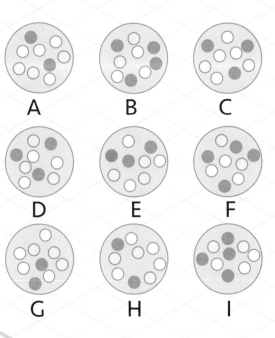

A   B   C

D   E   F

G   H   I

Answer see page 280

Answer see page 280

34 Following the logic of this diagram, what symbols should the triangle at the top contain?

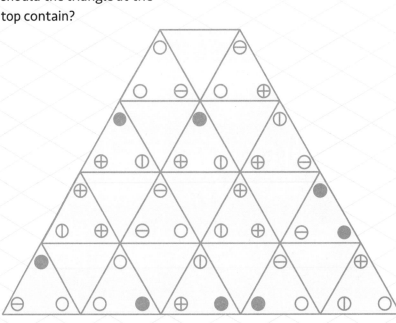

Following this set of simple instructions is supposed to turn any number of your choice into the same number. However, there is an error, and it doesn't work. What's wrong?

1. Choose any number and write it down.
2. Subtract 1 from the last number you wrote down and remember the result.
3. Write down the number you are remembering
4. Multiply the last number you wrote down by 3 and remember the result.
5. Write down the number you are remembering.
6. Add 12 to the last number you wrote down and remember the result.
7. Write down the number you are remembering.
8. Divide the last number you wrote down by 2 and remember the result.
9. Write down the number you are remembering.
10. Add 5 to the last number you wrote down and remember the result.
11. Write down the last number you are remembering.
12. Subtract the first number you wrote down from the last number you wrote down and remember the result.
13. Write down what you are remembering.
14. If the last number you wrote down was 8, say SUCCESS otherwise say FAILURE.
15. Stop.

193

Answer see page 280

Answer see page 280

These clocks obey a specific sequence. What time should the missing hour hand on the fourth clock be pointing towards?

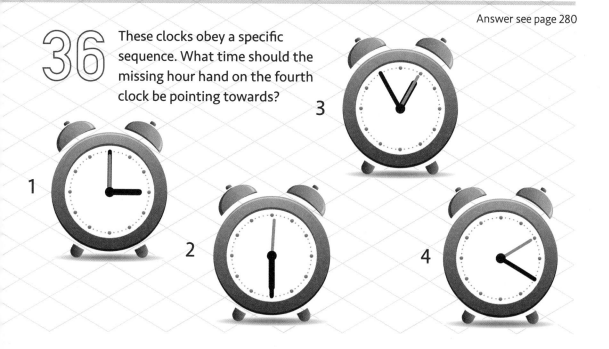

37 Four of these five pieces fit together to make a regular geometric shape. Which one is left over?

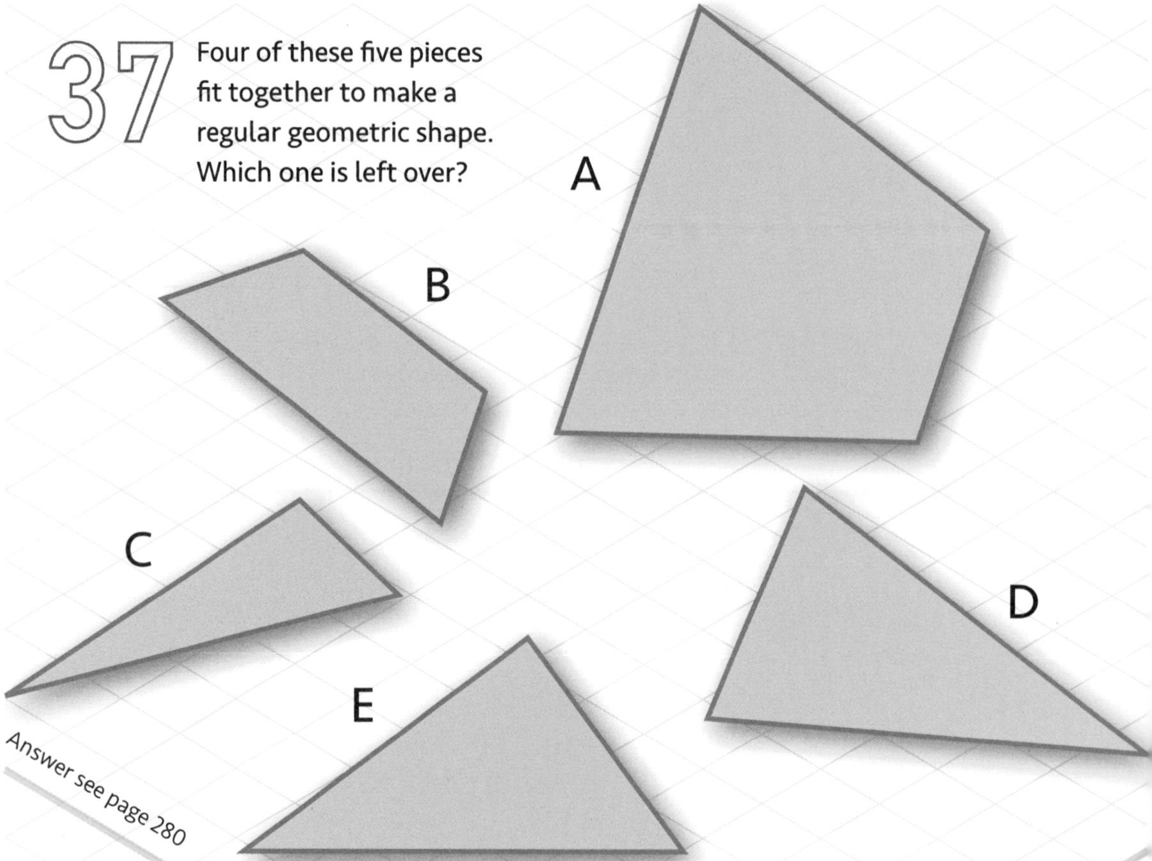

A

B

C

D

E

Answer see page 280

194

Answer see page 280

38 The matchstick diagram below shows three triangles. Can you move just two matchsticks to leave you with no triangles remaining?

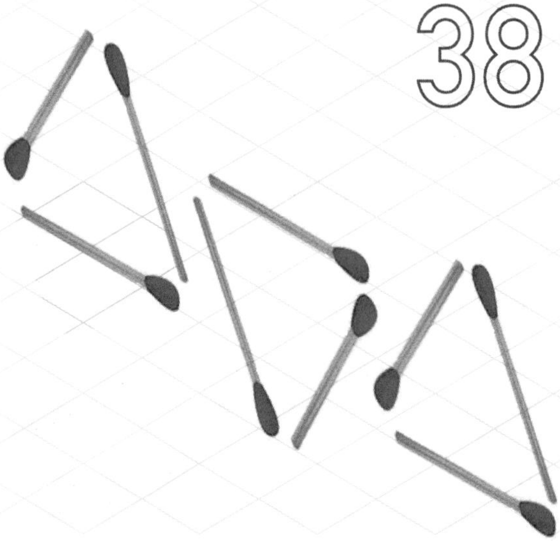

39 You are faced with three people, A, B, and C, who know each other. They are standing in that order, where A is on the left as you look at them. One of the three always lies, one always tells the truth, and one either tells the truth or lies randomly. You are allowed to ask three yes or no questions, each one to be answered by a single person of your choosing. Which three questions, directed to which people, will uncover the truthful member of the three?

Answer see page 280

Answer see page 280

 A highly competitive race was run in five legs. Given the distances in kilometres of each leg, and the average speed in meters per second for that leg for the top five contestants, can you work out who won, and in what total time?

Runner	Leg: Distance:	A-B 2.4km	B-C 2.6km	C-D 2.5km	D-E 2.7km	E-F 2.3km
V		4.65	4.52	4.32	3.81	5.23
W		4.67	4.51	4.35	3.79	5.22
X		4.71	4.49	4.31	3.80	5.24
Y		4.68	4.51	4.29	3.82	5.23
Z		4.72	4.52	4.30	3.79	5.21

41 Can you rearrange the digits in this equation to make it correct, without adding any mathematical operators?

$$6 \quad 6 \quad = \quad 2 \quad 3 \quad 4$$

Answer see page 280

Answer see page 280

42 Examine the following sets of scales, which are in perfect balance. How many balls are needed to balance the final scale?

196

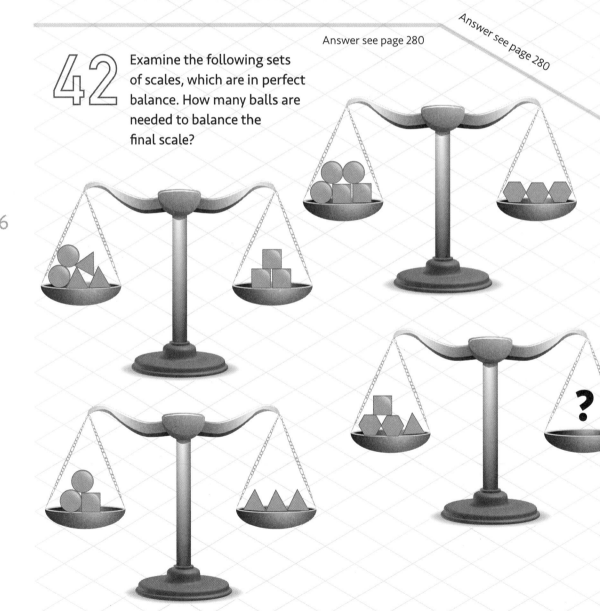

43

The following playwrights have had the vowels and spaces removed from their names. Can you untangle them?

JNCCT   GRGBCHNR

LBRTCMS   LFRHKRSMNRSN

SMNRZ   PRRDMRVX

MRTNMCDNGH   STPHNSNDHM

SNCTHNGR   TRCLTTS

SHLGHDLN   KLDS

Answer see page 280

44

Ten people are going to different locations in the city centre, and want to meet up afterwards. Which street corner should the tenth stand on in order to have the shortest possible walk to the meeting place that they pick to minimise their total combined journey?

Answer see page 280

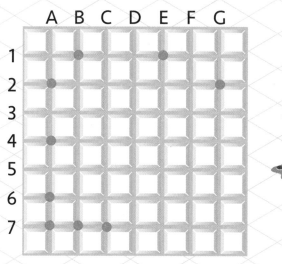

Five people found themselves waiting for sequential interviews at an information day for the Open University. Where did the would-be historian travel from?

The person from Norfolk worked as an estate agent, whilst the person from Rutland wanted to study philosophy, and Elvira was from Essex. The teacher, whose name was Milton, was the person immediately before the accountant. The person with red hair wanted to study sociology. The person who worked as a vet had black hair, whilst Lala had the middle spot. The resident of Hampshire had the first interview. The person with blonde hair was immediately before or after the person who wanted to study anthropology, whilst the person with black hair was immediately before or after the person wanted to study psychology. Anthony had grey hair, but the person from Cumbria had brown hair. The person from Hampshire was immediately before or after the person who worked as a life coach. Lillian was immediately before or after a person with blonde hair.

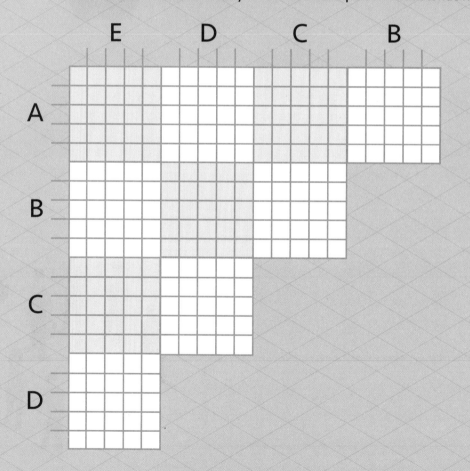

Answer see page 280

You are faced with three doors, two of which are wired to kill you as soon as you open them. Each door bears a sign. However, either one or none of the signs are true, you are not sure which. Which door should you open?

Sign A: This door is deadly.

Sign B: This door is safe.

Sign C: Door B is deadly.

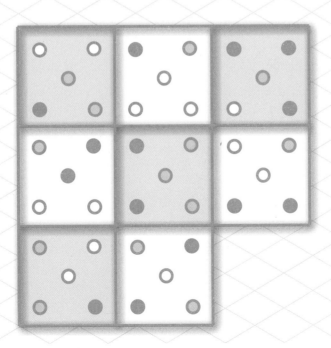

Answer see page 280

The diagram below operates according to a specific logic. What should the missing square look like?

Answer see page 280

48 These circles function according to a certain logic. What number should replace the question mark?

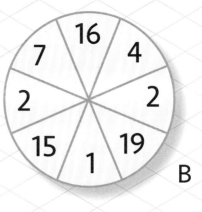

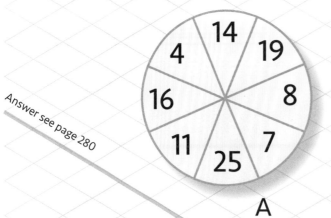

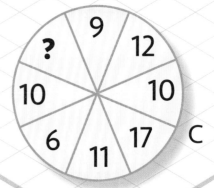

Answer see page 280

49 These columns observe a certain logic. What should the next column look like?

Answer see page 281

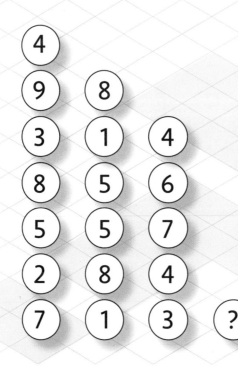

Can you uncover the logic of this grid of letters and replace the question mark with the right letter?

Answer see page 281

Answer see page 281

Signs – symbols in a specific position – which appear in the outer circles are transferred to the inner circle as follows: If it appears once, it is definitely transferred. If it appears twice, it is transferred if no other symbol will be transferred from that position. If it appears three times, it will be transferred if there is no sign appearing once in that position. If it appears four times, it is not transferred. In instances where signs with the same count are competing, then from high to low, priority runs top left – top right – bottom left – bottom right. What does the inner circle look like?

52 The word MAMMAL is located exactly once in the grid below, but could be horizontally, vertically or diagonally forwards or backwards. Can you locate it?

202

```
L L A L A A M A M A M A M A M
A M L M A L A M A A M M A M M
M L M A L M A M M M A A M A M
L L A A A M M L L M A A A M
A L M L L A M A M A A M M L M
M A A A L M A M A M L M A A A
A M A A L M M A M M M M L M L
M M M A M A L M M M A M A M M
M A L L A A M M A M M A A A A
A M L M A A M M A A M L M M M
A L M M M M A A A L L L M M A
A A L M M L A M L A A M M M L
A M M M A M L M M A A M A M M
M M M M M A A L A M M A A A L
L L M M A L M M A M L M A M A
```

53

A is to B as C is to D, E, F, G or H?

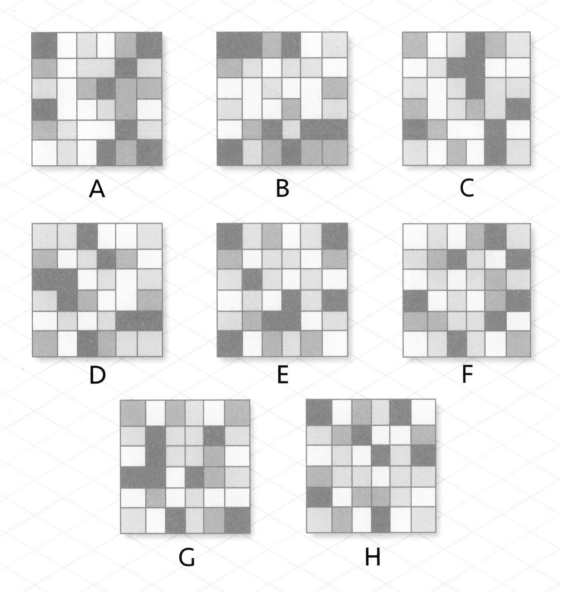

A

B

C

D

E

F

G

H

Answer see page 281

54 Imagine that there are a pair of level train tracks encircling the Earth's equator. A pair of trains are set running in opposite directions, so that they each complete a full circuit of the earth in one calendar day. Assuming that they don't fail, crash, or run out of fuel, which train's wheels will wear down first?

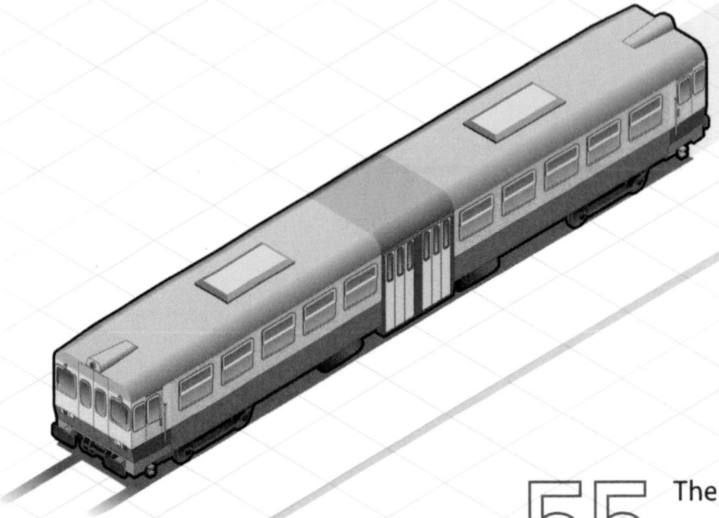

Answer see page 281

Answer see page 281

55 The letters and numbers in this square obey a certain logic. What letter should replace the question mark?

56

The following list of numbers represents uncommon colours whose letters have been encoded into the numbers needed to reproduce them on a typical phone dial. Can you decode them?

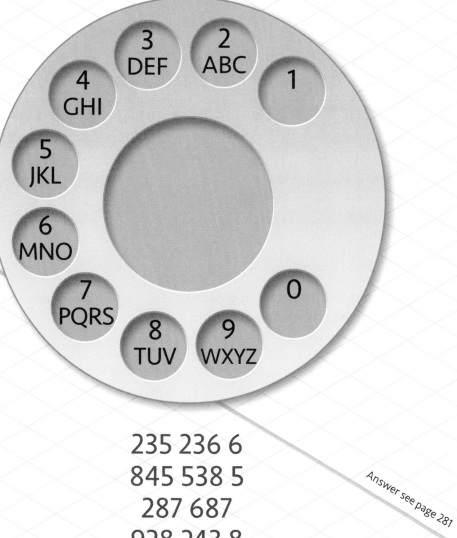

235 236 6
845 538 5
287 687
928 243 8
635 463
267 232 8
765 337 466

Answer see page 281

The following design works according to a certain logic. What number should replace the question mark?

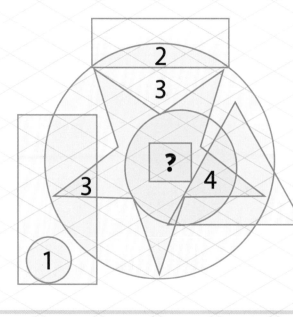

Answer see page 281

Answer see page 281

 Jack and John want to know Jill's birthday. She informs them that it is either:

February 5,	June 17,	September 9,
March 2,	June 6,	September 13,
April 7,	July 14,	October 11,
April 16,	July 16,	October 12,
May 15,	August 14,	October 14, or
May 16,	August 15,	November 10.
May 22,	August 17,	

She then whispers the correct month to Jack, and the correct day to John, after each promises not to tell the other the information she has confided. Jack says that while he can't tell the full date of Jill's birthday, he's confident that John can't either. John replies that in that case, he knows the date. Jack then says that this means he knows it too. What is Jill's birthday?

59 These triangles follow a specific logic. What should replace the question mark?

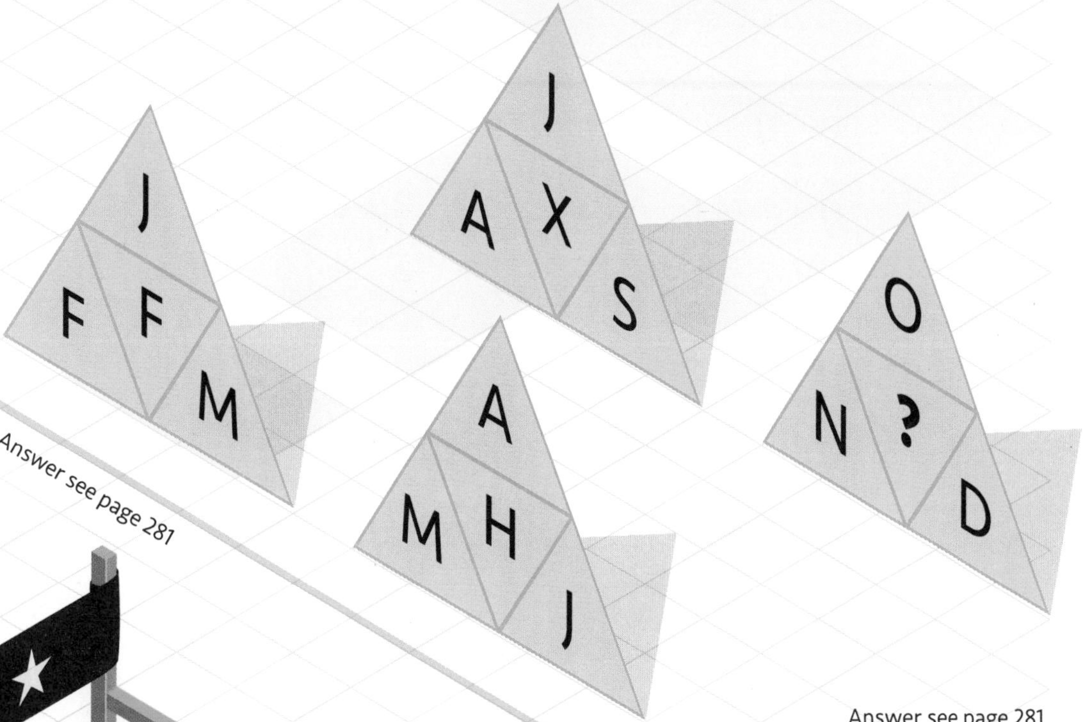

J

J
F F
M

J
A X
S

A
M H
J

O
N ?
D

Answer see page 281

Answer see page 281

60 Can you match the fragments to reassemble the names of several Hollywood celebrities?

OCK	ZE	NI	SAN	JA
DRA	GAN	RL	DREY	UT
MAN	LI	MOR	SEL	ETT
SCA	DA	JO	CHOL	HANS
MI	FREE	CHA	AU	DOU
GLAS	RON	SON	CK	THE
HAS	OU	HO	EL	FF
BULL	CHAR	SON	VID	TA

61

Can you divide up this board to correctly show the 28 dominoes listed below?

4	1	0	6	6	3	3	1
5	5	0	1	1	0	4	4
5	6	2	3	6	4	6	2
0	2	2	4	3	3	0	4
0	5	2	1	6	4	3	5
0	6	5	0	1	1	1	5
2	4	5	6	2	2	3	3

0	0

0	1	1	1

0	2	1	2	2	2

0	3	1	3	2	3	3	3

0	4	1	4	2	4	3	4	4	4

0	5	1	5	2	5	3	5	4	5	5	5

0	6	1	6	2	6	3	6	4	6	5	6	6	6

208

Answer see page 281

Answer see page 281

62

Five crooks are suspected of participating in a two-person robbery. Each gives a statement, but three of the statements are false. The three who lie are innocent. Which two are guilty?

A: B is innocent.

B: Both A and C are guilty.

C: D is guilty.

D: C is telling the truth.

E: C is innocent.

63

Complete the grid so that:
- Each 9x9 row and column contains each digit from 1 to 9 once only
- Each 3x3 box contains each digit from 1 to 9 once only.

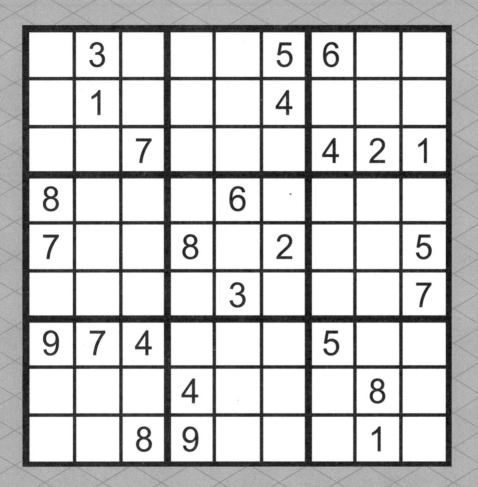

Answer see page 282

64

Examine the top three shapes. Which of the five options A–E continues the sequence?

Answer see page 282

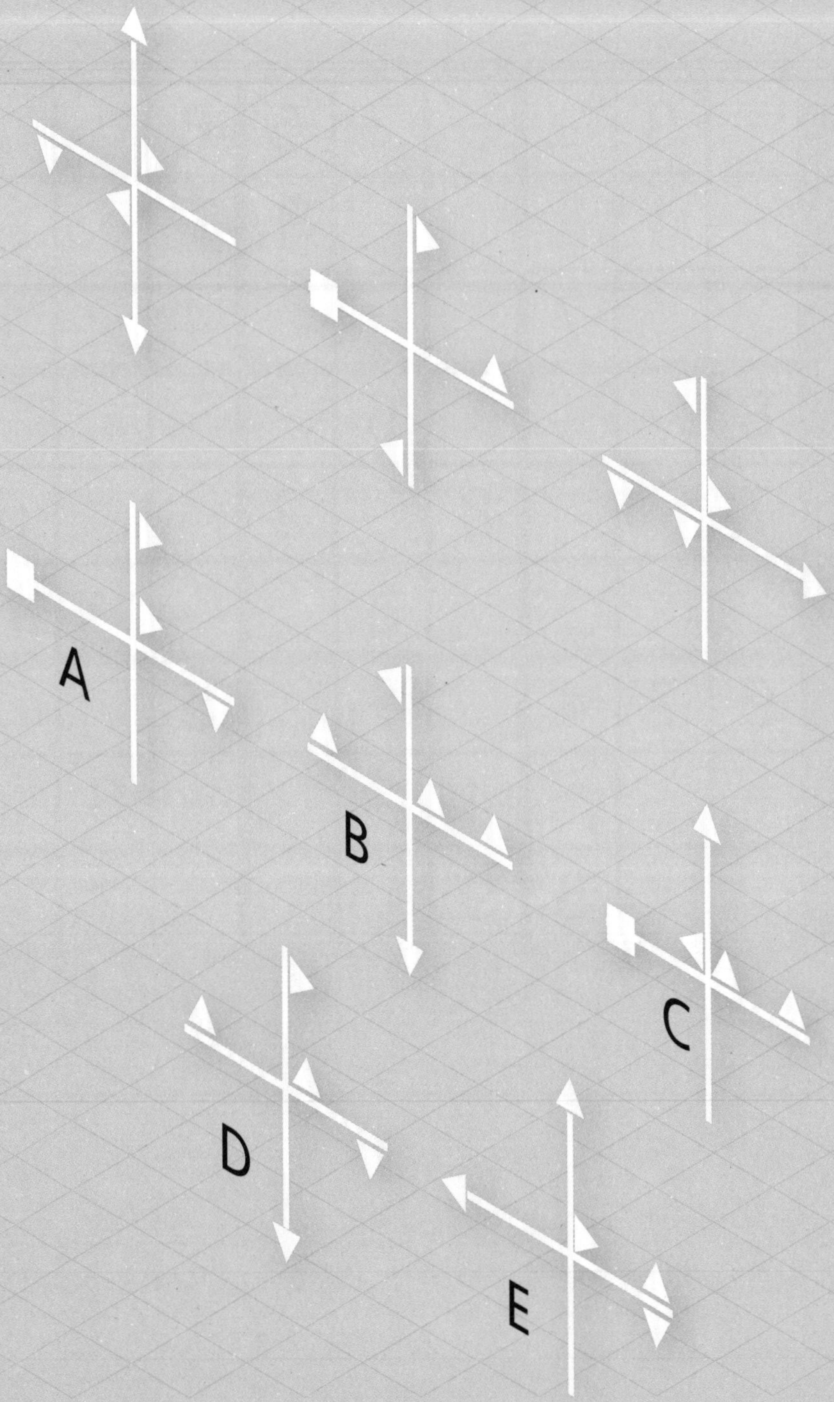

210

A

B

C

D

E

65

Each of the circles below contains the name of a work of literature and its author. Can you unscramble them?

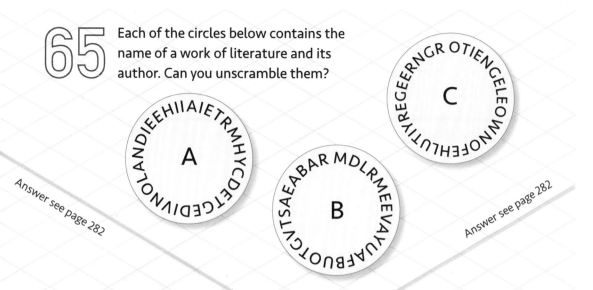

Answer see page 282

Answer see page 282

66

One of the squares in the 3x3 grid is incorrect. Which one?

211

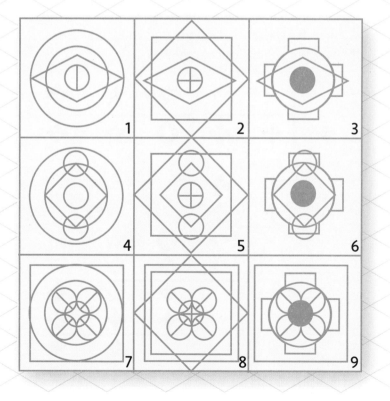

67

Jonathan was born on March 26, lives in Nashville, and is a minister. He likes Artichokes. Felicia was born August 5, lives in Galloway, and is a doctor. She likes Leeks. Magnolia was born on December 29, lives in Springfield, and is a scientist. She likes Cabbage. Steven was born on October 11th, lives in Danville, and is a lecturer. He likes Lettuce. Georgina was born on March 9, lives in Throckmorton, and is a financier. Which of the following vegetables does she like?

A. Kale
B. Peas
C. Spinach
D. Turnip
E. Broccoli

Answer see page 282

68

In this long division calculation, each digit has been consistently replaced with a letter chosen at random. Can you discover the original calculation?

Answer see page 282

The following tiles have been taken from a five by five square of numbers. When they have been reassembled accurately, the square will show the same five numbers reading both across and down. Can you rebuild it?

Answer see page 282

The following grid operates according to a specific pattern. Can you fill in the blank section?

214

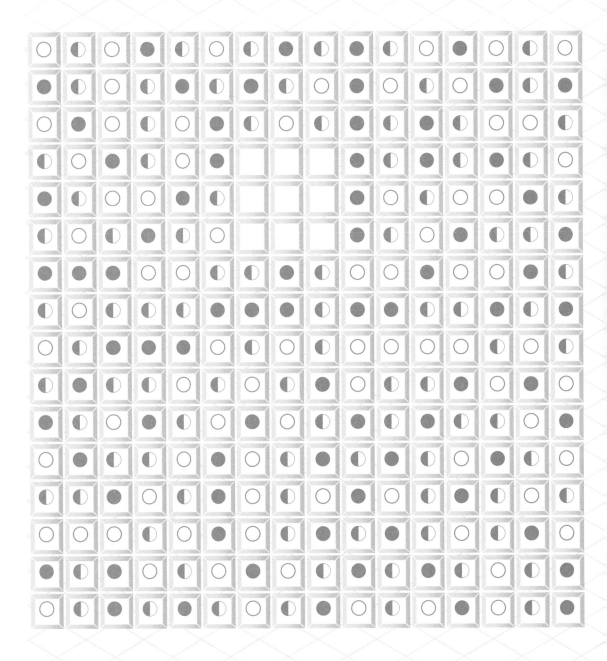

Answer see page 282

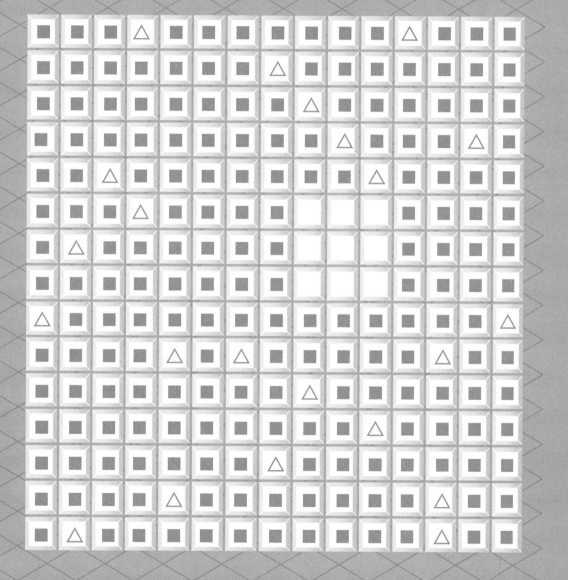

Answer see page 282

72 Complete the grid below so that each unbroken horizontal and vertical stretch of light cells sums to the total indicated in the cell to the left or above the stretch respectively. Each cell may contain only the digits 1 – 9, and no digit may be repeated in any given stretch of cells.

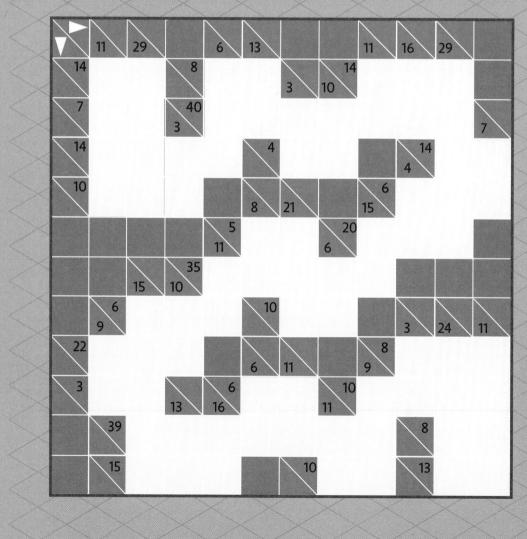

Answer see page 282

73 Complete the grid so that every row and column each contains the digits 1-6 precisely once. A cell with a chevron pointing into it is smaller than the cell on the other side of the chevron.

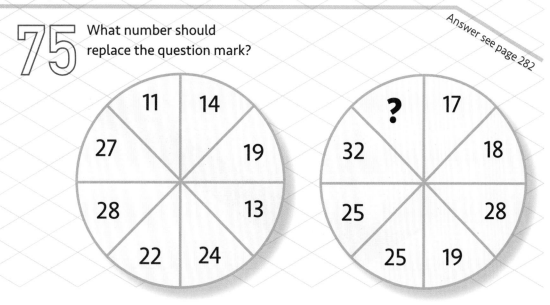

3

4

2

Answer see page 282

74 Taylor likes Arsenal but not Chelsea. Deanna likes Southampton but not Portsmouth. Jayce likes Celtic but not Rangers. Which of the following does Frannie like?

EVERTON   MANCHESTER UNITED
LIVERPOOL   TRANMERE ROVERS

Answer see page 282

75 What number should replace the question mark?

Answer see page 282

Left circle: 11, 14, 27, 19, 28, 13, 22, 24

Right circle: ?, 17, 32, 18, 25, 28, 25, 19

76 Ten vessels are hidden in the grid below, four one-cell ships, three two-cell ships, two three-cell ships, and one four-cell ship. Ships are positioned horizontally or vertically. No two ships are immediately adjacent to each other, including diagonally. The numbers next to each row and column show the total number of ship segments in that line. Identify the exact locations of all ten vessels. Some ship segments and/or spaces of empty ocean are shown to assist you.

218

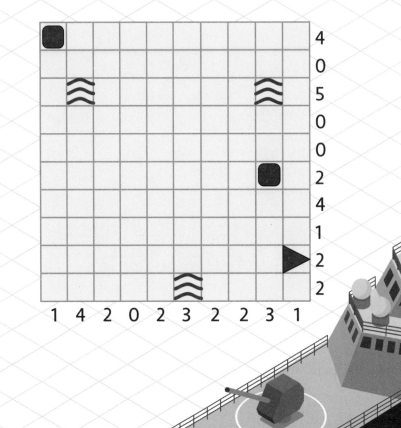

4
0
5
0
0
2
4
1
2
2

1 4 2 0 2 3 2 2 3 1

Answer see page 282

77 The pieces can be assembled into a regular geometric shape. What is it?

Answer see page 283

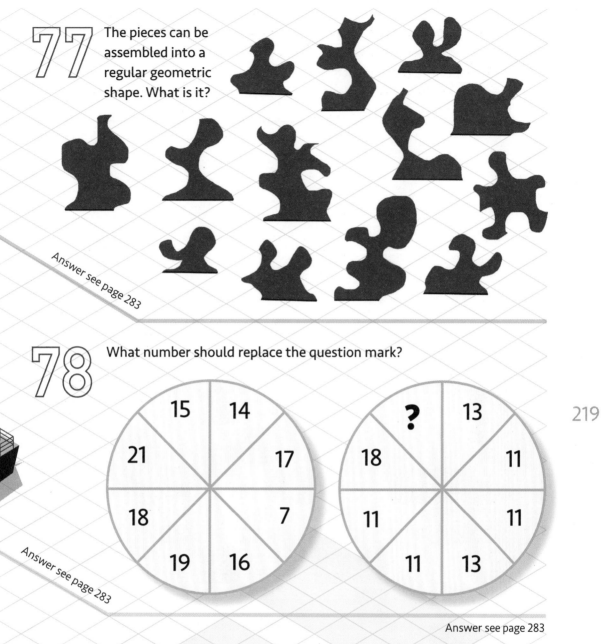

78 What number should replace the question mark?

219

15	14
21	17
18	7
19	16

?	13
18	11
11	11
11	13

Answer see page 283

Answer see page 283

79 Fill in the missing plus, minus, multiplication, division, and/or factorial signs to make the equation below correct, performing all calculations strictly in the order they appear on the page.

13　2　8　22　7　12　15　= 365

80 Complete the grid below so that each unbroken horizontal and vertical stretch of light cells sums to the total indicated in the cell to the left or above the stretch respectively. Each cell may contain only the digits 1 – 9, and no digit may be repeated in any given stretch of cells.

220

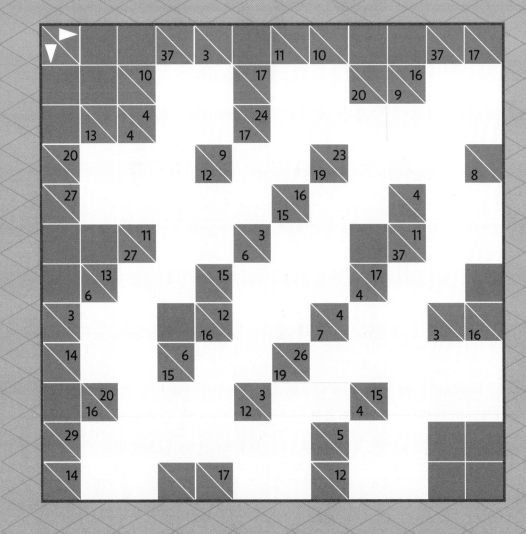

Answer see page 283

81

Connect each pair of identical numbers with a single continuous path running horizontally and/or vertically through the cells of the grid below. Paths may switch direction at the centre of a cell, but may not branch, loop back on themselves, or cross. When the grid is complete, each cell will contain a single path section.

Grid numbers:
10
2   13   6
8   2   10   11   3
12   7
9   8
11
5
4   5   3
4   12   7   1
1
6
9
13

Answer see page 283

82

Are the following statements true or false?

Answer see page 283

i. Argon is the fourth-most abundant gas in the Earth's atmosphere, after water vapour.
ii. Frogs have small tails.
iii. José de San Martin was the first President of Peru.
iv. Karpathos is a Greek island.
v. Morning glories all belong to the genus Convulvulus.
vi. Santa Fe is the capital of New Mexico.
vii. The constellation of Pavo represents a phoenix.
viii. The revolver was invented in the USA.
ix. The Sieve of Eratosthenes is a technique for finding prime numbers.
x. Yahtzee is played with six regular dice.

Which symbols are missing from the grid below?

222

Answer see page 283

Assemble the pieces shown below into a square grid which reads the same across as it does downwards.

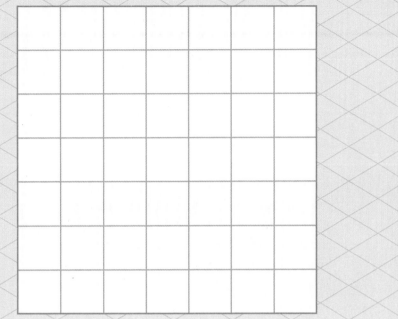

| 7 | 8 |
| 0 | 2 |

| 8 | |
| 0 | 9 |

| 5 | 7 | 0 |
| | | 2 |

| 4 | 8 | 3 |

| 2 | 4 |
| 7 | 8 |

| 3 | 1 |
| 8 | 4 |

| 8 |
| 9 |
| 1 |
| 8 |

| 3 | 8 |
| 8 | 7 |

| 4 | |
| 5 | 4 |

| 2 |
| 4 |
| 5 | 4 |

| 7 |
| 7 | 2 |

| 1 |
| 9 |
| 3 |

| 3 | 8 |
| 1 | |

| 4 |
| 0 |
| 9 |

Answer see page 283

85 Julie likes Milan but not Rome. Olivia likes Warsaw but not Krakow. Eric likes Kiev but not Odessa. Laurence likes Barcelona but not Madrid. Which of the following does Allan like?

SAINT PETERSBURG   MOSCOW
VLADIVOSTOK   PERM

Answer see page 283

86 Ten vessels are hidden in the grid below, four one-cell ships, three two-cell ships, two three-cell ships, and one four-cell ship. Ships are positioned horizontally or vertically. No two ships are immediately adjacent to each other, including diagonally. The numbers next to each row and column show the total number of ship segments in that line. Identify the exact locations of all ten vessels. Some ship segments and/or spaces of empty ocean are shown to assist you.

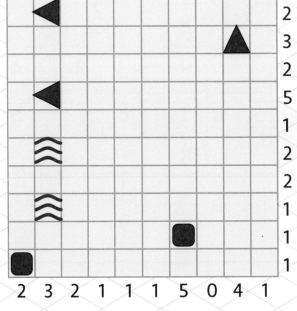

Row numbers (top to bottom): 2, 3, 2, 5, 1, 2, 2, 1, 1, 1

Column numbers (left to right): 2, 3, 2, 1, 1, 1, 5, 0, 4, 1

Answer see page 283

87 In the grid below, how much is each symbol worth?

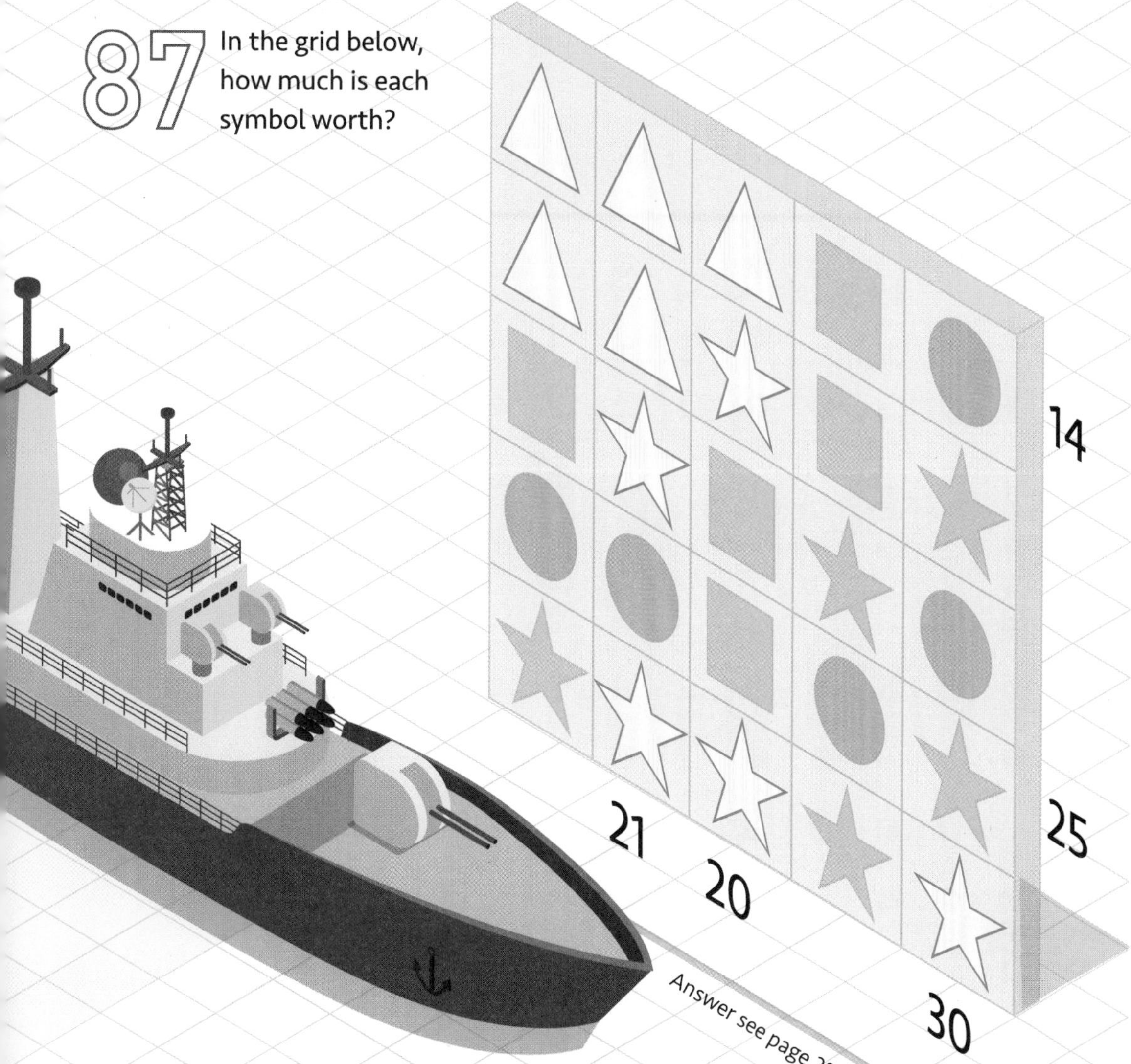

14

225

21

20

25

30

Answer see page 283

Answer see page 283

88 Fill in missing plus, minus, multiplication, division, and/or factorial signs to make the equation below correct, performing all calculations strictly in the order they appear on the page.

17 14 6 13 4 16 3 = 489

Which symbols are missing from the grid below?

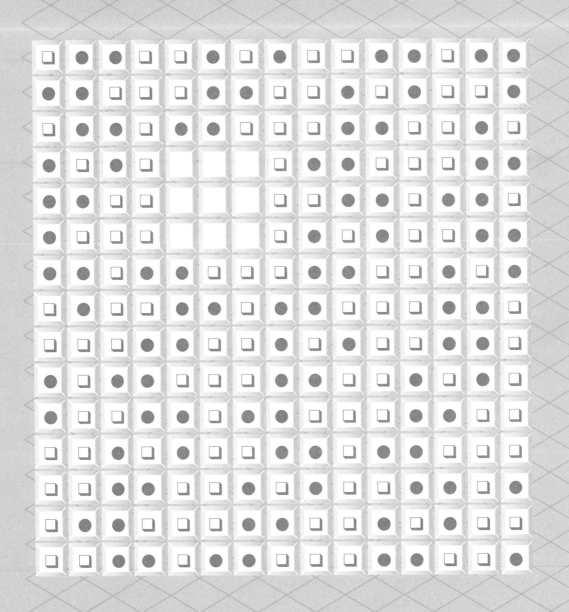

226

Answer see page 284

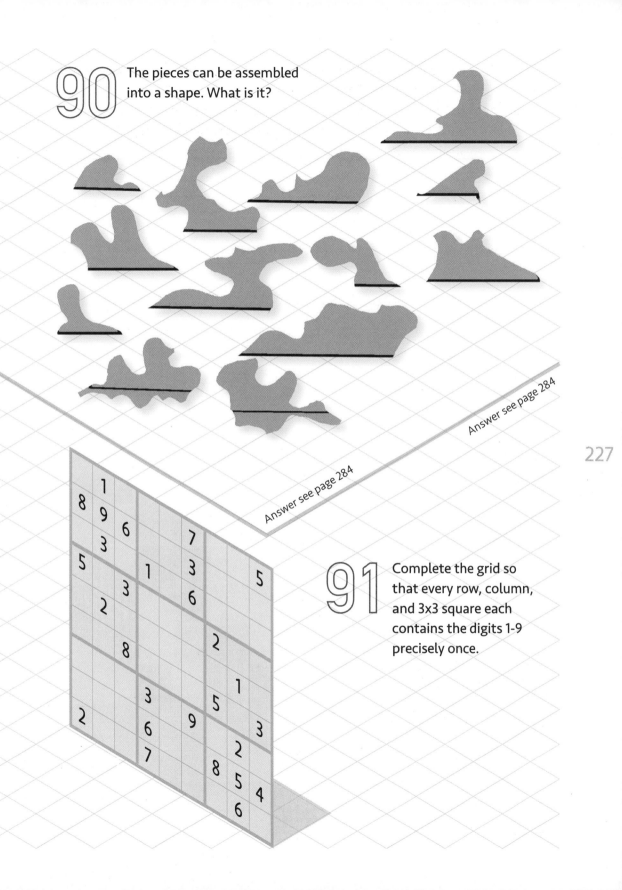

90 The pieces can be assembled into a shape. What is it?

Answer see page 284

Answer see page 284

227

91 Complete the grid so that every row, column, and 3x3 square each contains the digits 1-9 precisely once.

92

Complete the grid below so that each unbroken horizontal and vertical stretch of light cells sums to the total indicated in the cell to the left or above the stretch respectively. Each cell may contain only the digits 1 – 9, and no digit may be repeated in any given stretch of cells.

228

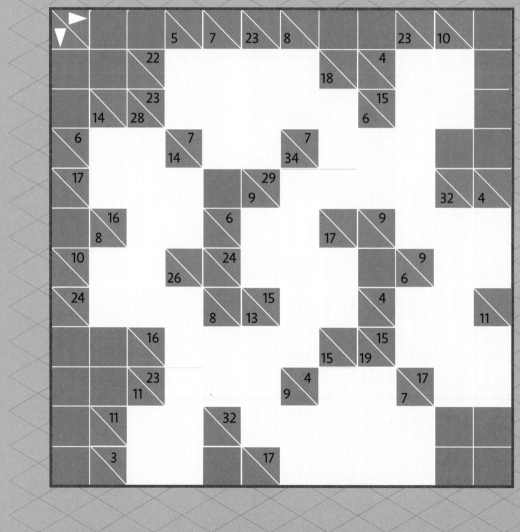

Complete the grid below so that every row and column each contains the digits 1-6 precisely once. A cell with a chevron pointing into it is smaller than the cell on the other side of the chevron.

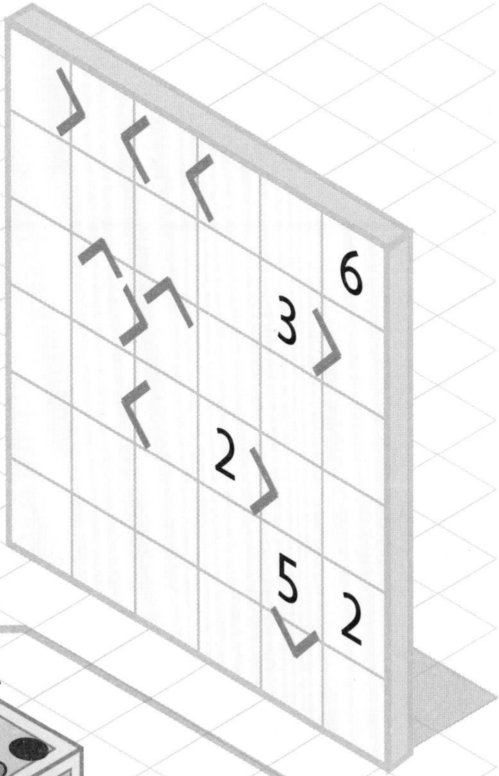

Answer see page 284

Two faces, on separate cubes, show identical symbols. To which cubes do they belong?

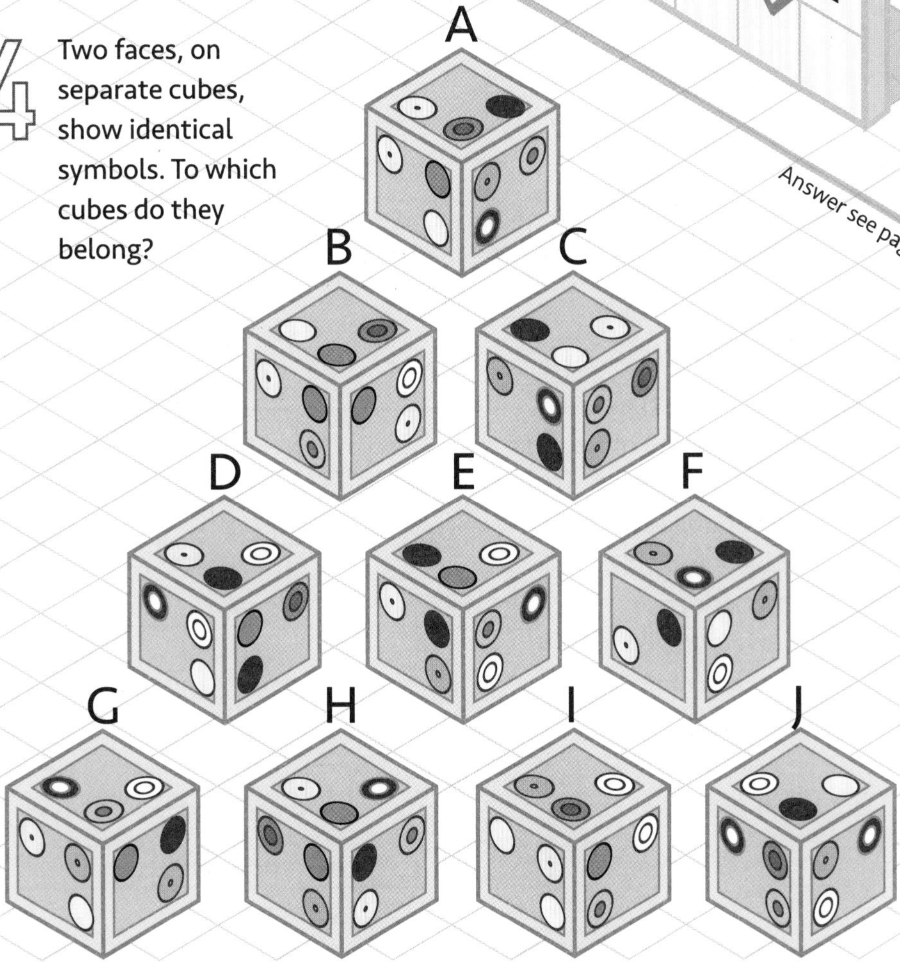

A

B   C

D   E   F

G   H   I   J

Answer see page 284

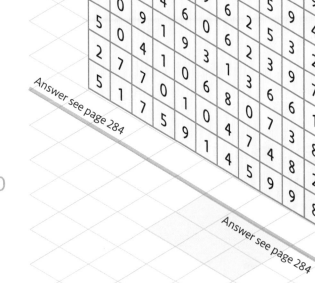

The grid below shows the numbers on a full set of dominoes, from 0-0 to 9-9 inclusive, that have been pushed together horizontally and vertically to make a solid rectangle. Complete the grid to show where each domino lies.

Answer see page 284

Answer see page 284

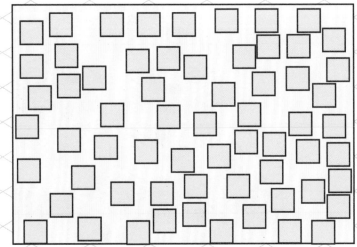

Using six straight lines, which must each touch at least one edge of the box, divide the design into seven sections, each containing one of 6, 7, 8, 9, 10, 11 and 12 squares.

97

Complete the grid below so that each unbroken horizontal and vertical stretch of light cells sums to the total indicated in the cell to the left or above the stretch respectively. Each cell may contain only the digits 1 – 9, and no digit may be repeated in any given stretch of cells.

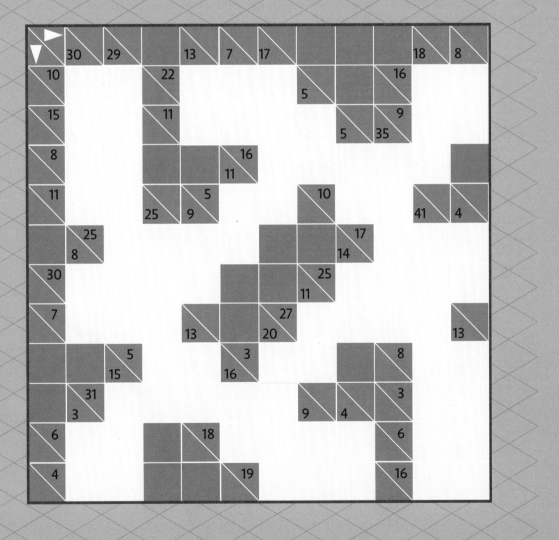

Answer see page 284

98 From the information below, where did the angler who used a jig lure in the competition come from?

The rancher, whose name was Sarah, finished immediately above the secretary. The angler from Tulsa worked as a singer, whilst the angler from Chicago used a spoon lure, and the angler from Portland was named Julie. The angler with a Toyota used a spinnerbait lure. The angler who worked as a taxi driver drove a Lexus, whilst the third-placed angler was named Laura. The resident of Derry was the first-placed angler. The angler with a Ford placed adjacent to the angler who used worms, whilst the angler with the Lexus placed adjacent to the angler who used a crankbait lure. The angler named Steven drove a Tesla, but the angler from Albuquerque drove a Chevrolet. The angler from Derry placed adjacent to the angler who worked as a manager. The angler named Mark placed adjacent to the angler with a Ford.

232

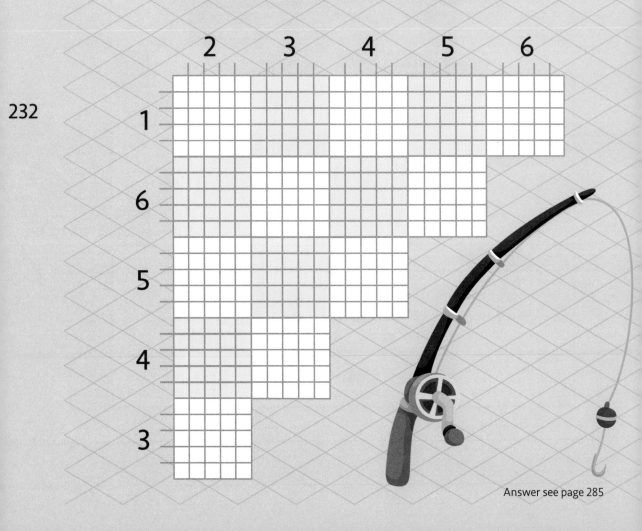

Answer see page 285

The pieces can be assembled into a shape. What is it?

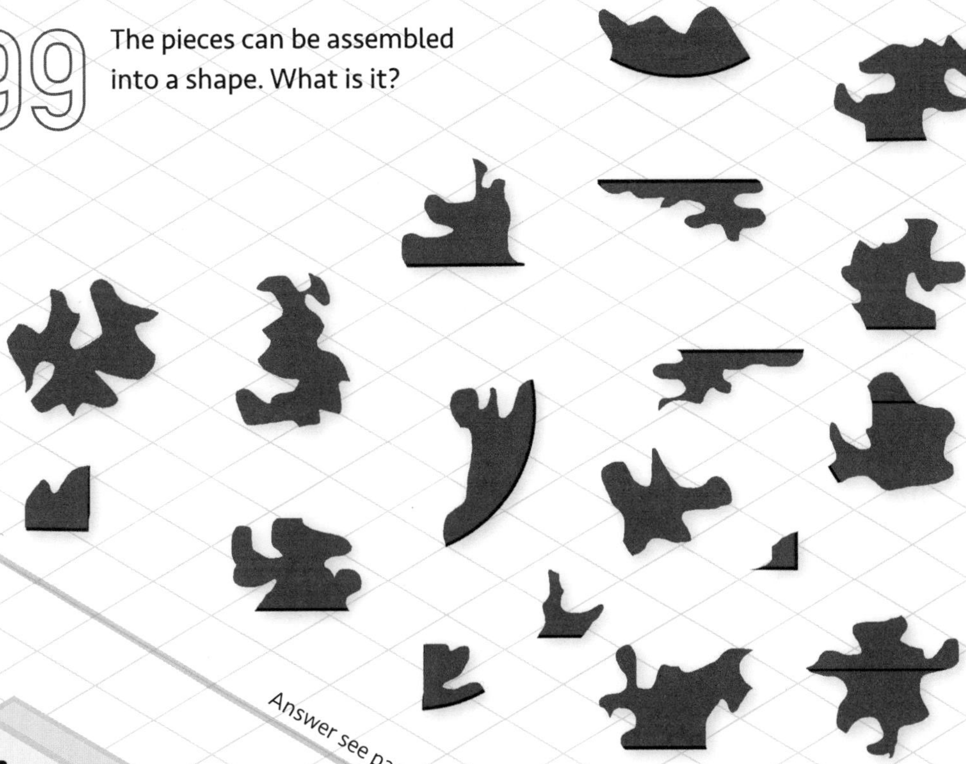

Answer see page 285

Answer see page 285

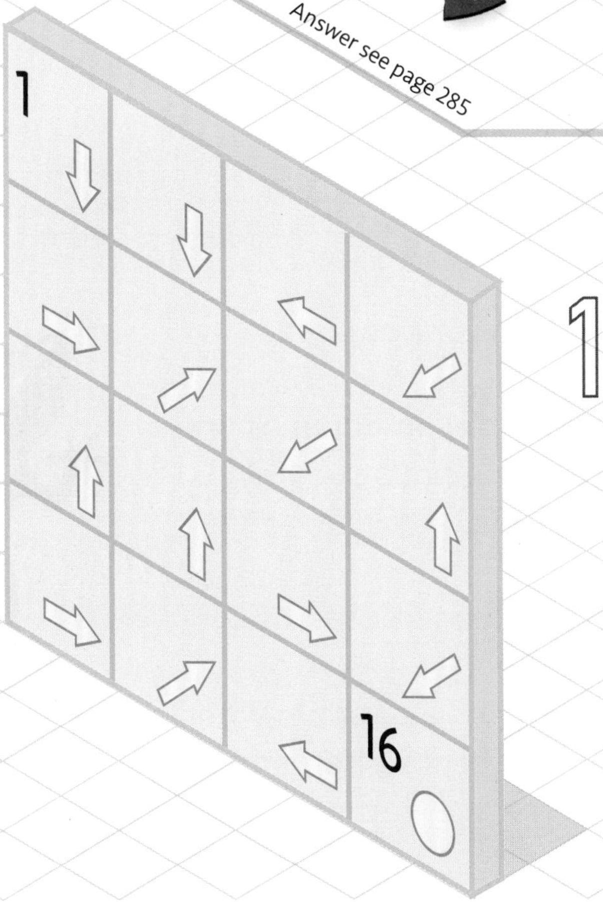

233

1

16

In each square, the arrow shows the direction you must move in. The numbers in some squares show that square's position in the correct sequence of moves. Move from top left to bottom right, visiting each square in the grid exactly once.

101

What number should replace the question mark?

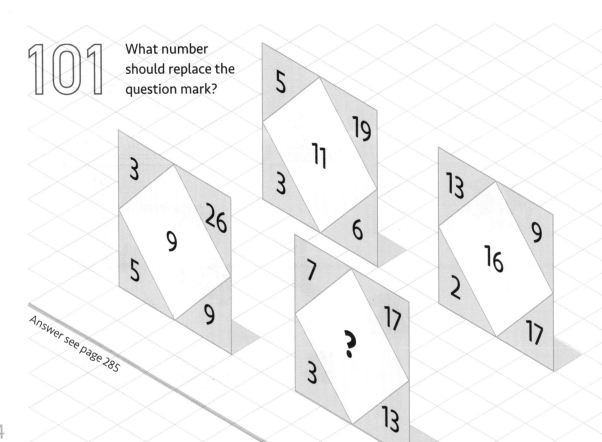

Answer see page 285

Answer see page 285

102

Are the following statements true or false?

i. Ion Iliescu is a former president of Romania.
ii. Krypton is green.
iii. The game of Liar's Dice originated in north Africa.
iv. Nether Wallop is a village in England.
v. Permutable prime numbers can only include the digits 3, 7, and 9.
vi. Pink carnations are said to represent motherly love.
vii. Portland is the capital of Oregon.
viii. Salamanders generally lay their eggs in the water.
ix. The constellation of Vela represents a herdsman.
x. The telescope was invented in the Netherlands in the 17th century.

103

Assemble the pieces shown below into a square grid which reads the same across as it does downwards.

Pieces:

- Vertical: 3 / 6 / 2
- Vertical: 6 / 3 / 4
- Horizontal: 7 8 1
- Horizontal: 3 2 5
- Vertical (2x2 block top row): 1 3 / 7 2
- Horizontal: 2 4 5
- Horizontal: 3 4 5
- Horizontal: 5 8 1
- Horizontal: 2 1 4
- L-shape: 5 1 / 2 / 4
- L-shape: 5 4 / 1
- Vertical: 2 / 5 / 8
- Block: 3 0 / 0 1
- L-shape: 8 2 3 / 3
- L-shape: 7 / 2 1

Decipher the names of several celebrities using the telephone dial as a guide.

585427623787
783832872364
8666953356637
7224356223267
2782377746478336
5225432426

Answer see page 285

105

Complete the grid so that each number shown forms part of a group of horizontally and/or vertically connected cells. The number of cells in the group must be the same as the number shown on the grid. So a '2' indicates a group that is a pair of two cells. No group shares a horizontal or vertical boundary with another group of the same size/number. Every group of cells has at least one number shown.

Answer see page 285

Using seven straight lines, divide the design below into eleven sections, each containing precisely twelve circles of at least two different shades.

Answer see page 285

237

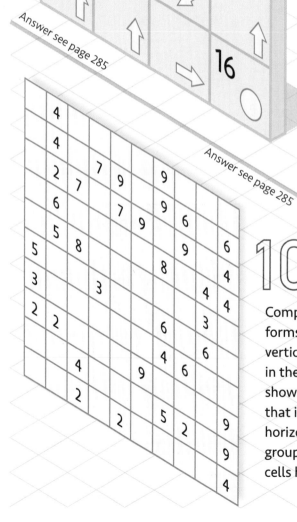

107

In each square, the arrow shows the direction you must move in. The numbers in some squares show that square's position in the correct sequence of moves. Move from top left to bottom right, visiting each square in the grid exactly once.

Answer see page 285

Answer see page 285

238

108

Complete the grid so that each number shown forms part of a group of horizontally and/or vertically connected cells. The number of cells in the group must be the same as the number shown on the grid. So a '2' indicates a group that is a pair of two cells. No group shares a horizontal or vertical boundary with another group of the same size/number. Every group of cells has at least one number shown.

109

Ten vessels are hidden in the grid below, four one-cell ships, three two-cell ships, two three-cell ships, and one four-cell ship. Ships are positioned horizontally or vertically. No two ships are immediately adjacent to each other, including diagonally. The numbers next to each row and column show the total number of ship segments in that line. Identify the exact locations of all ten vessels. Some ship segments and/or spaces of empty ocean are shown to assist you.

Answer see page 286

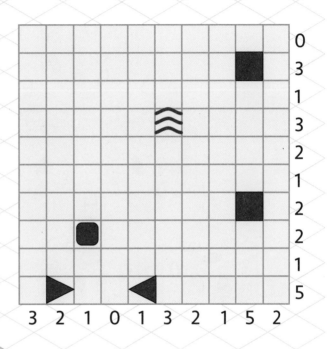

Row numbers (top to bottom): 0, 3, 1, 3, 2, 1, 2, 2, 1, 5

Column numbers (left to right): 3 2 1 0 1 3 2 1 5 2

239

110

Adeline likes A. A. Milne but not Beatrix Potter. Rudolph likes Virginia Woolf but not P. G. Wodehouse. Hakim likes J. R. R. Tolkien but not Henry James. Which of the following does Byron like?

Answer see page 286

JANE AUSTEN WILLIAM GOLDING

JOANNE HARRIS LEWIS CARROLL

111 Two faces, on separate cubes, show identical symbols. To which cubes do they belong?

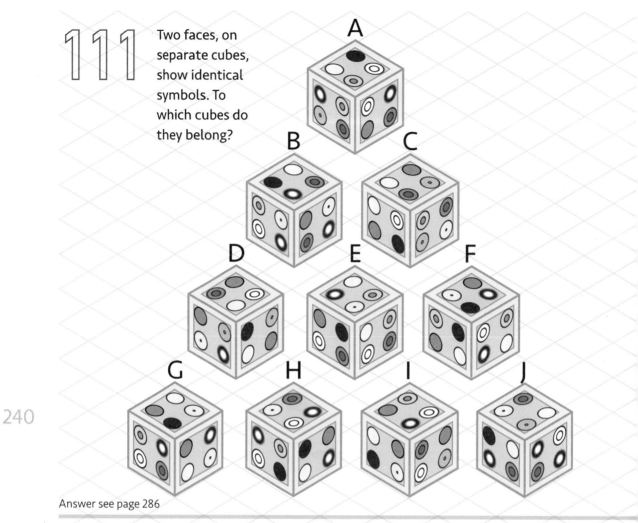

Answer see page 286

Answer see page 286

112 The pieces can be assembled into a regular geometric shape. What is it?

113

From the information below, where does Anthony live?

1. Shannon lives in Essex. Her favourite puzzle is neither Wordsearch nor Kakuro.
2. The Cornwall puzzler is a police officer, and is not the Crossword fan, who is named Christine.
3. The driver lives in Hampshire.
4. The maze fan is called Charles, and he is not a carpenter.
5. The programmer is not in love with either Sudoku or mazes, and does not live in Derbyshire.
6. Anthony does not live in Edinburgh.
7. The Wordsearch fan is an analyst, and is not called Tammy.
8. One puzzler lives in Derbyshire.

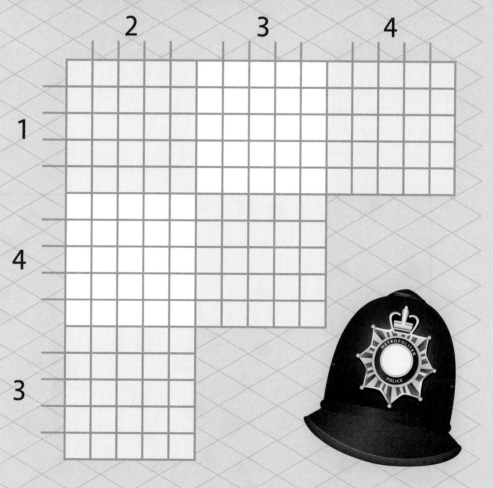

241

Connect each pair of identical numbers with a single continuous path running horizontally and/ or vertically through the cells of the grid below. Paths may switch direction at the centre of a cell, but may not branch, loop back on themselves, or cross. When the grid is complete, each cell will contain a single path section.

Answer see page 286

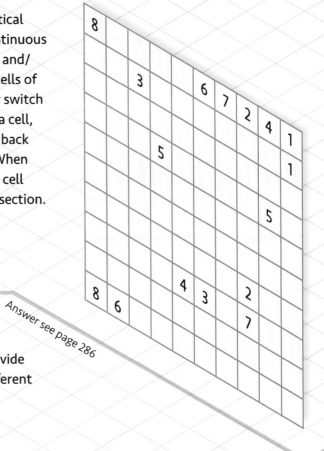

Answer see page 286

Using six straight lines, divide the design below into different sections, each containing precisely three circles.

242

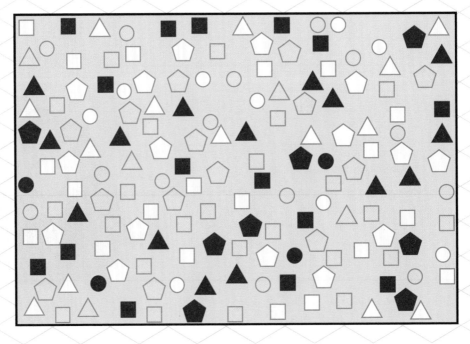

116 Which of the four pieces A to D fits to complete the shape?

A

B

C

D

Answer see page 286

Answer see page 286

117 Complete the grid below so that each number shown forms part of a group of horizontally and/or vertically connected cells. The number of cells in the group must be the same as the number shown on the grid. So a '2' indicates a group that is a pair of two cells. No group shares a horizontal or vertical boundary with another group of the same size/number. Every group of cells has at least one number shown.

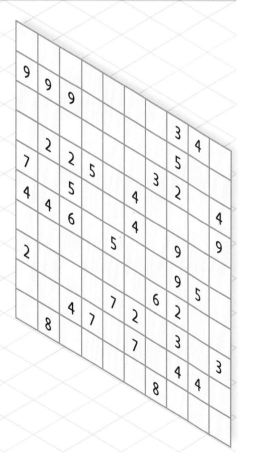

Decipher the names of several celebrities using the telephone dial as a guide.

244

8443796637
253248466377
527667828426
24747436796784
762378336476
536643372647866

Answer see page 286

119

Shade the cells in the grid below so that each row and column holds continuous lines of shaded cells of the lengths indicated by the numbers shown at the start of that row or column. Blocks are separated from others in the same row or column by at least one empty cell. A picture will emerge when the cells are shaded correctly.

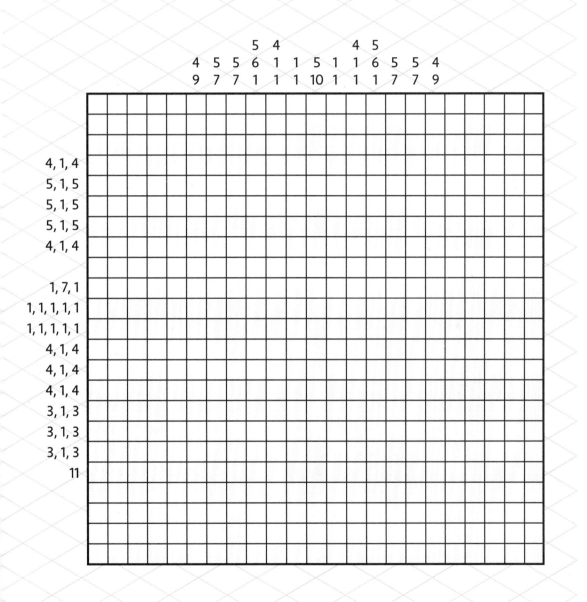

245

Answer see page 286

In each square, the arrow shows the direction you must move in. The numbers in some squares show that square's position in the correct sequence of moves. Move from top left to bottom right, visiting each square in the grid exactly once.

1

16

Answer see page 287

Answer see page 286

246

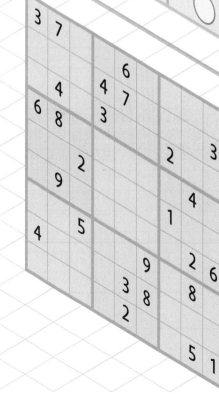

121

Complete the grid so that every row, column, and 3x3 square each contains the digits 1-9 precisely once.

What number should replace the question mark?

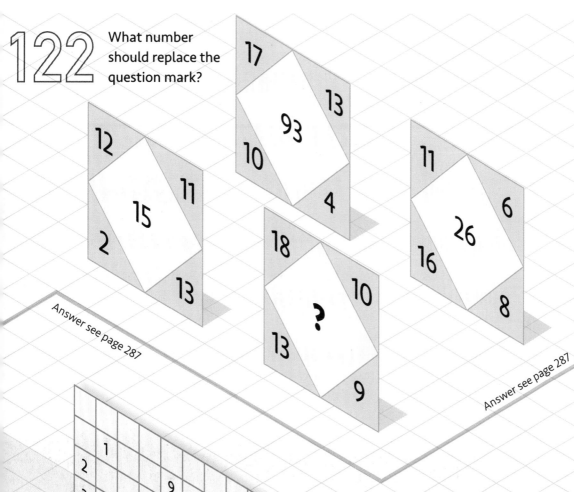

17
13
93
10
4

12
11
15
2
13

18
10
?
13
9

11
6
26
16
8

Answer see page 287

Answer see page 287

123

Connect each pair of identical numbers with a single continuous path running horizontally and/or vertically through the cells of the grid. Paths may switch direction at the centre of a cell, but may not branch, loop back on themselves, or cross. When the grid is complete, each cell will contain a single path section.

1
2
3
9
2 10 11 5 11
4 8
7
3 8 7 9
1 6
4 5 6
10

Fill in missing plus, minus, multiplication, division, and/or factorial signs to make the equation below correct, performing all calculations strictly in the order they appear on the page.

(25) (9) (10) (1) (14) (11) (19) (1) = (299)

Answer see page 287

Ten vessels are hidden in the grid below, four one-cell ships, three two-cell ships, two three-cell ships, and one four-cell ship. Ships are positioned horizontally or vertically. No two ships are immediately adjacent to each other, including diagonally. The numbers next to each row and column show the total number of ship segments in that line. Identify the exact locations of all ten vessels. Some ship segments and/or spaces of empty ocean are shown to assist you.

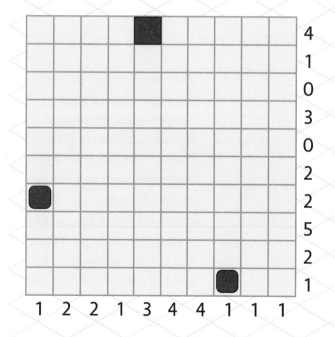

4
1
0
3
0
2
2
5
2
1

1 2 2 1 3 4 4 1 1 1

Answer see page 287

In the grid below, how much is each symbol worth?

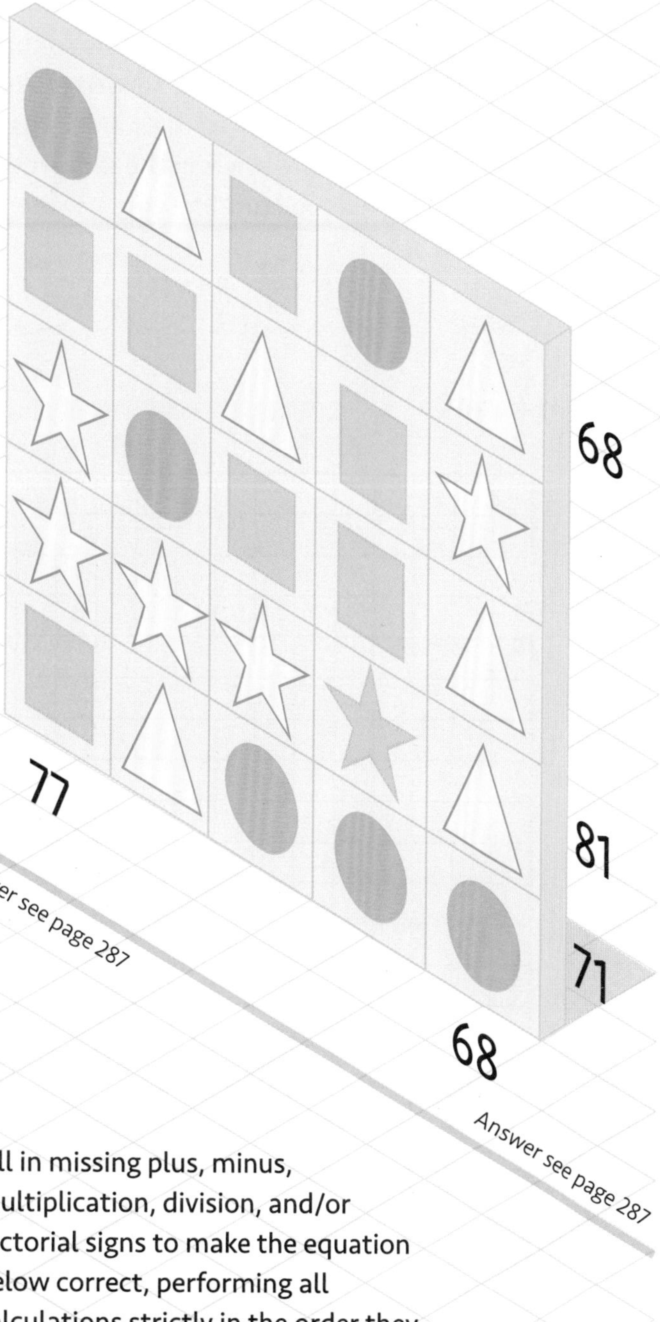

68

77

81

71

68

Answer see page 287

Answer see page 287

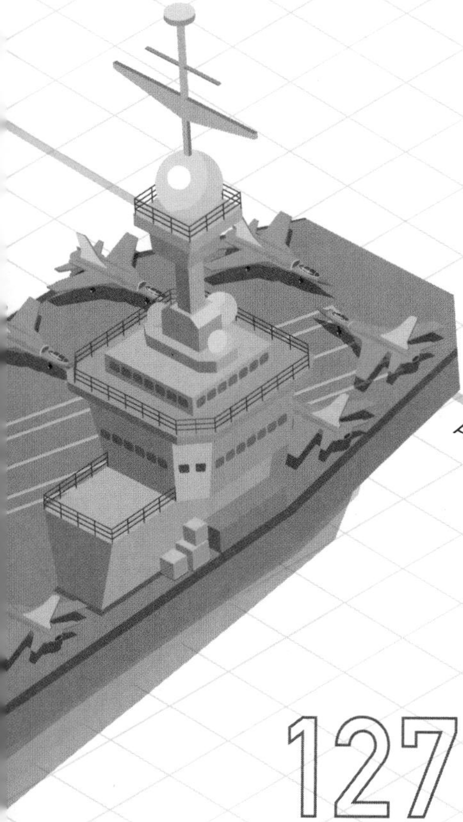

127 Fill in missing plus, minus, multiplication, division, and/or factorial signs to make the equation below correct, performing all calculations strictly in the order they appear on the page.

(5) (16) (20) (3) (25) (11) (2) (25) (8) = (944)

Shade the cells in the grid below so that each row and column holds continuous lines of shaded cells of the lengths indicated by the numbers shown at the start of that row or column. Blocks are separated from others in the same row or column by at least one empty cell. A picture will emerge when the cells are shaded correctly.

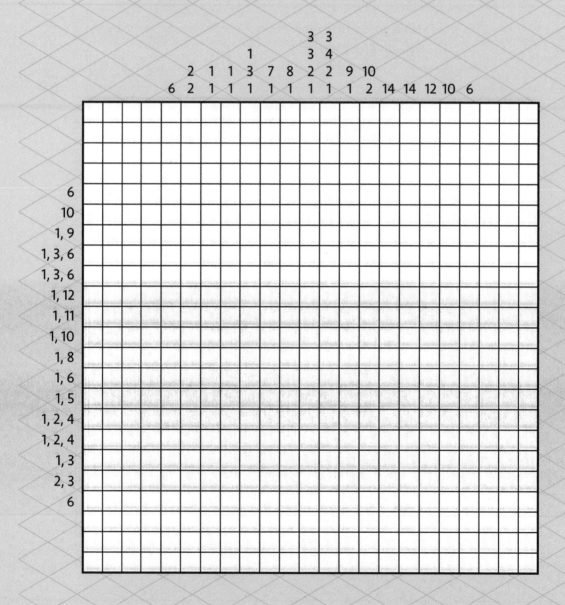

250

Answer see page 287

129 Complete the grid below so that each number shown forms part of a group of horizontally and/or vertically connected cells. The number of cells in the group must be the same as the number shown on the grid. So a '2' indicates a group that is a pair of two cells. No group shares a horizontal or vertical boundary with another group of the same size/number. Every group of cells has at least one number shown.

Answer see page 287

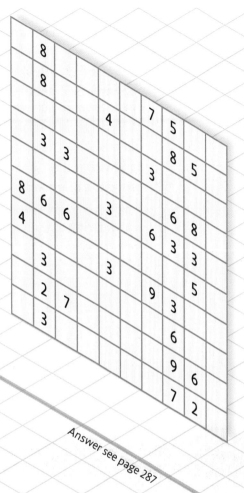

Answer see page 287

251

130 In each square, the arrow shows the direction you must move in. The numbers in some squares show that square's position in the correct sequence of moves. Move from top left to bottom right, visiting each square in the grid exactly once.

From the information below, which person had a sausage sandwich?

Jeremy had a turkey sandwich, but was not at the cat show to look at Bobtail cats – that person was wearing a red sweater. The person with a cheddar sandwich was wearing a blue sweater, and was not there to look at Siamese or Persian cats. One person was wearing a green sweater. Tanya did not bring the omelette sandwich. Joshua did not bring the omelette sandwich either, and wasn't there to look at Bobtail cats. The person who'd brought a brie sandwich was there to look at Shorthair cats, and was not wearing a white sweater. Lucy was there to investigate Manx cats. Ryan was wearing a mauve sweater, and was not there to look at Shorthair cats.

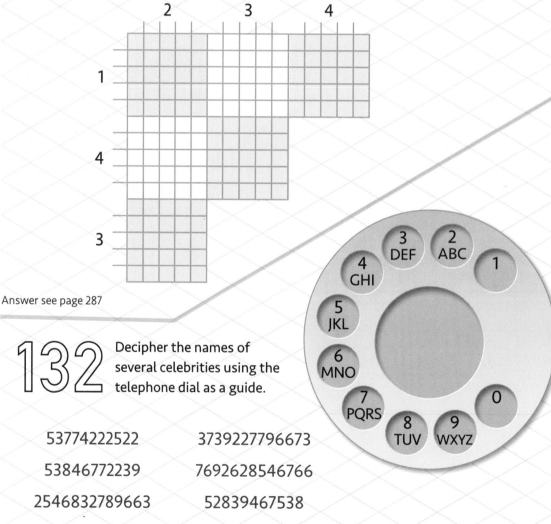

Answer see page 287

132 Decipher the names of several celebrities using the telephone dial as a guide.

53774222522   3739227796673

53846772239   7692628546766

2546832789663   52839467538

Answer see page 287

133

Complete the grid below so that each unbroken horizontal and vertical stretch of light cells sums to the total indicated in the cell to the left or above the stretch respectively. Each cell may contain only the digits 1 – 9, and no digit may be repeated in any given stretch of cells.

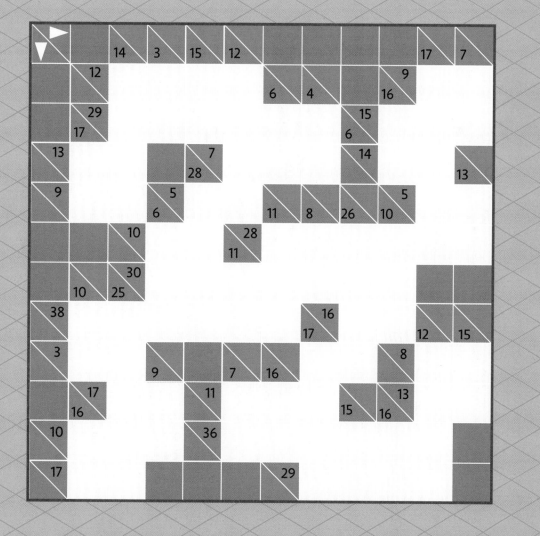

Answer see page 288

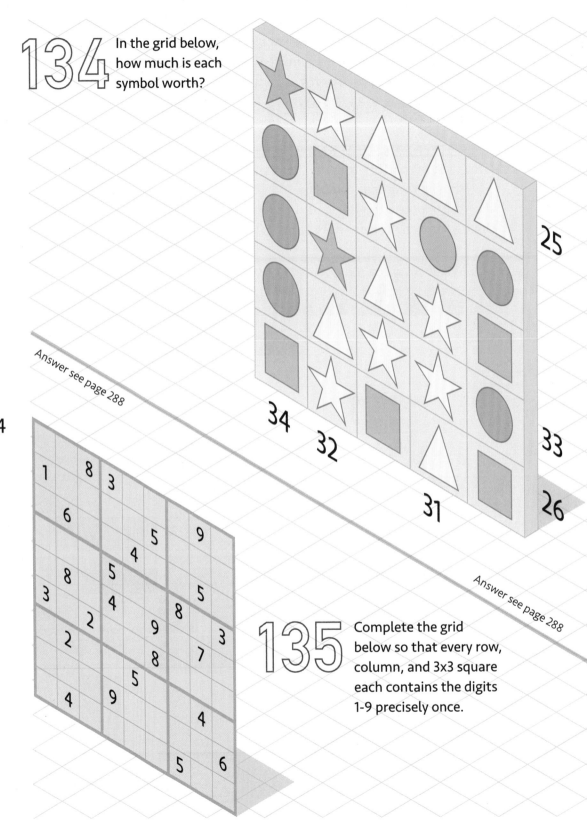

134 In the grid below, how much is each symbol worth?

25

34

32

31

33

26

254

135 Complete the grid below so that every row, column, and 3x3 square each contains the digits 1-9 precisely once.

Answer see page 288

1		8	3					
	6				5		9	
			4					
	8		5			5		
3			4		8			3
	2			9			7	
	2			8				
			5				4	
	4		9					
						5		6

136

From the information below, where did the person who wanted to adopt a Terrier come from?

The person from Hampshire was the first of the five to be interviewed at the centre. Kenneth had grey hair. The person from Norfolk worked as a chef. Tina was interviewed immediately before or after a person with blonde hair. The person from Strathclyde wanted to adopt a Corgi. The professor, whose name was Gregory, had his interview immediately before the marketer. The person with red hair wanted to adopt a Spaniel. The writer had black hair, whilst Lori had the middle interview spot. The person with blonde hair was interviewed immediately before or after the person who wanted to adopt a Labrador. Patricia was from Powys. The person with black hair was interviewed immediately before or after the person who wanted to adopt a Poodle. The person from Cumbria had brown hair. The person from Hampshire was interviewed immediately before or after the person who worked as an optician.

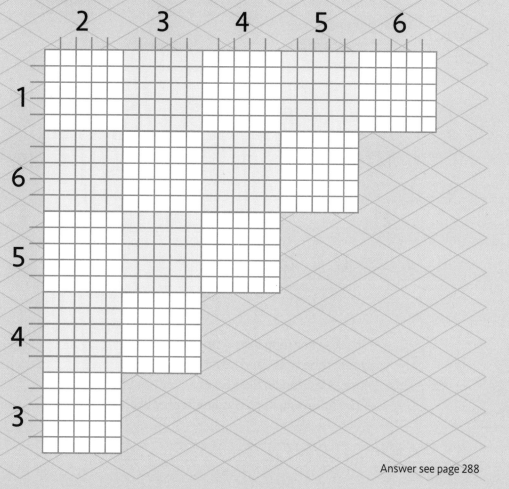

137

Complete the grid below so that every row, column, and 3x3 square each contains the digits 1-9 precisely once. The sum of the digits in each group of cells with a dotted outline must total the number in the group's top/left corner.

Answer see page 288

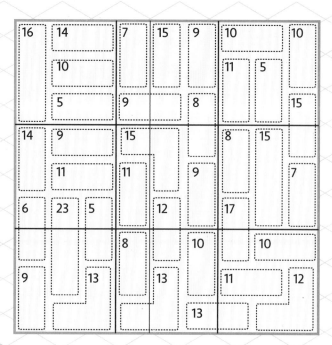

Answer see page 288

138

What number should replace the question mark?

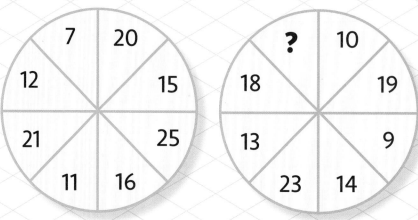

Answer see page 288

139

Patrick Armstrong likes Aston Martin but not Jaguar. Cyndi Stone likes Land Rover but not Rolls Royce. Morag MacDonald likes Bentley but not Lotus. Which of the following does Harding Tooley like?

ASCARI   RANGE ROVER   BRISTOL   MINI

1

2

Minnie Driver. Angelina Jolie. Alyson Hannigan. Julia Dreyfus. Rip Torn. Mel Gibson. Matthew McConaughey. Kiefer Sutherland. Owen Wilson.

3

In step 4, the instruction does not specify that vehicles need to be moving.

4

Our solutions: a. 7–((6*5)/15)+18 = 23. b. 9+(((7*7)+3)/13) = 13. c. ((8*9/12)+14)/5 = 4.

5

Pattern runs left to right in an 11-symbol sequence from top left.

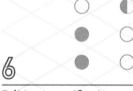

6

B (More specific sign must be the false one.)

7

S (Add arithmetical values of letter positions and convert total back to a letter, wrapping from Z=26 to A=27.)

8

5 (E = B).

9

A: 260 (Statement 3 is wrong).
B: 220 (Statement 2 is wrong).
C: 200 (Statement 3 is wrong).

10

Y.

11

0	2	8	5	4
2	3	5	7	9
8	5	6	3	4
5	7	3	0	2
4	9	4	2	3

12

13

B3.

14

Desk 4.

15

Vermont, Kentucky, Oregon, Nebraska, Oklahoma (The alphabet has been transposed by 8 letters).

16

17

17 (The terms are successive prime numbers).

18

They are not playing each other.

19

9 (= 7-2+4).

20

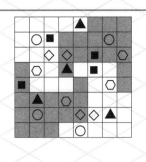

21

104 (The numbers increase by the prime numbers in sequence).

22

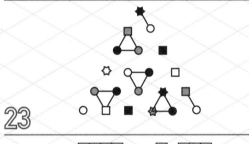

23

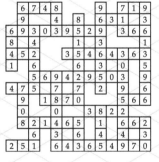

24

C (No liar could ever admit the fact).

25

26

18 (segment by segment, C = A * B).

27

2 ("Tumbler").

28

203840 / 14= 14560.

29

80%.

30

C.

31

32

B (66% vs 50%).

33

13 (Difference between H=8 and U=21).

34

A little under 1.5 billion kilometres.

35

Prague, Barcelona, Glasgow, Brisbane, Vancouver, Dubai.

36

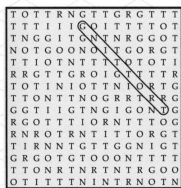

37

F (The letters represent the numbers 1-9 based on their position in the alphabet, in this instance forming a magic square which totals 15).

38

11:46.43. (Time decreases by 1:13.04, 2:26.08, 3:39.12, 4:52.16 minutes).

39

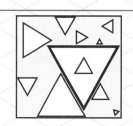

40

B.

41

6.

42

4 (Convert numbers to the letters at those positions in the alphabet. Spells out DISAPPOINTINGLY, reading top left -> bottom right through each block).

43

C.

44

1.

45

Otis (Otis, engineer, duck, Oregon. Bobbie, botanist, chocolate, Ohio. Hersh, farmer, cherries, Vermont. Margaret, doctor, bread, Louisiana. Angie, researcher, lamb, Arizona).

46

A light blue square with a white ball in the top left and dark blue balls in the other three corners.

47

7 (The difference between bottom left and sum of other 3 corners).

48

7	6	1	5	3	2	8	9	4
2	4	3	6	9	8	7	1	5
9	8	5	7	1	4	2	6	3
3	7	8	1	5	6	4	2	9
1	9	6	4	2	7	5	3	8
4	5	2	9	8	3	6	7	1
6	3	9	2	4	5	1	8	7
8	2	4	3	7	1	9	5	6
5	1	7	8	6	9	3	4	2

49

Stephen Poliakoff. Oscar Wilde. Johann Wolfgang von Goethe. Federico García Lorca. Lillian Hellman. George Bernard Shaw. Nikolai Gogol. Aristophanes. Christopher Marlowe. Sarah Kane.

50

9 (The small white balls are overwriting the large circle).

51

4 squared = 16.

52

85 (= 28+17+23+17).

53

The 1UR tile that's in row 4 and column 4, where 1,1 is the top left corner.

54

8pm (Total of numbers pointed at increases by 2 each time).

55

G (The others all have a functionally identical partner).

56

17 (Each ball is equal to the sum of the individual digits of the two balls to its right in the same line. The two rightmost balls in each line are that line's starting condition).

57

38 (= 5+9+7+8+9).

58

3 (Number of rectangles enclosing the value).

59

C (Triangle).

60

Y, with 0:45.20. (V=46:23, W=48:18, X=47:30, Y=45:20, Z=46:06).

61

Our solutions: a. 12+17−9+6−14=12. b. 26−10+4−17+11=14. c. −15+17+9−8+13=16.

62

A: In Search Of Lost Time, Marcel Proust. **B:** Finnegan's Wake, James Joyce. **C:** Don Quixote, Miguel De Cervantes.

63

D (The length of the sport is the same length as the name).

64

12.

65

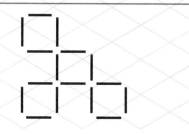

66

B.

67

9 (Each segment totals the same as its opposite number).

68

7 (= The prime numbers in ascending order, starting from 2. The two bottom points of the triangles taken as a single number are the square numbers in ascending order, and the top points are the digits counting down from 9).

69

A & I.

70

21+11−18+5+15+21+4 = 59.

71

3+7+2+6 = 18.

72

59. (Equivalent sectors in the second circle are 3.5* their counterpart in the first circle, rounded down.)

73

 = 1, = 2, ● = 4.

74

A square.

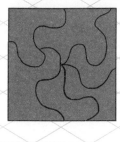

75

Daniel Radcliffe, Natalie Portman, Antonio Banderas, Bradley Cooper, Halle Berry, Kobe Bryant.

76

9	5	4	6	1	7	6
5	6	2	9	2	8	6
4	2	8	7	6	4	9
6	9	7	1	5	3	0
1	2	6	5	2	7	5
7	8	4	3	7	3	9
6	6	9	0	5	9	5

77

3+14+22-11+3-24+17 = 24.

78

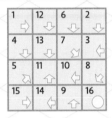

79

Carnation. (Same last letter.)

80

B.

81

9	7	5	1	8	2	6	4	3
2	4	8	3	6	7	1	5	9
1	6	3	5	4	9	8	2	7
4	2	7	9	5	6	3	1	8
3	8	6	2	7	1	5	9	4
5	1	9	8	3	4	7	6	2
7	5	4	6	9	3	2	8	1
6	3	1	4	2	8	9	7	5
8	9	2	7	1	5	4	3	6

82

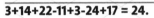

83

i. False (they're the only one). **ii. True. iii. True. iv. False** (it's hydrogen). **v. True. vi. True. vii. False** (it was Poland). **viii. False** (they were invented in Egypt). **ix. False** (it isn't). **x. True.**

84

85

A circle.

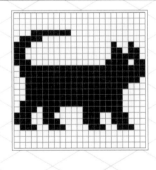

86

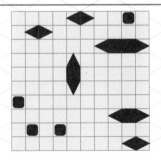

87

88

2	3	1	6	4	5
1	5	6	4	3	2
4	1	3	5	2	6
5	2	4	3	6	1
6	4	2	1	5	3
3	6	5	2	1	4

89

21. (Equivalent sectors in both circles sum to a total of 35.)

90

Michel.
Georges, a blacksmith from Bagnol, liked wines from Champagne. **Iva**, a whitesmith from Rouen, liked wines from Burgundy. **Jacques**, a greensmith from Aix, liked wines from Beaujolais. **Michel**, a goldsmith from Reims, liked wines from Bordeaux. **Veronique**, a tinsmith from Paris, liked wines from Alsace.

91

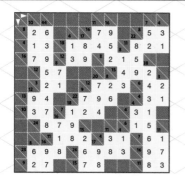

92

28. (Equivalent sectors in both circles sum to a total of 44 to 51, starting from the top right sector.)

93

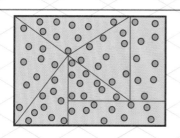

94

A.

95

33. (Equivalent sectors in the second circle are equal to their counterpart in the first circle with the digits reversed and from 2 to 9 subtracted, starting from the top right "12 o'clock" sector.)

96

D & F.

97

Diamond. (Same initial.)

98

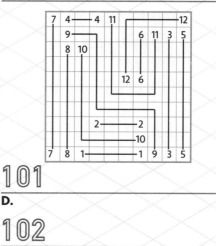

99

17+25-19-15*4-23*8 = 72.

100

(grid with numbers: 7 4 — 4 11 — 12; 9; 6 11 3 5; 8 10; 12 6; 2 — 2; 10; 7 8 1 — 1 9 3 5)

101

D.

102

Lavender. (Third letter of name same as initial of colour.)

103

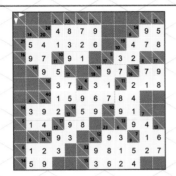

104

9+5-4+5 = 15.

105

i. **False** (it isn't). ii. **True**. iii. **False** (he ruled Burkina Faso). iv. **False** (it's Austin). v. **True**. vi. **True**. vii. **False** (they were invented in China, 2300 years ago). viii. **True**. ix. **False** (the columbines). x. **True** (the platypus and four types of echidna).

106

Al Pacino, Jake Gyllenhaal, Will Ferrell, Megan Fox, Samuel L. Jackson, Tom Hanks.

107

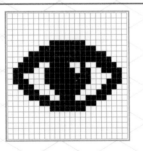

108

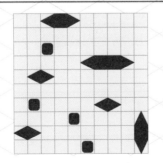

109

A triangle.

110

111

Swallows. (Same length.)

112

(9*7)+(6*5)=63+30 = 93.

113

6	3	7	1	2	5	8	9	4
5	8	2	6	4	9	7	1	3
9	1	4	3	8	7	6	5	2
1	7	5	2	9	4	3	6	8
4	9	3	7	6	8	5	2	1
8	2	6	5	3	1	4	7	9
2	6	1	8	7	3	9	4	5
3	5	9	4	1	6	2	8	7
7	4	8	9	5	2	1	3	6

114

9	5	6	4	2	1	7	8	3
3	7	1	8	5	9	4	2	6
8	2	4	6	7	3	9	5	1
1	6	3	5	4	2	8	7	9
7	4	2	9	1	8	6	3	5
5	9	8	7	3	6	2	1	4
6	1	9	2	8	5	3	4	7
4	8	5	3	6	7	1	9	2
2	3	7	1	9	4	5	6	8

115

▲ = 1, ■ = 3, ● = 4.

116

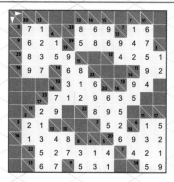

117

Pierce Brosnan, Macaulay Culkin, Orlando Bloom, Keira Knightley, Emma Stone, Russell Crowe.

118

119

i. False (it's in Cygnus). **ii. False** (it was Chile). **iii. True. iv. False** (it's in Belarus). **v. False** (there's also technetium, and most elements with an atomic weight >90). **vi. True. vii. False** (It's a matching card game). **viii. True. ix. False** (it does). **x. True.**

120

Tofu.
The teacher liked tofu, was born in California, and had grey hair. The nurse liked chocolate, was born in Wales, and had auburn hair. The therapist liked cherries was born in Cyprus, and had black hair.
The trainer liked fresh bread, was born in Provence, and had blonde hair. The counsellor liked lamb, was born in Tuscany, and was bald.

121

Yushan. (If the length of the first name is X, then the Xth letter of the surname is the same as the initial letter of the mountain that the person likes.)

122

54. (The sectors in each circle sum to a total of 114.)

123

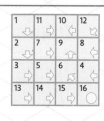

124

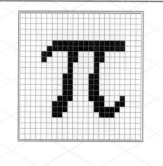

125

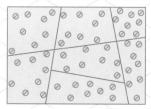

A 14-symbol sequence runs horizontally from left to right, starting from the top left.

126

Bill Murray, Christian Bale, Ian McKellen, Peter Sellers, Nicolas Cage, Tom Hiddleston.

127

(8*5)-(2*9)=40-18 = 22.

128

7.

129

130

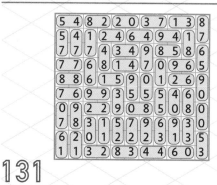

266

131

D.

132

2	5	8	8	3	0	0	2	7	5
0	8	4	6	6	4	5	4	3	2	6
1	7	3	3	1	6	5	9	2	3	5
9	5	5	0	5	5	3	9	2	7	0
1	8	6	0	7	9	8	1	3	8	4
6	9	6	0	4	1	9	0	6	1	4
3	8	5	8	8	7	1	1	7	5	0
2	7	9	6	4	9	4	7	3	1	1
4	7	4	0	7	1	8	2	9	7	3
6	2	0	3	9	2	6	4	9	2	2

133

2	4	1	3	6	5
3	1	4	2	5	6
5	3	6	4	2	1
6	2	5	1	3	4
1	6	2	5	4	3
4	5	3	6	1	2

134

1	4	2	6	7	9	3	8	5
8	9	6	3	4	5	1	7	2
7	3	5	2	1	8	4	9	6
2	1	4	7	9	6	8	5	3
3	7	9	5	8	1	6	2	4
5	6	8	4	3	2	9	1	7
6	5	1	8	2	4	7	3	9
4	8	7	9	5	3	2	6	1
9	2	3	1	6	7	5	4	8

135

i. True. ii. False (Pollux is brighter). **iii. False** (it's a type of solitaire). **iv. True. v. True. vi. True. vii. False** (not in the Americas). **viii. False** (they evolved into the birds). **ix. True. x. False** (it's in Wales).

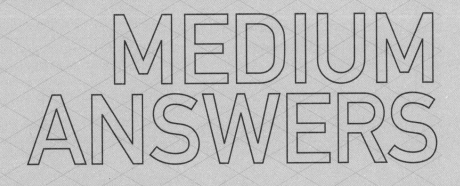

01

The **1U tile** that's in row 4 and column 3, where 1,1 is the top left corner.

02

W (The letters spell out the quote "Who is down needs fear no fall," starting from the question mark and running first inwards then counterclockwise around the circle.)

03

8. (Convert numbers to the letters at those positions in the alphabet, starting with A=26. Spells out EXISTENTIALISTS, reading top left -> bottom right through each block).

04

58.33% (7 chances out of 12).

05

17.

06

07

Anna.

08

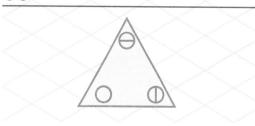

09

F (The letters represent numbers based on their position in the alphabet, where the first column * the second = the third).

10

The 12-symbol pattern zig-zags up then back down, from bottom left.

11

23 (The numbers come in pairs, in the form XY and YX. 32 is unpaired).

12

Dry Martini. Manhattan. Old-fashioned. Margarita. Daiquiri. Gin Fizz. Mint Julep.

13

Infinitely (You've already used all the time up).

14

Take a second pill from the first bottle, and break all four pills in half, setting the halves carefully into two separate piles. Then take one pile today, and one pile tomorrow.

15

4	8	6	1	9
8	2	8	5	6
6	8	3	4	2
1	5	4	1	1
9	6	2	1	7

16

C (The others all have a functionally identical partner).

17

Countertop, Playpen, Antimacassar, Credenza, Sideboard, Tallboy.

18

X.

19

1 (The top left small ball is missing its horizontal stroke).

20

15 (The numbers indicate the position in the alphabet of the intial letters of the months, starting with January. J=10, F=6, M=13, A=1, etc.)

21

A.

22

23

A: Moby Dick, Herman Melville. **B:** Hamlet, William Shakespeare. **C:** War and Peace, Leo Tolstoy.

24

412804 / 23 = 17948.

25

It should read **3 7 1 9** from top to bottom (Remove top digit, reverse).

26

C (Initial letter of the disliked location is the sixth letter of the name; and of the liked location, the fifth – she likes Inverness).

27

6 (Difference between (Top left * top right) and (bottom left * bottom right)).

28

9 (Number of sides belonging to all regular polygons, both proper and improper, enclosing the value).

29

Magdalena (Magdalena, cheese, red, geraniums. Thad, tuna, pink, azaleas. Matt, egg, purple, pansies. Hayden, ham, white, camellias. Liza, chicken, blue, delphiniums).

30

The 3D tile that's in row 2 and column 7, where 1,1 is the top left corner.

31

32

Y (Words spiral in clockwise from top).

33

8.16 (Hour increases by 1, 2, 3; minutes decreases by 12).

34

37 (Sum of arithmetic value of alphabet positions of R and S).

35

It should read **2 4 1** from top to bottom. (Add top and bottom numbers and place result downwards in next column, then work inwards).

36

D (A and C are lying).

37

W, with a total time of 1:15.06 (V=1:16.38, W=1:15:06, X=1:15:45, Y=1:19.48, Z=1:16:59).

38

A light blue square with white balls at bottom left and top left, and dark blue balls at bottom right and top right. (The squares in the middle row have been rotated 90 degrees clockwise, then combined with the top row to create the bottom row. The middle row is dominant).

39

61 (= 13+16+15+17).

40

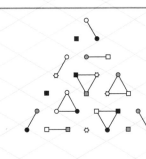

41

D (Rectangle).

42

B (Both signs are false; sign 1 cannot belong to Door A without causing a paradox).

43

35 (From 15, add 2, 3, 4 etc. to alternate segments).

44

1	0	9	8	5		9	4	2		3		
8		1		2	9	3		5	1	2	0	0
7		1		4		7		3		6		
1	1	2	1	7	9	6	6			6	7	8
2				5		6				0		
7	4	9		5	6	0	7	1		2		
	7			2		9		1	8	2	9	1
3	7	2	5	5		8		6		6		4
6		7		2	1	5	6	2	8	0	7	2
4		7			7			4			3	
3	0	8	9		8	3	4		6	3	9	
8		9				9				7		8
2	3	2			7	3	4	7	3	8	5	

45

Catherine Deneuve. Halle Berry. Jennifer Lawrence. Miley Cyrus. Sacha Baron Cohen. Denzel Washington. Peter Stormare. Rowan Atkinson.

46

C (A & C oppose. C's self-reflective statement means C either random, or statement true, but C random makes A & B paradoxical. So C is true, and B is random, and since C is true, C must be honest, leaving A as liar).

47

C.

48

5 (To see why, consider the case of just two statements. Odd numbers of statements are insoluble).

49

B.

50

04:56.27 (Sum of digits increases by three).

51

4³ = 64.

52

1113122113 (Each term is equal to the vocal enumeration of the digits in the previous term – "3"; "one 3"; "one 1, one 3"; "three 1s, one 3", etc.)

53

A (10+3+25+25+15. B=50+25+1+1+1. C=50+10+10+5+3).

54

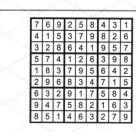

7	6	9	2	5	8	4	3	1
4	1	5	3	7	9	8	2	6
3	2	8	6	4	1	9	5	7
5	7	4	1	2	6	3	9	8
1	8	3	7	9	5	6	4	2
2	9	6	8	3	4	7	1	5
6	3	2	9	1	7	5	8	4
9	4	7	5	8	2	1	6	3
8	5	1	4	6	3	2	7	9

55

7463524131 (Step 6's result is not recorded).

56

3 (● = 1, ■ = 2, ▲ = 3).

57

8 (● = 2, ■ = 3, ▲ = 5).

58

Henrik Ibsen. Alexander Ostrovsky. Mikhail Bulgakov. Harold Pinter. Miguel de Cervantes. Tom Stoppard. Thornton Wilder. Pierre Corneille. John Osborne. Juan Ruiz de Alarcón.

59

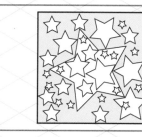

60

23.

61

```
H T T O T T R T T A T R A H R
O A A R H T O T R O A O R T R
T T H A T A T T H A H T H A T
O R R T R T A T R O H R T H O
T T O T T O A T O R T T H O T
H A A R T A O A R T R T O O R
T R T R O T T R T T H H R A O
T H T R H T R H O H T R O H O
T O R H R R R A T O H O O T O
R O H T T A O A H H T H O R T
R T T R A T O O R H O T T R H
R A T T T T T O R O T T O T O
R T T T R H R O T T H A O T A
R T T A O A A H T A T A R T H
A H O A H T T T O A H T R R T
```

62

Three instances of 1, two instances of 2, three instances of 3, one instance of 4, and one instance of 5. (Five space + five digits, so total must be 10. Try all 1s and iterate to find the solution).

63

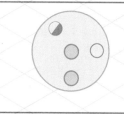

64

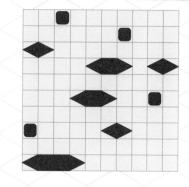

271

65

▲ = 3, ■ = 4, ● = 7, ★ = 9.

66

185.

67

3	8	1	7	5	2	9	6	4
6	7	5	4	1	9	3	2	8
2	4	9	3	8	6	7	5	1
7	6	8	2	9	4	1	3	5
9	5	3	8	7	1	2	4	6
4	1	2	6	3	5	8	9	7
1	9	7	5	4	3	6	8	2
8	2	4	9	6	7	5	1	3
5	3	6	1	2	8	4	7	9

68

i. False (it's divisible by 3). **ii. True. iii. False** (it was invented in China). **iv. False** (he was a tyrant of Sparta). **v. False** (it's Albany). **vi. False** (it's in Croatia). **vii. True. viii. True. ix. True** (A few know more than a thousand words, and understand the concept of time as expressed by different tenses). **x. True.**

69

i. True. ii. False (there are actually around 8*10^67 orderings). **iii. True. iv. False** (it's in Russia). **v. False** (it's Sacramento). **vi. True. vii. False** (it's a metalloid, with some metallic properties). **viii. False** (it's in Canis Major). **ix. True. x. True.**

70

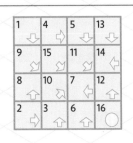

71

6th square number = 36. (Numbers on corners irrelevant.)

72

1	5	2	9	6	7	3	8	4
9	8	6	1	4	3	2	5	7
7	4	3	8	5	2	9	1	6
2	9	5	6	8	4	7	3	1
8	6	7	5	3	1	4	2	9
3	1	4	7	2	9	5	6	8
5	7	8	2	9	6	1	4	3
6	3	9	4	1	5	8	7	2
4	2	1	3	7	8	6	9	5

73

James Franco, Johnny Depp, Kate Beckinsale, Vin Diesel, David Tennant, Angelina Jolie.

74

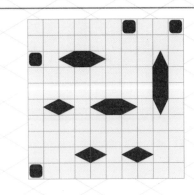

75

0	3	5	8	3	1	9
3	9	8	5	4	9	3
5	8	2	7	0	2	5
8	5	7	9	2	5	3
3	4	0	2	6	4	5
1	9	2	5	4	3	6
9	3	5	3	5	6	1

76

11 + 5 / 4 * 7 - 23 * 7 - 16 = 19.

77

i. False (26AL is radioactive). **ii. False** (Not on Antarctica). **iii. False** (it's Tallahassee). **iv. False** (it was Pakistan). **v. False** (it's irrational). **vi. True. vii. True** (they're called d12s). **viii. True. ix. True. x. False** (It was invented in India).

78

B + H.

79

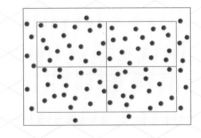

80
▲ = 2, ■ = 3, ● = 5, ★ = 8.

81
12.

82

4	4	5	5	2	2	5	5	5	5
4	4	5	5	5	3	5	2	2	8
3	3	3	2	2	3	3	8	8	8
5	5	5	5	5	9	9	8	8	8
8	8	3	3	9	9	5	5	5	8
8	8	8	3	9	5	5	6	6	6
8	8	8	9	9	6	6	6	5	5
6	6	6	9	9	7	7	7	7	5
8	8	6	6	6	7	7	7	5	5
8	8	8	8	8	8	4	4	4	4

83

1	7	4	8	9	2	5	6	3
6	8	3	5	4	1	9	7	2
2	9	5	7	6	3	1	8	4
8	2	1	3	5	7	4	9	6
9	5	6	1	2	4	7	3	8
4	3	7	9	8	6	2	5	1
5	6	8	2	1	9	3	4	7
3	4	2	6	7	5	8	1	9
7	1	9	4	3	8	6	2	5

84
20. (Diagonally opposing pairs of sectors in each circle sum to a total of 23.)

85

9	5	8	6	7	1	3	2	4
7	2	1	5	3	4	8	6	9
6	4	3	8	2	9	1	5	7
5	9	2	4	6	3	7	1	8
4	1	7	2	5	8	6	9	3
8	3	6	9	1	7	5	4	2
3	6	4	1	8	2	9	7	5
2	8	5	7	9	6	4	3	1
1	7	9	3	4	5	2	8	6

86

A 17-symbol sequence runs horizontally from left to right, starting from the top left.

87

88

1 ⇨	10 ⤡	9 ⇦	2 ⤢
11 ⇨	7 ⤡	12 ⇩	8 ⤢
6 ⤢	5 ⇦	14 ⇩	15 ⇩
3 ⇨	4 ⇧	13 ⇧	16 ○

89
C.

90
Rupert Grint, Edward Norton, Jack Nicholson, Channing Tatum, Bruce Willis, James McAvoy.

91
▲ = 1, ■ = 2, ● = 3, ★ = 5.

92
A rectangle.

93

5	2	7	4	1	9	6	8	3
4	8	3	2	6	7	9	1	5
6	1	9	5	3	8	4	2	7
3	5	6	9	2	1	7	4	8
8	9	4	7	5	6	1	3	2
1	7	2	8	4	3	5	6	9
9	4	1	3	8	5	2	7	6
7	6	8	1	9	2	3	5	4
2	3	5	6	7	4	8	9	1

94

A star.

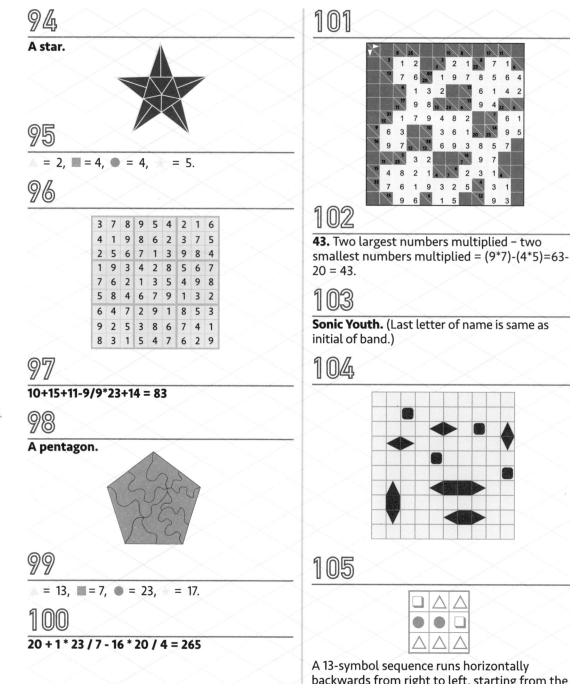

95

▲ = 2, ■ = 4, ● = 4, ★ = 5.

96

3	7	8	9	5	4	2	1	6
4	1	9	8	6	2	3	7	5
2	5	6	7	1	3	9	8	4
1	9	3	4	2	8	5	6	7
7	6	2	1	3	5	4	9	8
5	8	4	6	7	9	1	3	2
6	4	7	2	9	1	8	5	3
9	2	5	3	8	6	7	4	1
8	3	1	5	4	7	6	2	9

97

10+15+11-9/9*23+14 = 83

98

A pentagon.

99

▲ = 13, ■ = 7, ● = 23, ★ = 17.

100

20 + 1 * 23 / 7 - 16 * 20 / 4 = 265

101

102

43. Two largest numbers multiplied − two smallest numbers multiplied = (9*7)-(4*5)=63-20 = 43.

103

Sonic Youth. (Last letter of name is same as initial of band.)

104

105

A 13-symbol sequence runs horizontally backwards from right to left, starting from the bottom right. Each time a new row is started, 5 symbols from the sequence are skipped.

106

Gymnastics.
Elizabeth, who had a forearm scar, was former gymnast, and worked as a librarian. Rebecca, who had a torn hamstring, was a former footballer, and worked as a teacher. Daniel, who had a sprain, was a former sprinter, and worked as a pharmacist. Kevin, who had a broken arm, was a former pole vaulter, and worked as a cook. Kelly, who had been in car crash, was a former snowboarder, and worked as a barrista.

107

108

42.5.

109

A 13-symbol sequence runs vertically from top to bottom, starting from the top left.

110

5	7	0	3	4	7	4
7	0	4	5	8	4	3
0	4	6	9	6	1	5
3	5	9	7	9	8	6
4	8	6	9	2	3	9
7	4	1	8	3	5	6
4	3	5	6	9	6	1

111

(9*1)-7 = 2.

112

130.

113

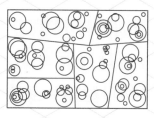

114

i. True. ii. False (they have four). **iii. True. iv. False** (they're used to wrap a cheese). **v. False** (it's in Spain). **vi. True. vii. True. viii. True. ix. True. x. True.**

115

A 12-symbol sequence spirals inwardly clockwise, starting from the top left.

275

116

8	5	3	6	9	1	2	4	7
9	2	4	7	3	5	1	6	8
6	1	7	4	2	8	5	9	3
4	8	6	2	5	7	9	3	1
2	7	9	1	6	3	4	8	5
1	3	5	8	4	9	6	7	2
3	4	1	5	8	6	7	2	9
5	6	8	9	7	2	3	1	4
7	9	2	3	1	4	8	5	6

117

A.

118

Cappuccino. Richard had a croissant with an americano, for $4.00. Scott had a pain au chocolat with latte, for $4.50. Mary had a black forest gateau with cappuccino, and paid $6.00. Jeffrey had a red velvet cake with an espresso, and paid $5.50. Amanda had a blueberry muffin with ristretto, and paid $5.00.

119

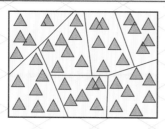

120

14. (The top two and bottom two sectors in each circle sum to the same value as the left two and right two sectors, 60.)

121

A.

122

Ben Stiller, Matt Damon, Owen Wilson, Anne Hathaway, Tim Allen, Robin Williams.

123

1	2	5	1	9	4	2
2	9	4	7	3	9	3
5	4	8	9	4	6	1
1	7	9	5	8	1	2
9	3	4	8	0	5	4
4	9	6	1	5	2	9
2	3	1	2	4	9	1

124

3	2	1	5	6	4
1	5	6	4	3	2
6	3	2	1	4	5
5	6	4	2	1	3
2	4	3	6	5	1
4	1	5	3	2	6

125

11. (11+4)-(3+7)=5.

126

9	5	2	5	0	7	2	7	9	3
1	6	1	8	9	8	8	3	2	5	0
9	6	1	4	3	8	2	3	7	5	2
2	6	8	8	0	8	0	6	3	5	0
4	5	4	1	6	8	7	6	9	5	8
0	1	7	6	1	5	9	0	0	9	1
7	3	0	4	9	1	9	3	3	4	0
6	1	8	6	0	4	7	4	2	1	3
6	4	2	2	5	1	4	2	6	7
5	8	5	3	7	4	3	4	7	9	7

127

5	6	2	4	3	1
2	3	5	1	6	4
3	2	1	5	4	6
1	4	3	6	5	2
4	5	6	2	1	3
6	1	4	3	2	5

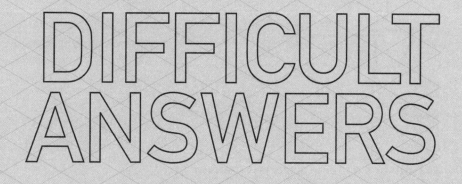

DIFFICULT
ANSWERS

01

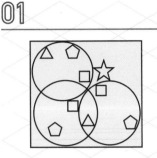

02

$1/\sqrt{1}=1$

03

Desk 7

04

28 (Segments with even numbers in the inner and middle rings total 50).

05

Flip a coin ($\frac{1}{2}$ chance versus $\frac{5}{12}$ chance).

06

0 (D = the last digit of bc - A, treating bc as a two-digit number).

07

34 (= 5 + 8 + 5 + 9 + 7).

08

Battenberg cake, Oatmeal, Escalivada, Quorn, Corned beef, Jambalaya, Ratatouille, Jerky.

09

C.

10

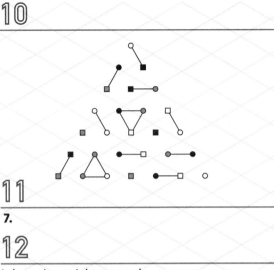

11

7.

12

I threw it straight upwards.

13

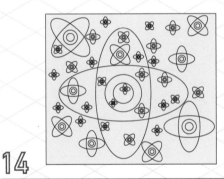

14

Our solutions: a. 4^2*3/4-8 = 4.
b. ($\sqrt{25}+4$)^2−(4^3) =17.
c. ((5!+5)*.5−.5)−5−((5+5)/5) = 55.

15

16

1225 (Christmas day).

278

17

5 (taking each wheel as a single number clockwise from 12 o'clock, C=A-B).

18

6 (=bottom right and centre, taken as a first and second digits of a single number = top * bottom left of the previous triangle).

19

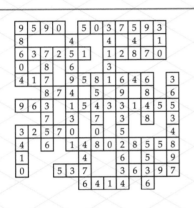

20

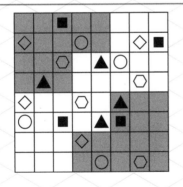

21

40.

22

37 (=7+8+7+8+7).

23

E4 or E5.

24

Brigadier Sun (Lieutenant Colonel Nomi, Major Capheus, Major Will, Lieutenant Riley, Lieutenant Kala, Corporal Lito).

25

D.

26

Flora and Susie (Anna: mathematics, engineering, micro-electronics, Japanese. Flora: Physics, programming, micro-electronics, Japanese. Susie: mathematics, physics, programming, engineering).

27

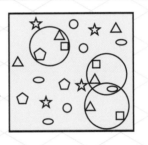

28

01:46.18 (Time alternately increases by 9h 47m 17s, then increases by 5h 22m 37s).

29

E.

30

3 (AB = CD * E, treating AB and CD as two-digit numbers).

31

3.

32

107 (= 14 + 39 + 14 + 26 + 14).

33

C (One white ball should be yellow: the others all form part of a trio with the same numbers of balls of each colour).

34

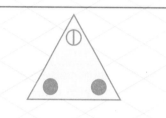

35

In step 8, the instruction says to divide by 2. It needs to say to divide by 3.

36

3pm ("LIVE").

37

D (Pentagon).

38

39

Ask A if the liar is to the immediate left of the random person, as they face you. If A is honest, then "Yes" means that C is random, and "No" means that B is random. If A is the liar, then "Yes" means that C is random, and "No" means that B is random. If A is random, then neither B nor C are random. Thus if you get "Yes," B is definitely non-random, and if you get "No," C is definitely non-random. Ask the identified non-random person if one of the three is a liar (or some other obvious question). If you get the answer "No," the non-random person is the liar. If you get the answer "Yes," the non-random person the truth-teller. Ask the same person "Is A random?" to be sure of the disposition of all three.

40

X, at 46:58.12 (V=46:58.49, W=46:58.14, X=46:58.12, Y=46:58.64, Z=46:58.95).

41

$6^4 = 36^2$.

42

8 (● = 3, ▲ = 4, ■ = 6, ⬟ = 7.)

43

Jean Cocteau. Albert Camus. Yasmina Reza. Martin McDonagh. Seneca the Younger. Shelagh Delaney. Georg Büchner. Ólafur Haukur Símonarson. Pierre de Marivaux. Stephen Sondheim. Tracy Letts. Kālidāsa.

44

B4.

45

Cumbria (Int. 1, Lillian, Hampshire, vet, black hair, anthropology. Int. 2, Elvira, Essex, life coach, blonde hair, psychology. Int. 3, Lala, Norfolk, estate agent, red hair, sociology. Int. 4, Milton, Cumbria, teacher, brown hair, history. Int. 5, Anthony, Rutland, accountant, grey hair, philosophy).

46

A (B & C are mutually exclusive, so A has to be lying).

47

A light blue square with light blue balls at top left and bottom right, white balls at top right and bottom left, and a dark blue ball in the centre. (Sequence runs horizontally through the grid as WWDLDDLWLDLW).

48

9. (nC = difference between (n-2)A and (n-1)B, where (n+1) is one segment clockwise).

49

It should read **0229** from top to bottom (Treat column as a number and multiply by three, recording last digits in next column, decreasing column height by 1).

50

O (The letters spell out the word TOOTHLIKE).

51

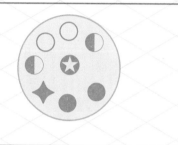

52

53

D (Repeating 13-colour pattern mbWlbBmblbWlbBWlbBW goes from clockwise spiral at top left to vertical rows upwards from bottom left).

54

The one going opposite to the planet's spin (No centrifugal force lightening its weight).

55

R ("MYTHOGRAPHER").

56

Celadon, Tilleul, Atrous, Watchet, Meline, Corbeau, Solferino.

57

4 (Number of separate lines immediately surrounding the value).

58

July 16th (Jack knows her month has no unique candidate dates on the list. John then realises only July and August fit, and that he knows which it is. Jack then realises that eliminating common candidate dates in those months gives him the full answer, so it has to be July, with only one unique candidate, the 16th).

59

G (Central letter has position in alphabet equal to the sum of the positions of the months initialled around that triangle, wrapping from Z=26 to A=27).

60

Audrey Tautou. Scarlett Johansson. Sandra Bullock. Charlize Theron. David Hasselhoff. Michael Douglas. Morgan Freeman. Jack Nicholson.

61

62

A & E.

63

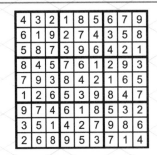

64

D.

65

The Divine Comedy, Dante Alighieri. Madame Bovary, Gustave Flaubert. Nineteen Eighty Four, George Orwell.

66

1 (Extra vertical line in the small central ball).

67

B (Each person likes a vegetable that has the same initial letter as their star-sign).

68

978368 / 32 = 30574.

69

```
3   5   1   9   5
5   5   7   7   5
1   7   4   6   0
9   7   6   4   3
5   5   0   3   2
```

70

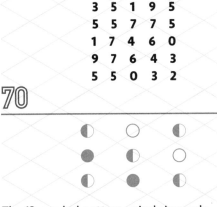

The 13-symbol pattern spirals inwards, clockwise, from the bottom right.

71

A 19-symbol sequence spirals inwardly clockwise, starting from the bottom left.

72

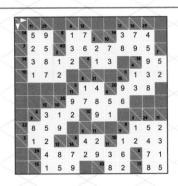

73

74

Everton. (4th letter of name is same as last letter of football club.)

75

50. (Equivalent sectors in both circles sum to a total of 31, 37, 41, 43, 47, 53, 59 and 61, the primes >29 in ascending order, starting from the top right "12 o'clock" sector.)

76

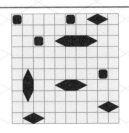

77

A hexagon.

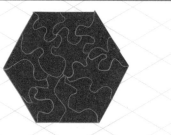

78

13. (Diagonally opposing pairs of sectors and their equivalent sectors in the second circle collectively sum to a total of 57.)

79

13 * 2 + 8 + 22 * 7 - 12 - 15 = 365

80

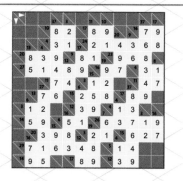

81

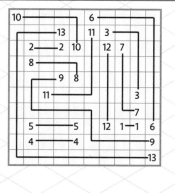

82

i. False (it's third, twice as abundant as steam). **ii. False** (they don't). **iii. True. iv. True. v. False** (they belong to many other genera as well). **vi. True. vii. False** (it's a peacock; the constellation that represents a phoenix is, well, Phoenix). **viii. False** (it was invented in Germany). **ix. True. x. False** (it uses five dice).

83

A 17-symbol sequence runs vertically from the bottom right and retreats leftwards, changing from upwards to downwards at the end of each line.

84

2	4	5	7	0	3	8
4	5	4	8	2	1	4
5	4	1	9	3	8	0
7	8	9	1	8	7	9
0	2	3	8	7	2	4
3	1	8	7	2	7	8
8	4	0	9	4	8	3

85

Moscow. (People whose names start with vowels like capital cities.)

86

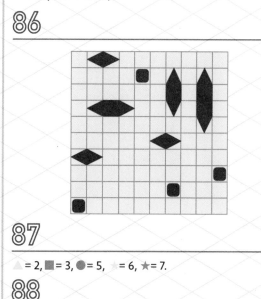

87

△ = 2, ■ = 3, ● = 5, ◆ = 6, ★ = 7.

88

17 - 14 ^ 6 - 13 / 4 - 16 * 3 = 489

89

A 17-symbol sequence runs horizontally from left to right, starting from the top left and jumping every other line to the bottom half of the table, starting from the ninth row, so that the rows run in the order 1, 9, 2, 10, ... 15, 8.

90

91

4	1	2	8	9	7	6	3	5
8	9	6	4	5	3	1	7	2
7	3	5	1	2	6	9	4	8
5	4	3	9	6	1	2	8	7
9	2	7	5	3	8	4	1	6
1	6	8	2	7	4	5	9	3
6	5	4	3	8	9	7	2	1
3	7	9	6	1	2	8	5	4
2	8	1	7	4	5	3	6	9

92

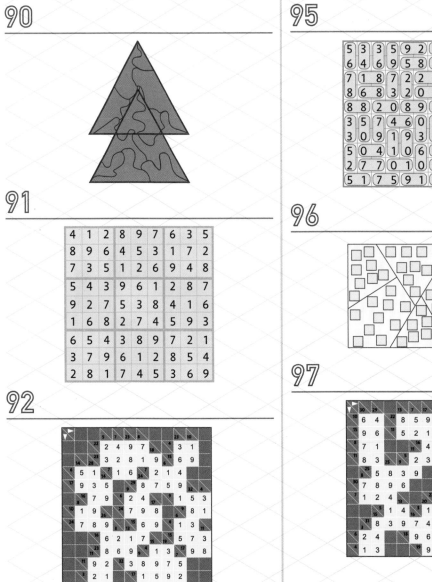

284

93

4	1	3	5	2	6
5	4	2	6	3	1
2	5	4	1	6	3
6	3	5	2	1	4
3	6	1	4	5	2
1	2	6	3	4	5

94

E (right) **& G** (top).

95

5	3	3	5	9	2	0	7	4	1	4
6	4	6	9	5	8	2	1	4	6	4
7	1	8	7	2	2	7	3	5	6	9
8	6	8	3	2	0	0	1	5	9	4
8	8	2	0	8	9	6	2	5	3	2
3	5	7	4	6	0	6	2	3	9	7
3	0	9	1	9	3	1	3	6	6	1
5	0	4	1	0	6	8	0	7	3	8
2	7	7	0	1	0	4	7	4	8	2
5	1	7	5	9	1	4	5	9	9	8

96

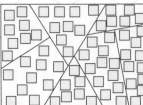

97

98

Albuquerque. In sequential order: **1.** Mark, a Derry taxi driver, who drove a Lexus, and used worms. **2.** Julie, a Portland manager, who drove a Ford, and used a crankbait. **3.** Laura, a Tulsa singer, who drove a Toyota, and used a spinnerbait. **4.** Sarah, an Albuquerque rancher, who drove a Chevrolet, and used a jig. **5.** Steven, a Chicago secretary, who drove a Tesla, and used a spoon lure.

99

100

1 ⇩	10 ⇩	9 ⇦	5 ⇦
3 ⇨	8 ⤢	6 ⤡	4 ⇧
2 ⇧	7 ⇧	12	13 ⤡
15 ⇨	11 ⤡	14 ⇦	16 ○

101

7^3 - (17 * 13) = 343 - 221 = 122.

102

i. True. ii. False (it's colourless). **iii. False** (It comes from Latin America). **iv. True** (it's in Hampshire). **v. False** (they can also include 1s). **vi. True. vii. False** (it's Salem). **viii. True. ix. False** (it represents sails; the constellation that represents a herdsman is Boötes). **x. True.**

103

3	2	5	1	3	6	2
2	1	4	7	2	3	5
5	4	7	8	1	4	8
1	7	8	2	3	5	1
3	2	1	3	3	0	2
6	3	4	5	0	1	4
2	5	8	1	2	4	5

104

Julia Roberts, Steve Buscemi, Tommy Lee Jones, Rachel McAdams, Bruce Springsteen, Jackie Chan.

105

4	4	2	3	3	3	4	4	2	2
4	4	2	8	8	4	4	7	8	8
2	2	8	8	5	5	7	7	8	8
8	8	8	8	5	5	7	7	7	8
2	2	9	9	9	5	7	9	9	8
4	4	4	4	9	9	9	9	8	8
6	6	6	6	3	7	7	7	7	7
6	6	5	5	3	7	7	2	2	4
4	4	5	5	3	2	2	4	4	4
4	4	5	2	2	5	5	5	5	5

106

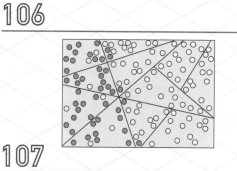

107

1 ⇩	9 ⤡	14 ⇩	13 ⇦
8 ⤢	4 ⤡	10 ⤡	12 ⇧
3 ⇧	7 ⤢	5 ⤡	11 ⇧
2 ⇧	6 ⇧	15 ⇨	16 ○

108

4	4	7	7	9	9	9	6	6	6
4	4	7	7	9	9	9	6	6	6
2	2	7	7	7	9	9	9	4	4
6	6	6	6	6	6	8	8	4	4
5	5	8	8	8	8	8	8	3	3
5	5	5	3	3	3	6	6	6	3
3	3	3	4	4	4	4	6	6	6
2	2	9	9	9	9	9	9	9	9
4	4	4	5	5	5	5	2	2	9
4	2	2	5	2	2	4	4	4	4

285

109

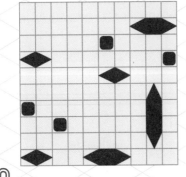

110

Lewis Carroll. (Middle letter of name is same as middle letter of author's surname.)

111

B (top) **& J** (left).

112

An oval.

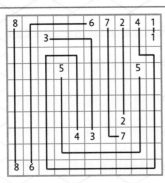

113

Derbyshire. Christine loves Crosswords and lives in Edinburgh, where she is a programmer. Anthony loves Wordsearch and lives in Derbyshire, where he is an analyst. Shannon loves Sudoku and lives in Essex, where she is a carpenter. Tammy loves Kakuro and lives in Cornwall, where she is a police officer. Charles loves mazes and lives in Hampshire, where he is a driver.

114

115

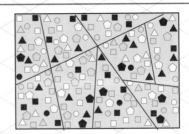

116

C.

117

9	9	9	9	9	3	3	3	4	4
9	9	9	9	5	5	5	5	5	4
7	7	7	7	3	3	3	2	2	4
7	2	2	5	4	4	9	9	9	9
7	7	5	5	4	4	9	9	5	5
4	4	6	5	5	9	9	9	5	5
4	4	6	6	6	6	6	2	2	5
2	2	7	7	7	2	2	3	3	3
4	4	4	7	7	7	7	4	4	4
4	8	8	8	8	8	8	8	8	4

118

Tiger Woods, Alec Guinness, Jason Statham, Chris Hemsworth, Robert De Niro, Jennifer Aniston.

119

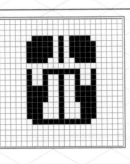

120

121

3	7	8	9	6	2	5	1	4
9	2	1	4	7	5	8	6	3
5	4	6	3	8	1	2	7	9
6	8	3	2	1	7	9	4	5
7	5	2	6	9	4	1	3	8
1	9	4	8	5	3	7	2	6
2	6	5	1	4	9	3	8	7
4	1	7	5	3	8	6	9	2
8	3	9	7	2	6	4	5	1

122

154. Top two numbers multiplied – bottom two numbers from adjacent square multiplied, taking squares as two pairs = (18*10)-(2*13)=180-26 = 154.

123

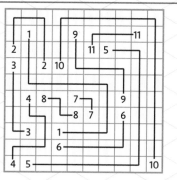

124

25 * 9 / 10 + 1 * 14 - 11 - 19 * 1 = 299

125

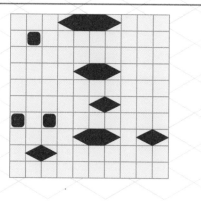

126

$\triangle$ =12, $\blacksquare$ =14, $\bullet$ =15, =17, $\star$ =18.

127

5 + 16 - 20 ^ 3 + 25 * 11 / 2 - 25 * 8 = 944

128

129

8	8	7	7	7	7	7	5	5	5
8	8	7	4	4	8	8	8	5	5
8	3	7	4	3	3	3	8	8	8
8	3	3	4	6	6	6	6	8	8
8	6	6	6	3	6	6	3	3	3
8	6	6	6	3	5	5	5	5	5
4	4	4	4	3	9	9	3	3	3
3	3	3	9	9	9	6	6	6	6
2	2	7	7	9	9	9	9	6	6
3	3	3	7	7	7	7	7	2	2

130

1	11	6	7
14	15	3	8
13	10	9	4
2	12	5	16

131

Tanya. (Tanya had a sausage sandwich and a red sweater, and liked Bobtail cats. Joshua had a brie sandwich and a green sweater, and liked Shorthair cats. Ryan had an omelette sandwich and a mauve sweater, and liked Siamese cats. Jeremy had a turkey sandwich and a white sweater, and liked Persian cats. Lucy had a cheddar sandwich and a blue sweater, and liked Manx cats.)

132

Jessica Alba, Kevin Spacey, Clint Eastwood, Drew Barrymore, Rowan Atkinson, Kate Winslet.

133

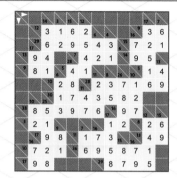

134

 =3, ■ =5, ● =7, ★ =8, ★ =8, ● =9.

135

5	7	8	3	1	6	4	9	2
1	3	4	2	9	5	6	8	7
2	6	9	8	4	7	3	5	1
4	9	7	5	6	2	8	1	3
6	8	1	4	3	9	2	7	5
3	5	2	1	7	8	9	6	4
9	2	6	7	5	3	1	4	8
8	1	5	9	2	4	7	3	6
7	4	3	6	8	1	5	2	9

136

Cumbria. The first interviewee was Tina from Hampshire, a writer with black hair, who wanted to adopt a Labrador. The second interviewee was Patricia from Powys, an optician with blonde hair, who wanted to adopt a Poodle. The third interviewee was Lori from Norfolk, a chef with red hair, who wanted to adopt a Spaniel. The fourth interviewee was Gregory from Cumbria, a professor with brown hair, who wanted to adopt a Terrier. The fifth interviewee was Kenneth from Strathclyde, a marketer with grey hair, who wanted to adopt a Corgi.

137

1	5	9	4	6	2	3	7	8
8	4	6	3	9	7	5	1	2
7	2	3	8	1	5	6	4	9
5	7	2	9	4	3	1	8	6
9	3	8	6	2	1	7	5	4
4	6	1	5	7	8	9	2	3
2	9	4	1	5	6	8	3	7
6	8	5	7	3	4	2	9	1
3	1	7	2	8	9	4	6	5

138

27. (The numbers across both circles form a sequence, starting from 20, that runs +7, -12, +3, and that switches back and forth from circle to circle, starting from the top right "12 o'clock" sector, going from first circle to the mirrored equivalent sector in the second circle, then progressing clockwise one space back in the first circle.)

139

Bristol. (The numeric position of the last letter of the first name is equal to the length of the car marque that the person likes.)

288